From Roadrunner to Showrunner

THE CREATIVE MASTERMIND MIND

How to Make it in Showbusiness and Content Creation

Author: Daniel Cubillo

Independently published by Daniel Cubillo

ISBN: 979-8-9935868-0-9

Cover design by Joaquin Jordan

Edited by Kate Williams

Printed in the city of Los Angeles, California, United States of America.

www.danielcubillo.tv

thecreativemastermind.com

THE CREATIVE MASTERMIND MIND

FROM ROADRUNNER TO SHOWRUNNER

HOW TO MAKE IT IN SHOWBUSINESS AND CONTENT CREATION

BY DANIEL CUBILLO

This book is dedicated to my son Daniel, and to the rest of the dreamers and doers of the universe. I hope you all will put your talent and energy into something good.

I want to thank God and Miles Davis (if they are not the same person) for their participation in this effort. They made it easier and joyful. Thanks also to CG, TB, and JB for their love and for the way they pushed me to move forward in life.

INDEX

INTRODUCTION

How To Achieve Your Creation Dream?

INTRODUCTION

I was 12 years old when I saw the first Star Wars movie in a small-town theater called 'Cine Xucar.' The city is located about an hour away from the European metropolis where I grew up. Like every summer when we were kids, at the beginning of the break, my parents sent us out of Madrid to give them some well-deserved freedom, and for us to enjoy time with our grandparents, uncles, aunts, and two dozen cousins under 12 years old. I was interested in Star Wars from the moment I first read about it in a magazine. But back then, going from the hood to the premier theaters of Calle Gran Via (our Madrid's little Broadway Avenue) was an adventure we couldn't afford without adults. One of the advantages of a small town is that kids can walk to the theater on their own. We would find our way there three or four times a day, pressing our faces against the theater's walls to see –again and again– the collections of stills used by past century marketers to promote movies. But we still needed an adult to pay for our entry.

Finally, after a lot of begging, Tía Loren took the older kids to see the film, as she had with Jaws, the Airport saga, and many other cult and not-so-cult classics. She was an angel I miss every day. The night after watching Star Wars for the first time, unable to sleep and completely entranced by what I had experienced, I started writing my first piece of audiovisual content with my older cousin. Today, we call them "podcasts," but back then, my aunties called them radio-novelas. We started recording the next morning with two of Tío Gori's cassette recorders and a hand microphone. We were only allowed to use one, so we had to sneak the second and return it before Tío Gori noticed. Several times. The audio piece we made was full of homemade space-related sound effects, created in the bathroom, kitchen, closets, and some other unconventional places. I'm not sure if the recording still exists—I doubt it—but I'd love to hear it again. We picked up where the first Star Wars movie left off, producing a 20-minute audio sequel of the saga that has marked generations.

That was the first piece of content I created, and I had no idea then that telling stories would be my life ride–the craft that has made it possible to experience things that were impossible to dream of.

What do you dream about, reader? Do you see yourself doing what you love and making a shit lot of money? What do you imagine when you think of a future where your craft brings success, wealth, joy, and even love? I'm talking about those moments when you daydream—relaxed, with your thoughts soaring in a high like no other— what are your dreams then? Hold on to those thoughts; you'll need them later.

In my case, it was impossible to even conceive the reality I live in now. I never dreamed of the things I have or the things I've done thanks to my ideas. I dreamt of making my living from storytelling, but I never dreamed of moving to Hollywood, diving with sharks, flying over the Alps with my body out of a chopper, dancing with Debbie Allen, traveling through the Basque country cooking Michelin-starred chefs, or directing Antonio Banderas in a musical number. None of that was in my dreams. What my dreamed career has brought me is twenty times better –and weirder– than anything I could've imagined. If you look at the most successful people in showbiz today, you'll see this pattern often. The lives they live, the things they have, the experiences they enjoy; none of them were part of their initial daydreams. I'm certain they never dreamed of becoming what they are today, nor achieving it in the way they did.

The same is true for you. This book will be your guide to converting your dreams into freaking awesome realities—realities you couldn't even have imagined, all because of your capability to create things out of your imagination. Creation is a drug. And—like any drug—it's a double-sided bitch. It brings incredible highs, but also deep lows. You have probably dreamed of the highs that come from creation. But have you thought about the lows? Like how to handle the pressure of becoming a creative mastermind? The constant demand for perfection? The unpredictable hours? The brutal competition? The fear of failure? The people who va a hablar mierda (will talk trash) about you or your work? You probably didn't consider these "B-sides" when daydreaming. Nobody does. Not me, not you, not the showbiz celebrities. But the B-sides are very real. Everyone who pursues a creative career will face pressures no one can imagine.

So, if nobody thinks of the B-sides of showbusiness, why should you? Because they will give you a framework. Not just any framework, but one adapted to your situation and your dream-making plans. The process of creation is different for a movie, a marketing campaign, a piece of pottery, or an innovative business; we all know that, but guys, trust me on this one, the basic framework is pretty much the same. This dream-making route that I'm talking about gives specific actions to become a creative mastermind and to see your ideas in real life, but it all starts with your curiosity.

That night after watching Star Wars my dreams of creations started como una cosa de crios (as kiddie crap) and they haven't finished yet. Eleven Star Wars movies later, I'm still playing and telling stories. Please go back now to the source of your own dreams. Back to the creative daydreaming. Picture your work, connect with that feeling of satisfaction, success, and wealth that comes from your craft, and travel through these pages with candidness.

Welcome! And enjoy the reading.

CHAPTER 1

What Is It About The Top 1% Of Successful People?

UNLOCKING THE MYSTERIES BEHIND DREAM MAKING

Notes

CHAPTER 1

Unlocking The Mysteries Behind Dream Making

Dreams are a tricky territory. Let's start with the basics: There's no single formula, but there are common characteristics that show up in people who succeed big in dream-making. Certain personality traits, experiences, or even accidents -Universe Timing in my dialect- can play a role in whether someone is able to see their visions realized or not.

There are cases of effortless success in creation. I know a couple, the same way I know a couple of lottery winners. But this book is not about hitting the raffle of the perfect-universe-timing. It is for the rest of the cases, those that come from intention and work. Reader, think big for a second, think about top celebrities who started from scratch and have succeeded in more than one discipline. Names like Serena Williams, Dwayne "The Rock" Johnson, Jessica Alba, Childish Gambino, or Rihanna, who have found massive success in multiple fields. Feel free to add more. Think about their dreams when they were kids. Think about their surroundings, too. When I do it, when I picture their teenagers' dreams, the same question pops into my mind every time: How the hell were they able to transform their visions into realities not once, but twice? What is it that these people have that I don't? How can someone make it into the very exclusive 0,1% of humans absolute masters in a craft, and then change the craft and repeat? People who, despite their origins and backgrounds, have had the same capability to succeed big in their dreams, twice. Shit, I applaud them. I always asked myself what they are made of. Making my storytelling dream possible was complicated enough, but to do it twice? It can feel impossible.

But achieving top success -or dreams achievement- is not impossible. It comes down to a combination of personality, adaptability, boldness, and pain. Yeah, let's call it by its name, pain. An expert would say 'the willingness to learn', but I'm not an expert, and I've gone through a lot of pain. I'm kind of slow on the uptake, especially in soul-related subjects. It doesn't matter if success in dream-making is coming through dejarse los huevos (relentless work), pure branding, a gift from the gods, or pure talent; pain is always invited to the party. That these pop icons found success even through pain proved to me that it is possible for anyone's dreams to come true. But would I be able to find success? Would a similar path work for me? And more importantly, am I suited for the journey?

DO I HAVE WHAT IT TAKES?

Have you considered these questions already? If so, you might fear the answers. They kept me frozen for a long time. I preferred not to ask myself these important questions because I thought my passion was enough, and I didn't want to crack into my personality traits, or lack of them. Digging into your defects is painful. But avoiding it is not a very smart attitude. The lesson? If you want to create stuff out of your imagination, know that passion is not enough. Passion is good as an energy source, but it suffers with time and experiences. You need a lot more than passion for the dream-making journey. And what is that exactly?

Trying to figure out those answers for the purpose of this book, and maybe because I'm old enough and I don't give a shit, I made the effort of comparing myself with those superstars who made it big. Like really big. Like Rihanna big. I started researching those celebrities and exploring what -if anything- I could have in common with them. Curious what I discovered? Me too! Here are the basics of my head-to-head with those A Listers. What do they have in common? What do I have in common with them?

Let's start with the stars: For those that are into astrology, among those five names -Serena, The Rock, Rihanna, Gambino, and Miss Honest Company -Lady Alba- there are two Taurus, two Libras, and one Pisces. I am an Aries, so, my score is cero in the first possession. The two Taurus (Johnson and Alba) and the two Libra (Williams and Gambino) could suggest some kind of alignment in persistence and balance. Ok, I have a lot of the first, and a fragile amount of the second. I can score in this one. Field goal, not the best outcome possible, but we share something already.

What if it is faith that made their dreams possible? Why not consider it? Regarding spiritual beliefs, they are all into some kind of deep connection con el mas alla (with the unseen). In some cases, they are attached to religion, but mostly without the presence of dogmas. Another field goal, not enough.

The next one is about personality types, which of them are better suited to succeed? What is it that they have that the rest don't? Allow me a moment to thank the shrinks -and the marketers- for their contribution to storytelling. The Myers-Briggs personality system is one of the best writing tools ever, it has been helping me to create solid characters and to understand part of my own shit, it really works. A-listers first: Dwayne Johnson is an ESFJ charisma and ability to connect, a natural leader -proved; Rihanna is seen as ENTP or ENFJ who combines creativity with strategic thinking -also proved!; Serena is about discipline, determination, and focus, an ESTJ or ISTJ -proved!; Childish Gambino is an INTP who shines in creative and intellectual fields -proved again; Jessica Alba is likely an ENTJ strong leadership qualities, risk-taking, and strategy. -proved too.

Oh shit, no way. The results are against me. Again! Whatever those letters mean in terms of 'predisposition for dream making', not one of the combinations fits me. Another possession with no score.

Quick note for you lazy future storytellers: If you don't know what the hell I am talking about with those capital letters mixtures, do your homework and research. Not only if you are into storytelling -great instrument, trust me in this one-, but also if you are really committed to your dream of creation. The better you know yourself, the easier it is going to be out there.

Here is the conclusion of my research: at the end of the day, I am not like them, and they are not like each other. What those successful celebrities share is not astrology charts or personality types, it is a combination of cojones, trabajo, y vision de la jugada (balls, work, and vision). In other words, making dreams come true –one or twice, doesn't matter– takes a blend of drive, vision, adaptability, and willingness to risk. That's the whole mystery. For those of you counting the words, the term cojones in *Spanish* means a variety of things, in this case they are drive and willingness to risk, all together. I happen to have a bit of cojones, vision, y capacidad de tabajar. Do you have them reader? Obviously, amounts can fluctuate, but if you do, it's time to put them to use. Of course, I don't have the cojones all the time, nor the energy to work all the time, and my vision is blurred occasionally, but in certain moments, I have enough of all to make a try. I can answer the 'do I have it?' question with a real 'kind of', knowing that the answer will be my life sentence. The real work starts now.

What about you, reader? Do you 'kind of' have a bit of what it takes? Do you think you can put some effort in training your muscles for better drive, vision, adaptability and risk-taking? If that is the case, if the answer is 'kind of', you are on the right path. The rest is irrelevant now. I am talking about your doubts, your fears, your title, your past, your background, your age, your location, your traumas, your resources, even your health! Do you think those five celebrities didn't have traumas? Turbulent past? Doubts? Weaknesses? Of course they did, probably they still do, but they made it, twice. It is possible, there is a way, but in order to succeed, you reader must be part of the journey. You need to apply the tools and the stories in these pages to your success, real or imagined.

HANDS ON DECK: THE DARK LISTS

As an artistic and creative person, you have two long lists of reasons not to start pursuing your dreams. But some advice: the reasons in those dark lists are here to stay with you. They will evolve with the times. Para siempre! No end date. The pop-culture icons in the top .1% still share the lists with us humans, despite succeeding in dream-making twice. The freaking lists are freaking consistent. Those negative arguments work the same when you're trying to start, trying to evolve, and needing to restart. 'Shit' was the expression I used when realizing it.

Let's work on the first dark list: What are the external concerns that keep you saying, 'it's not the right time'? Are they issues like market saturation, political climate, financial crisis, social expectations, limited time, disruptive technology, or shitty changing algorithms? Yes, they are, of course. There will always be 'outside' reasons to not to move our creative asses. The other dark list does not take into consideration anything outside of you; it is all about the one in the mirror. What are the internal reasons you won't follow your creative path? What is the inner conversation? What do you not want to hear in your mind when you stand in front of the mirror? Btw, get used to the espejo (mirror) thing and keep it close. It's an indispensable item for any creative mastermind.

We are going to keep focus on the list where you have more control: the internal reasons, and guys, don't BS the mirror please, it won't work. Time for honesty: What's holding you back in the dream-making task, for real? Fear of failure? Not enough skills yet? What this person would say? Self-doubt? Fear of rejection? Lack of resources? Unclear path? Low confidence? What are the voices inside your head saying? What would make you downsize when the opportunity to showcase your creativity comes? When would you finally move your ass for your own creative persona and not because of others' expectations? Be freaking honest reader.

It feels like a contradiction, but the dark list exists to be used to your advantage. Maybe I should consider changing the name because, while they are dark, they bring light. Here's how: Information is power, and pinpointing the exact fear –failure? criticism? making mistakes?– gives you the opportunity to tackle it. If your internal talk carries phrases like "I'm afraid people will think my work is amateurish" or "I feel like a fraud," you are doing great in the mirror. Keep talking and start analyzing those fears with more perspective. Try to recalibrate them. What happens if you adopt a growth mindset? If you accept the truth –and the truth is that nobody starts out as a master, o no?– instead of using an excuse like "people will think my work is amateurish"? What happens if you embrace the fact that creativity is an evolving skill and spend your energy on progress over perfection? What happens if you tell yourself 'You are growing as a creator every time you create'? Limit the self-sabotage by limiting the self-bull-shit. Those are all verdades como puños! o no? (Spanish dicho that means 'Straight-up truth bombs').

If you accept and recalibrate the truths coming from digging deep into your dark lists, you will see the answers are often unfounded, exaggerated, or completely made up in your head. One after the other, all those internal excuses will look ridiculous after some real talk with the mirror. I didn't forget about the list of external excuses. You will learn how to transform those issues into doable actions through strategy. You are reading this book to know how. The effort is worth it. Practicing the dark lists will give you the road map for the first stages of the dream-making journey. La charla con el espejo (the talk with the mirror) tells you what to work with, what actions you'd need to take first. Facing the lists reframes your mindset and puts your ass into action. Not that dark at the end of the day!

FREEING THE DREAM TO ACHIEVE THE UNDREAMT

I don't know what Rihanna's or The Rock's dreams were when they were teens, but I can guarantee reality has surprised them. The good thing about pursuing dreams is the realization of the 'dreams behind the dream', which most of the times are way better. Before reaching the summit of their dreams, those two A listers –like you and me– also felt those dreams were impossible to accomplish. Their circumstances were probably as shitty as yours or mine, maybe more, and here they are, as it is the rule: Once you apply the cojones, trabajo, y vision de la jugada, the dream is going to take its own shape, and guide you also during the hard times.

If you have completed the dark lists exercise, congrats, you are officially in the dream-making journey. That simple conversation with yourself acknowledged the obstacles to shift your mindset. Now, it's time to free your dreams.

I am using the expression 'free', but I could have used the words 'liberate' or 'release.' What is key is to understand the reason behind the concept. The moment you set a basic plan in pursuing your creative dream, your focus and energy must shift from the 'dream' part to the 'making' part. But even as you focus on the 'making,' the 'dream' is always there, flying on top of you, looking at you working on the 'making' from the sky, free, growing, evolving. The dream becomes an autonomous stealth flying entity connected to your 'making'. There's no way of breaking that connection. The more you put in the making, the further away the dream flies. The further it travels; the better undreamt crazy stuff will bring. I know, it is one of those weird inexplicable mysteries of dream-making, but it is freaking real.

Time for the specific actions for the 'free the dream' part of the equation. Here is how the 'making' part starts:

- **Addressing skill gaps & practical concerns.** Learn the basics of whatever you lack the most. In my case, the subjects were English, business, and tech. Understanding the stuff you fear will turn anxiety into something sustainable. I know you have practical concerns now, but you don't need the fanciest gear to create. Explore any low-cost tool that could serve your 'making'. Don't spend money first; spend time exploring. Set realistic timelines and budgets; Finances are always a concern, so find your way and build up slowly. I started practicing some kind of balance between new gear VS life-cost while sweeping soccer stadiums for a cleaning company. If I did it, you can too. Audio and video devices were 10 times more expensive then.

- **Building accountability & support.** The 'making' part also includes finding some kind of creative community: Local groups, writing circles, online forums, or aliens, just do it. Seek mentors too; look for established creatives to talk freely about your thing. I showed my first video ever as independent creator to my professor in Zaragoza. The piece was for a nonprofit corporation, and I am going to remember my professor's words until my last breath. I haven't opened an audiovisual piece the way I did ever again; for good, I am sure. Sharing your work with other creators is key, even if it's just with one teacher, a close friend in the craft, or a small online writers group. Get used to sharing your incomplete and imperfect shit. Period.

- **Fostering resilience.** Do whatever you need, but don't burn out. Your energy is your main asset. In the hard times, keep the big picture in mind, embrace the journey, and remember las verdades como puños (the straight-up truth bombs): Artistic growth is never linear; peaks of inspiration and self-doubt are part of the deal. The solution is adaptation; revisit your goals and your efforts frequently and adjust your 'making' routines to the circumstances.

- **Keeping your ass updated.** Technology and trends shift too quickly. Action is required. Keep learning new tools, exploring, watching, and testing new stuff, and staying excited and relevant. Keeping up with trends is another significant 'making' part, as relevant as the rest, and a good resource when our inspiration is in a break. I do that task especially when the inspiration is not around.

The moment you start anyone of those actions, the dream becomes active. It transforms from the intangible thing to the stealth flying entity. The more energy you put in the 'making', the more capable the entity becomes, and the wildest undreamt shit will come afterwards. I wish I could one day ask Serena, Dwayne, or Rihanna what their dreams were about and how they are different from what they have accomplished, experienced, and done. I wish they would share with me the dream they freed, and the shocking undreamt they got.

The undreamt part is where the magic of creation resides. If you haven't experienced it, yet you will. When I started in the craft as an apprentice, I dreamed of directing Real Madrid soccer games, high-budget commercials, MTV live concerts, and fabulous dramas that I would also write. Little by little, I have accomplished those dreams, but the undreamt part will give you an idea about how far away the stealth flying device can go, while you focus on the 'making'. Here are the highlights of my undreamt storytelling journey so far:

I started shooting and editing wedding videos fresh out of rehab, and I can tell you that wasn't my dream at all. I set up my first production company a few months later -never dreamed, never planned. Without dreaming about travel shows, I self-financed a pilot and commissioned my first cable show. I also dreamed of working with scripted content, and I made it. Without dreaming about it, I became an expert in unscripted storytelling, being part of the most iconic franchises. I've also grown a never-dreamed-of career in America, thanks to content globalization. I never dreamt of documenting the lives of the biggest soccer stars in Real Madrid or working with Jennifer Lopez, Pitbull, Daisy Fuentes, Residente, Eric Estrada, Camilla Cabello, or Antonio Banderas. I never dreamt about interviewing Michael Jackson, nor about meeting with Eva Longoria or Zoe Saldaña. I never dreamt of having my 15 minutes of fame in the very exclusive big-big offices of Hollywood, and meeting everyone from the -dark is the right word- Harvey Weinstein to the industry big shots.

Yeah. Mind-blowing stuff for a kid from a hood placed 7,000 miles away from LA. That is the kind of power of a freed dream. But, how can you free a dream if you won't allow yourself to dream? For those of you living under the shittier circumstances ever, for those who do not permit themselves to dream, and when you do, you tackle it fast, let me clarify something. Conditions are important, but they can't limit your dreams. You need those dreams to set them free and start the journey. I was one of those. I self-limited my own dreams because of the difficult circumstances I lived in. I stopped dreaming when I saw myself homeless. I did it also when I depended on substances, and I did it when I was in jail and rehab. In my case, dreaming got completely banned when I discovered that I had HIV. Cancelled. There was no dream that showed me happy and healthy writing these words from Beverly Hills. Nope. So, for those of you under extremely s****y circumstances, please relax, guys, just try to dream and keep reading, your time for the 'making' will come.

THE RINGS OF POWER FOR DREAMS ACCOMPLISHING

Once your dream is freed and the making is underway, there are four almost mythological rings that guarantee success and happiness in the creation journey (and other areas of your life). Like in a videogame, the rings are protected in the top of four pillars, and you will get the rings after winning the battle with the pillar's defenders. Which ring you choose to start with is very important. You will read about them in the order I obtained the rings. If I would've chosen differently, I could've easily been writing now from a nice villa in Zermatt or over Malibu, but nope, I'm still in a two-one apartment. You got it? Do you really want to go fast? Then prioritize the last ring I won.

The Ring of Clarity: Knowing What You Want

I know this is a tricky subject to start with. You probably still have no freaking idea about what you precisely want other than making a good life out of creation. Good, but how? With what kind of 'creation'? In what position in the creation process? You need clear, specific targets in mind. If you already have them, this ring is already yours, but remember to keep a wide-angle approach to your goals. Be flexible in the pursuing because tunnel vision is dangerous. Showbiz is a dream maker, but also a dream killer. Important clutch hack for this ring screen! In some cases, the clarity ring straight up transmogs into something else. Here's what I mean: As an apprentice, I had no clarity. I knew I wanted to have as much fun as possible, I knew I should avoid being another brick in the 9 to 5 wall, and I knew that whatever I ended up doing for money, it wouldn't feel like a job. But I had nothing related to the specifics of the path. No clarity about what area or what kind of storytelling, no idea about exactly what would allow me to reach my confused creation dreams. How the hell have my storytelling career and current life happened with that little conocimiento del marrón (understanding of the challenge)? This ring has a special power for those who are still not clear. If you don't know exactly what you want but have fire inside; the 'clarity' ring becomes the 'trying' ring. Exploring the different fields you like will score the same as having clarity. In my version of the game, the ring was about 'trying.' Don't worry, clarity will enter the stage on cue. Let's look at the other rings for now..

The Ring of Stopping the Comparison Game

It is well known, el que se compara, pierde (those who compare themselves with others, always lose). That is a universal truth, as comparison is a waste of precious energy. I guess I got the foundations of this ring inside me since I was a kid. My parents were different from the rest. Their jobs were exceptional, as was the way they educated us. Among my buddies at school and the hood, I was different inside -my mind was crowded with ideas and voices- and outside -rules and procedures at home. I learnt not to compare myself too much to anyone my age. I did it when playing soccer, or when not having the coolest pair of globes in the winter, but I never did regarding what other kids aspired for their lives. Reader, embrace your alienness. Every time you start comparing yourself with another person, just redirect your thoughts and energy. You are wasting time and money comparing. Put that effort into analyzing what you like about that person you admire instead of comparing yourself with the person whose opinions you fear.

The Ring to Become the Creative Mastermind

We all like the stories of those behind big creations. The bigger the creation, the more we would've like to be the one behind it, the mastermind who has the cojones, vision, y capacidad de tabajar (drive, vision, adaptability and risk-taking). The person behind the idea and the execution: The real showrunner. That is our ultimate goal: becoming not just a mastermind but the mastermind mind behind, in front, and all around the creation. It looks challenging, but mastering this ring is easier than you think. It comes naturally. We all must become the showrunners of our dream-making process.

To see how it works, let's play a little game. Imagine for a second that you were able to get total control of your life. You decide at what time you wake up tomorrow, in what mood, and with what goals for the day. Then you decide where to put your energy, how to recharge it, and what to do for fun with the rest of it. It's the end of the day, and you've spent it doing lo que te salio de los cojones (whatever you wanted). You either show-runned or show-ruined your day, depending on your decisions, but no doubt you were the mastermind mind behind those. If you showrun your day properly –with all the things under your control,– magic will happen soon. Be the mastermind mind of your 'making' days and nights, and you will get dream-making light speed.

The Ring of the Power of Knowing Yourself

This ring is la ostia (the shit). Knowing yourself is a formidable superpower, for many reasons. One of them is because you ignore enough stuff already. You don't know the future, you don't know the rest of the humans, nor your boss's hidden agenda. There's enough uncontrolled stuff to reject control of yourself. But imagine for a second that you knew exactly what to do to improve your strengths, to overcome your weaknesses, and to become better with every drop of energy you spend. Would that put you in a serous advantage over your competitors? Yes, or no? The answer is clear, regardless of craft: Know yourself as much as you can. Period.

SHORTCUTS FOR CREATION: WHAT ARE YOU AN EXPERT IN?

Another mystery behind dream-making is that there are shortcuts. Yes, you can skip a lot of stops. Here is the glitch in the dream-making system, a massive time and energy saver. Ojo! That doesn't mean you won't need the cojones, trabajo, y vision de la jugada (balls, work, and vision) part. You still need that, and the rings, but everything else will come easier and faster.

Reader, here's a little real-life sample to optimize your future energy investment in the 'making'. See my numbers and think about your own future in terms of time and efficiency: In the +1,000 hours of audiovisual content that I am responsible for –no news, no sports included– no more than 15 or 20 hours were about what I knew best. That means that I needed to research and learn a lot to create the other +980 hours. A very big lot. Would you like to avoid all those hours learning stuff? There is a way. The shortcut in creation is creating with what you know best. The shortcut in storytelling is writing about your real shit, no matter how painful. In the two things I know the best, in my two specialties, there were secrets, stigmas, shame, and a lot of fear involved. That is why I didn't take the shortcut. If I had, who knows what the undreamt part would've brought me.

A few months after watching Star Wars, I asked my parents for a specific 14th birthday gift: A ticket to a concert of the band The Clash in Madrid. I was probably the youngest person in that packed venue, placed where today you see four horrible skyscrapers flying over Madrid. Between Star Wars and London Calling, something went off badly. My own seeker personality -and some completely ignored mental health issues in the family- brought me to homelessness by fifteen. The streets led to an unknown freedom and an addiction to heroin. After that, I did a trip that I call the 'The home-run tour'. First base the streets, second base the hospital, third base jail, fourth base rehab. Instead of being the MVP, my home-run-tour also brought me HIV. That is what happens when you are 16 years old and you share needles. The ignorance of the times.

A decade living on the wild side and another decade on the healing side, give you unique perspectives for creation. Because of all that experience, I am an expert in mental health, addiction, HIV, and pain in general. I am also an expert in storytelling, and I wonder now, from those +1,000 hours of content I've created, if my first 10 hours would've been about those topics, how far the dream and the undreamt would've gone. The few times I had a project related to those topics; I was able to connect with the soul of the story as anyone else. I knew things that others couldn't even dream of. I knew the insides perfectly, and that makes the difference in content creation. Are your secrets also the things you know the most about? If they are, consider re-evaluating what your content is about. It's a tough shortcut, but worth it to try. The skip that fast-tracks you to the next level is made of a kind of courage I didn't have then. If you do, go for it!

I've come a long way in my dream-making journey. To be honest, having the balls to start this book talking about an intangible thing like dreams still surprises me. I've learned that the most solid way to unlock the mysteries of dream-making is investing in your cojones, trabajo, y vision de la jugada. Whatever you need to do to get those rings: Know what you want —even in an abstract way–, know yourself, do not compare yourself with others, and become the mastermind mind of your own show. The making of your dream is a fun trip; I can guarantee that. Buckle up!

CHAPTER 2

What Are The Secrets Of Becoming A Creative Genius?

HOW TO BECOME THE CREATIVE MASTERMIND MIND

Notes

CHAPTER 2

How To Become The Creative Mastermind Mind

The continuation of the first *Star Wars* movie was the first thing I wrote consciously; I was 13 by that time. A couple of years passed and, as an apprentice teenager with only a few days in the business, I had already decided what I wanted to be: The brain and the voice behind everything. The leader of the content creation pack. There is a line a I love in the second season of the series 'Halo;' Masterchief –the badass hero of the story– is closing an amazing dialog with his smart-and-dangerous new superior –his antagonist,– telling him exactly what his higher is not: *'I know a leader when I see one, sir'.* Well, I'm not Masterchief John 117, but I do too. Since I first stepped foot on a shooting, I knew what I wanted. Just to be the freaking leader. The Masterchief of the content, the ruler of the shooting, the editing, the decisions, the whole show. Not less, probably more if I'd do things right -it didn't look that difficult then. That was an ambitious goal that fueled me early in the game; that, and the fact that it is a really cool industry, is it not? But in those times I couldn't realize how freaking hard the journey is for the one in charge. Masterchief and any other hero knows exactly what it means. And yes, let's face it, sometimes the journey sucks.

Being the one with the whole picture in mind –the boss, the ruler of whatever you are creating– is a blessing and a nightmare. This chapter is about the common elements needed to become the mastermind mind, the one who has the vision, leads the process, and makes it happen, despite activities, crafts, or industries. To be the architect behind anything new in the world is a major task. It doesn't matter if you are building a house, lifting clay, launching a skin product, killing covenants, or creating a piece of content. This chapter has the keys to become a mastermind mind in any creation.

There are three major elements that will make you not only survive but succeed in the mastermind business: **knowledge, skills,** and **attitude**, in such a high amount that only a few will make it. Skills and knowledge are the easy part; attitude is the tricky one. To make the dream possible, there are lessons you can only get by walking the walk. Pick a hero and see their journey; it is pretty similar to the one you are facing. Heroes like Masterchief will chase opportunities with and without success, reinforcing that mastermind attitude until the opportunity to hit again arrives. In your case, you can change the covenants for the creation journey, and if you develop that mastermind mind, your success is guaranteed.

FIRST STEPS, SIMPLE STEPS, LIFELONG LEARNINGS

Less than two summers after the first Star Wars premiere, my mum -teacher- told my dad -photographer- '*Daniel, the kids need to learn a trade this summer, you never know what life is going to bring...*' Smart woman, mum. When technology made it possible to record video on a tape without being wired to a studio or a truck, my father acquired a professional portable video system, like many other photojournalists in those times. We were able to go anywhere and tape anything, as long as it was no longer than 20 minutes, which is all the tape allowed. Can you imagine what that meant for a 15-year-old kid who, not long ago, was creating a Star Wars sequel with two audio cassettes? I was so crazy exited. I learnt so much during those times. We taped a lot of weddings that paid for the expensive equipment, but we also documented unique things, like one of my dad's family businesses. Clay craftsmen from generations. They used a mule to grind the clay and their own legs to move the potter's wheel to create '*cacharros*' (pots and pans) exactly as the Romans did 2,000 years ago. I played in their workshop as a kid and video recorded their art as a teen. A side note about passions, art, and family: Some members of the family sometimes used the term '*botijeros*' to describe their humble activity in a not very positive way. Today my dad's two cousins who pursued that passion are some of the most valuated clay artists in the world. Again, the mastermind mind worked.

Anyone who can see their creations executed as a real thing is a mastermind. Period. Anyone! Fashion designers, set designers, app developers, musicians, artists, entrepreneurs, philanthropists, rocket builders, marketing executives, too! Despite how they got there, the challenge remains the same: making things happen out of pure imagination. Yes, supposedly we all can do that, but you know that is not true. Only a few can showrun not only their lives, but also their creations. Here are the simple, easy, and lifelong steps you must take to become the mastermind mind, the John 117 of your story.

One: **Observe**, learn as much as you can, pay attention to everyone's roles everywhere you go, and never stop doing it. Two: **Search for opportunities**. Within the box, out of the box, or just finding a new box. Don't stop searching. And three: **Always deliver high-level performance**. On every occasion and every task. More important than that: Like in fiction, the heroes must face themselves and also deliver in front of the mirror.

The creator mastermind mind starts with yourself. Yeah, it's hard, and it's demanding, but it is worth it. Creating things straight out of your mind will give you a high you cannot compare to anything, if you learn, try, and perform properly.

YOUR CRAFT, THEIR CRAFT, ALL CRAFTS

Once I realized I wasn't to be a pro-soccer player -*probably by the age of seven or so*- I only wanted to be a boss. Not an astronaut, not a scuba diver, just a boss. I would never be a bureaucrat, or another *oveja mas del rebaño* in a 9 to 5 shift. Nope. I have liked freedom and television since I became conscious. Lucky for me, I started in the business as a 16-year-old apprentice. Back then, I didn't know what a showrunner was, but I paid a lot of attention to those in control, including every department leader. The masterminds behind every team became my obsession. The best among the best I worked with: directors, producers, writers, cinematographers, editors, talent, or production designers, all people who understood the complexity of every part of the process perfectly. All of them! This was not a coincidence. Each one has a story about how they got such a broad view of the business.

When you are in the starting phases of mastermind mind development, take this advice: Pursue your main goal, but be smart. Learn about every position in the creation process, and especially about the way every department deals with their challenges. Start from the bottom. Learning how to behave at any stage is key. From the green room to the set, the editing suite, the executives' offices, and everything in the middle. Say 'yes' to every possibility of contact with any department, and any second-class gig for free on your sight. Yes to short films, video tutorials, and infomercials too. I'm not saying *'do-it-all', I'm saying 'understand-it-all.'* Who is right now around you that you can learn from? Put some energy there. *Piensa un poco y mueve el culo!*

One interesting fact of the Mastermind mind process; maybe you won't notice that you are learning, but you are, despite the lack of sleep, the long shooting days, the waiting hours on set, or whatever your craft requires. While I was acquiring that special wisdom, I wasn't conscious of it, not only because of the long hours and the heavy gear, but also because my life was in survival mode. I was sick then, and the daily dose of medicine was mandatory, but despite that, I got good learnings. Especially if you are starting, you probably still have doubts about what direction to go. Not a problem, that doubt is an asset if used properly –Remember the mutant ring.– One good thing of our business is that every project is different. Be prepared for the lessons in each one of them, observe, and try to explore every angle of your craft; your doubts will become paths.

LEARN IN THE GOOD AND IN THE BAD TIMES

Becoming a mastermind mind requires the ability to get the lessons faster and better than others. Your journey is going to have ups and downs; take advantage of both. Seeing all those smart senior pros during my first apprentice days was a brief taste of what I could achieve in the future if I was smart enough and had enough dope for the journey. Obviously, it didn't work. That decade, I ended up in jail, rehab, and shitty jobs. But despite that, I got valuable learnings from every shitty job and every wild situation. Learnings for storytelling, for survival, and for future creative success.

The art of getting the lessons faster –especially in the bad times– requires practice. Nobody is born as a master in any craft. Here it is again, *otra verdad como un puño* (another straight-up truth bomb). Your first experiences in the creation process are key. They will bring lessons that will remain stubbornly in your creation habits. You won't be conscious of any of those learnings in the moment, because you will be more than busy with the basics.

After high school, I went to the first private audiovisual school in Madrid. For two years, I was both an assistant intern working for free and a pupil not paying a fee. Win-win, but hard as shit. During that time, I went into the empty, well-organized studio in the early mornings and set everything up from top to bottom. From lighting to cameras, mics, connections, control room, dressing rooms, props, and others. Whatever the hell was needed for the daily shooting plan. Of course, I had to put it all back in place every night. It was the best training camp ever designed for future entertainment masterminds. I ended up also assisting in real productions, but that involved traveling, and when your body and performance depend on a daily stop into your dealer's place, you have a problem. I left the school/production house after running out of medicine on a few occasions. My dependent body and mind didn't permit me to enjoy my passion while travelling my country. It is going to sound contradictory, but the following gig implied travel again. I accepted it not because I was healthy, but because I was traveling with my homies, which meant dope was guaranteed. Besides the omnipresent weddings, my next paid job was in the music industry. A blessing gig that taught me **The Golden Rules of Showbusiness**.

For two summers, I toured with some of the biggest mainstream artists in Spain: Sabina, Mecano, Gabinete, Alaska, Danza Invisible, La Frontera, or Heroes del Silencio, among others. We did it with the very first 'turbo sound system' ever sold in the country. Allow me a little *live music archeology* moment, it is relevant. That turbo-sound shit was the highest PA volume gear ever used on tours, and the heaviest too. Music taught me a lot about how to move weights in every condition –stages in castles over hills with narrow streets that no f**king truck can go through– but it also taught me about showbiz, live events, talent, planning, stage lighting, and rock'n'roll life. Feel free to use your imagination and *"Trainspottingize"* the scenes we experienced in those tour trucks and venues' back-stages. *Una banda de descerebrados de barrio* from that side of the highway, some still in high school or recently dropped out. Too much, too soon. The mastermind mind behind the live sound company was the super smart oldest brother of my close friends Francis and Jesus, the Bracero brothers. They led the squad of young passioned seekers from the hood. Teens, addicts, party animals, and dangerous, but we were also freaking good in our shit, devoted workers, and good people. The rock'n'roll life didn't last too long, of course; heroin won again, this time also taking the lives of some musicians and close friends. Despite the good and bad times, the pain, and the losses, I got to learn with my homies **The Three Golden Rules of The Entertainment Business**. These are the most important procedures anyone must follow:

1. **You show up on time,** no matter how wild the previous hours were.

2. **You deliver**. Period. Showbiz comes with the most challenging demands and long waiting times. It is pure creation, it is slow. When it is your time to perform, you and your team rock it. Important side note! If you are the mastermind mind, you deliver 24/7. Period again.

3. **The show must go on.** You adapt to the circumstances and make it happen. Do you need a *period* here?

It's not that complicated a set of rules to call them 'Golden', don't you think? It feels like it's common sense in every activity under the sun: be on time, do your work well, and adapt when needed. The problem is that showbusiness is not under the same sun as everyone else. It is a parallel universe you can't compare with any other. When a novice mastermind mind swears those three basic rules, it is for life, and no novice has freaking idea what that carries.

After that short presence on stages, I found my way back to work in town. I did some gigs in news, mostly sports and celebrities. Not as fun as a real production shooting, but still content. I did also some pro editing gigs in super-expensive post-prod suites. For a lot more money, I have to say. The money became heroin. It disappeared in hours, but everything else I took advantage of during the bad times is still here. It took me decades to get out of that drama and to realize this: If you really want to achieve your goals, to pursue your dreams, to finally get there, it doesn't matter how shitty your current situation is, only how much you want it.

Like in the fictional hero's cases, to become a mastermind mind requires winning a lot of battles. Be smart and start with those you can win easily. Get to work and remember this while you advance slowly towards your objectives: Despite good or bad times, the day is full of small victories. Make them count. Even if your main goal is temporarily stopped, or if you are, as I've been many times, trapped by depression, anxiety, addiction, or grief, the tiny victories are key. Keep one thing in mind: credits with the small victories are only valid if YOU are the one in control. Getting felicitations from your boss about the last meeting is not the real victory. The real victory is all the things you did before. What you did to deliver in that meeting are your small victories. From jumping out of bed with the first alarm to that last change in the closing paragraph. In the bad and in the good times, small victories are doing both: training you for what is coming, and giving you the strength to win in the future big battles. And they will come! Train yourself. Winning in the little things under our control is any mastermind mind's first mission.

TECHNOLOGY & OPPORTUNITIES: RISKY BUSINESS

Believe it or not, technology was the final step in my transformation from a grab-any-gig roadrunner storyteller to a real showrunner –let's say from regular mind to mastermind mind. Can you believe it? Technology!! One of the skills on my dark list that I never mastered made me a content creator with a content house. *Manda huevos* (wtf) Despite my fear of tech, I got one of those revolutionary tech waves, I learnt how to surf it, and I succeeded. What is coming now is like that, on steroids. It is not bullshit, the world is going to change drastically, and the changes are based on something that most of us can even understand. I never liked technology, nor science, nor math. In high school, I chose *letras puras*, which means Latin, Greek, history, literature, art, and Spanish language. No numbers at all! No math, no physics, no electronics. When the moment of facing the electronic devices used for video and audio came, with only experts around me, I felt small and stupid. *Attitude* was the tool for me to overcome my machine-fear, and *passion* for storytelling was the engine that fueled that attitude.

Among all the shitty things I have had to endure to become a content creator, getting into electronics and physics was one of the hardest. For John 117, catching up with technology is as simple as a system update. For me it was a nightmare. Engineering is not my thing, never was, but I went from total ignorance and refusal to qualified expert, so, you can do it too. The current invasion of super artificial intelligence (AI) technologies will overwhelm us for years. It is already impossible to keep up, let alone to understand it all. The good news is that there is no need to get distracted by that. Find and pursue your passion, and the technology will come to you naturally. Have the right attitude, and the technology will not only serve you, but give you amazing opportunities. There is no way the showrunners of the future, the mastermind minds behind the forthcoming narratives, media business, and future awards winners shows, will make it without technology. Find your way.

Stop for a second and think about the opportunities that are coming with AI specifically for your craft. Research, read, think, and dream about the future. Tele-transport the next few lines to the current times, and you will see how broad and bright your future is, with just pursuing your passion with the right approach. In regard to machines, passion gave me the attitude, and the attitude gave me the skills. Even with no education on physics and electronics, I understood what the machines did and how to use them creatively to my advantage. Thanks to my dad, the school, and my first boss, I became one among the handful of people in Madrid than knew how to dissolve from video source A to video source B. It's easy nowadays, but in those times, you needed a super expensive technology that only a few freaks understood. What differentiated me from the other 99'9% of the kids around was the fact that, in the eyes of the employers, at least I knew something about storytelling and operating a machine, even without any understanding. They hired me and tech-trained me. I grabbed every learning opportunity, despite needing to keep feeding my receptors with dope. To overcome my tech fear, here are the gigs I did in those 'uneducated' times: I sold and installed professional video cameras, editing systems, and complete studio control rooms –with video mixers, digital effects consoles, time base correctors, and more obsolete shit. Crazy guys, considering I had no previous education. What is shocking is that the same technology I was fighting with brought me the biggest 'firsts' of my career. A bit later, in the digital revolution, how I used the new equipment available made such a difference that I also got my first show on air. From intern to the mastermind mind thanks to some *hierros* (devices) that couldn't do shit without power. Crazy. Unanimated objects made my career possible. Most of the biggest steps in my livelihood are linked to technology, something I feared in the beginning. Overcoming your fear requires effort, but the effort is built on passion. Don't be afraid. Make the move, explore, research, be the rookie, be bold, risk your chips on exploring tech instead of flooding your dopamine with fast food, social media screens, porn, dope, or whatever your thing is.

Despite all our contradictory cycles, the lack of education, and the fears about technology, it is as simple as making the first step. Once the first electronic device had power and show me what kind of things the machine was able to do, I was in. My storytelling dream was closer with those tools. The outcome for you? We are living in a fast-paced time where only **passion** and **attitude** can help you to navigate both the times and its consequences. Time to be bold.

SHOWRUNNER BOLDNESS

Anyone ambitioning a mastermind mind needs another ingredient for the 'creating-things-out of-their-brains' part: A certain amount of the right boldness. Where can you find it? Let's assume you already have the passion. How can you get the courage needed for the journey? How can you work out the perfect intrepid attitude? It's a hard topic for someone like me, who never liked to think too much about myself and always hated personal commitments and New Year's resolutions. Attitude is a very intimate thing. It is a 'me' thing, which is about me. Shit, too much 'me' for me. But again, somehow, I developed a way. When making a plan, a to-do list, an important pitch, or an executive decision, you first face your own inner stuff. What you think about yourself; the fears, the insecurities, the bad and good experiences, and of course, how you have reacted so far. That is a heavy weight to carry when approaching a task. And the task of finding opportunities in this business is outstanding. It doesn't matter how good you are; there is no way you are going to survive as a creator without a little bit of the proper 'me' attitude.

Reader, you are already a storyteller. Now, let's exercise and visualize a scene: Create a character, your own hero, a rising content creator who has been kept out of society for some time. How old is your hero? What's their basic background? Imagine your protagonist is being freed out of a couple of years of isolation. It's your hero, pick something: Alien abduction, sickness, jail, cult, or spiritual retreat. They spent years completely cut off from society, with no contact with anything. Imagine your hero was a streamer before, or an actor, an editor, a music producer, an artist, a journalist... pick yours and think about it. Totally gone. Imagine your hero's first contact with the current world, given the current tools. Think about their feelings when seeing the ways technology and life have evolved. Keep that feeling of your hero being 'lost' for a while and remember it for later.

My created hero is myself. The moment I got out of rehab, my situation was real, and it looked ugly. Courage and stigma won't mix well. It is difficult to find the boldness needed to put yourself out there when you are carrying a heavy load. I was so committed to the cause of creation that I put the stigmas from all that mental health shit –and their consequences– in the bottom of my backpack and made the decision: nobody should ever know. The decision was the right one then –I mean putting the load in the backpack. But then the 'nobody ever' part was a mistake.

Let me ask you about your hero now. What weight do they carry from the past? What experience or secret does your hero need to put in their backpack? Is there any heavy weight to consider? I'm talking about all those things we carry but won't share. That is the first act of boldness they must face. The time I put my backpack over my shoulders and went straight towards my ambitious goals, I feared failing more than anything, and I had only the very basics; a girlfriend I hadn't seen in two years, a very modest roof prepaid for two months, and a few ex-addicts and addiction therapists as my contacts in town. I'm telling you: Your hero can make it, regardless of how bad things look right now. Mine looked quite challenging from today's perspective, and now I am writing these words from the south side of the Beverly Hills. Is your character starting or re-starting? What is their first act of boldness? Are they in a small town or in the buzziest city? Does it look difficult? Feel impossible? Let me share with your hero some survival tricks that have helped reinventing myself a few times. There is discomfort in the process, but you and your hero –passioned creators both– already know that discomfort is better than pain, so let's focus on the task: When you desperately need to start or re-start career or life in a short period, you rather use your boldness –and energy– wisely. But where?

YOU

Your self-care, the real one, from exercise to eating, to 'me time.' Please don't get confused about what qualifies as 'me time.' Abuse of screens, comfort food, porn, shopping, or getting high are consider shady medicines to subsist when in survival mode. That is not considered 'me time'. Advice: Push your hero to start shifting towards the proper 'me time' thing.

THE MIRROR

I use this trick a lot. Advice: There is pain –not only discomfort– but it is soooooo effective! Any mastermind mind must go through it. Any fictional or real-life mastermind needs to confront themselves in the mirror sooner or later. Save time and pain! Your hero and their opinion of themself in front of the mirror matters. My recommendation is to make your hero look at the mirror calmly at least once a week. Are they on track towards their goals? If the answer is 'just a little', good news, it is enough. If the answer is 'not now' because your star is busy surviving, it's ok too. It doesn't need to be all perfect. If your hero is in survival mode, make them use the mirror daily. When looking at those familiar eyes, your hero needs to see that they still want to pursue creation and a better life.

We are how we are. We 'the makers,' the creators, are ambitious, lazy, tough, talented, resilient, weak, stubborn, fragile, and way more. Every contradiction possible exists inside each one of our bodies. We all know that depending on the times, doing our 'best' looks tiny comparing with the size of our goals, but if it is there, it exists, and it's you. So, go on, keep walking! You are moving towards those goals, even if it is just a quarter of an inch per week in a 5-mile run. The time for longer steps will come.

I bet some of your heroes are thinking: *'Boldness means spending energy on 'me' and looking in the mirror to see failure? Ok, great, next?* When you struggle for basic survival, managing your energy is tricky. To put food on the plate and pay the rent, I was working daily in a cleaning company, breaking my back sweeping a soccer stadium, among some other similar challenging, nasty locations. It was tough to grab my resume and visit the production companies in town after work. But I did it. I met the owners and gave them my CV in person. It was even harder to get an appointment with one of the three local networks' HR personnel, but the boldness was there.

THE VOICES INSIDE

Here's another useful trick to cultivate your mastermind mind. You'll need the mirror for this one, too. Remember the character Masterchief John 117 and think about your hero while reading these words: **When you think you have nothing, you still have yourself.** It's an important lesson that any protagonist will only get after losing everything. Having enough resilience to make it in the mastermind mind's arena starts and ends in the mirror. When the times are good, the voices inside are cool. You can even ignore them. But when the shit comes, the ignored voices inside you are not cool at all, and *cuando la mierda te llega al cuello* (when the shit is in your ears) the only solution will be only paying attention to the voices inside.

In one of those moments where things weren't easy, I took the mirror shortcut. After a first round of interviews trying to find a job, there were no answers, and I ran out of boldness. I didn't have enough time, enough freedom, enough money, nor enough energy to pursue what I wanted: a job in a production company or a network. I was not happy at all. Not with me, not with them. The solution? Using the voices inside. I went back to the inner dialog in front of the mirror: *'Cubi, just focus on the most achievable goal. You want to produce commercials, industrials, and television! And not wedding videos, ok. So, should I continue trying the impossible? Or the most probable?'* Who do you think won the debate? Well, I have married hundreds of couples since the voices inside gave me the answer: *'Nobody does wedding videos like you. You know you are going to rock it. The time for the rest will come.'* After listening to the voices, my strategy shifted towards trying whatever opportunity would bring me some creative job asap, with the goal of stopping sweeping soccer stadiums. Tell your hero that even during discouraging times, when they are not that connected with their goals, they can trust the mirror and the voices coming from inside. I did, and it worked.

PERFORMANCE

The road to becoming a mastermind mind is built with performance. For you and your hero, the sooner you apply high levels of performance to every task, the faster things will happen. Yes, every task. And I mean it! When the voices of 'creative job failure' in my head joined the voices of 'consistency' that remained from rehab, they kept the conversation open for some time. It wasn't easy. The voices made me squeeze my broomstick harder and continue the task with a level of precision nobody else would reach in that team. The cleaning contractor loved to hire fresh out of rehab workers because we were very detailed and self-demanding. Where you put your energy is key; how you spend it is also relevant. If you perform at your top while managing your energy properly, regardless of the task and/or good/bad days, your energy is not only going to grow exponentially with every hated task well finished, but it will also amaze you. It doesn't matter what you do. Focus and do it as good as possible. It is the best training for content creation and life. Yes. I assure you, when the moment comes, you will deliver in a way that it would blow your own mind. If you are interested in the brain chemical details of this weird paradox, watch the Huberman Lab guys! It's neuroscience.

I didn't learn that shit from YouTube though. I experienced it during rehab. I applied it afterwards, not because of the energy improvements –I didn't even know about them then– but for my personal high standards. I had the passion, I was properly shaping the attitude, and I was performing. F**k, I still laugh today remembering that I had *ni puta idea* that I was doing everything right. I promise you this: You do your part and the opportunity will come. Mine came as most do. Not as my favorite gig, of course. But everything started from there.

THE FIRST CALL AND THE MAGIC AROUND IT

Take into consideration that while learning how to become a mastermind, the current mastermind minds you will meet on your journey will also pay attention to you. They are already running shows for a reason. They have already learnt how important it is to surround themselves with the right team. Sooner or later, an experienced mastermind mind in search of help will know about you and will offer you an interview. Please don't lose your shit as I did! A few months fresh out of rehab, after disappointing meetings with local networks and production companies, I reached the wedding studios in town. Soon enough, a local photographer called me: if I passed the interview, I'd get my first wedding event, but only as a test of my abilities. It was the first gig after years. The opportunity I was sweeping for! Nerve breaking, but beautiful. As most of us do when facing this kind of situation, I spent tons of energy before the interview and the test dealing with contradictory, painful, and unstoppable inner conversations. One of the voices pictured a bunch of negative outcomes, while the other dreamed with the most beautiful –and impossible– happy endings. It is crazy how fears and dreams collide in those key moments. Lucky enough, I found a way to ignore the inner voices, stay focused on the task, and succeed.

During the interview, I discovered a solution to ignoring the voices' beef and just being myself. Interestingly, it went well. The key to open the 'just be who you are' door came –unconsciously– when the photographer walked me through his studio. As soon as I stepped in, I immediately noticed the differences from his set up to any other photo studio I visited –way too many.– The way he laid out the sets, the type of lighting gear, the unexpected props made me think 'this guy is not like the rest, *como yo*.' Listening to his extremely deep words about lighting, I got trapped by the flow of passion, and my body and mind relaxed for good. That was it! He was as passionate as I was. Holy shit! We were closer than I thought. That realization was like an anti-anxiety pill. The moment I felt our shared passion for visual storytelling, everything changed. Minutes later, he gave me the schedule for the test and showed me the gear.

The shooting test was a bit more challenging, mostly because it is difficult to find a shared passion with the priest, bride, groom, and hundreds of guests looking at you. Under that Spanish summer temperature, in the altar of a medieval church, in front of a crowd, with the anxiety of three years without touching a video camera, the battle in my head was won by the Spanish summer heatwave, and the negative voices took advantage of it. Right before the bride made her walk in the church, the photographer and his team looked at me with concerned eyes. I think it was more about me not fainting from dehydration over the bride than about the quality of my shots. Their expression somehow woke me up. For some reason my mind decided to put away all the negative thoughts. All the shit inside my mind –wet outfit and body odor included– got transformed into building the most beautiful wedding scene I could imagine. That was the call: just focus on the story you want to tell. The heat, the fears, the voices, all disappeared. While I was physically recording, I was mentally editing each shot, imagining the slow motions, the music, the cutaways, the inserts, when to use the priest's words, or what kind of pause I'd include here. I was creating, I was in the moment, and I was executing. I imagined, shot, and edited in my mind, and that was the way to overcome both the sweats and the negative voices inside. I performed.

Some days after the photographer watched some edited minutes of the wedding, and right away he offered me the whole season (around 40 events that year), but I still had to continue sweeping. It wasn't enough money, nor continuity. Sweeping a soccer stadium is not content creation related, but the place where I swept was. For a time, I married couples, sweated, and swept a lot. In a few weeks, the reduced landscape of video professionals in town knew about that guy from Madrid, and the magic came, almost like in an old Disney tale, no princesses and no kisses, but tons of fairy tales.

During that wedding season, and still being a soccer stadium cleaner, I got a call on a lazy Sunday morning from a sports producer having a panic attack. A crew member got sick and they needed someone to operate a camera in a La Liga match in the same freaking stadium I was sweeping. Could I do it?

Was it magic? Yes, and hard work, performance, consistency, and long shitty conversations with the mirror. But it all worked. Since that day, and because of that first performance, I went back to the stadium, but to create content! I couldn't believe how my life was changing. I was finally doing soccer games on live TV, as I always wanted to do. Tell your hero that the magic of creation also affects other areas. One day, I was enjoying the game –and the amazing modern camera I was operating from the side of the field– when the match paused for substitutions. A young kid got into the field with the Real Madrid shirt, another amazing mastermind mind named Raúl. It was his debut with *La Blanca* in a historic game in Zaragoza. Raúl won 17 titles with Real Madrid, among them three UEFA Champions Leagues. Yes, my storytelling soccer dream became real during the Galácticos time. I was working with the biggest stars in the soccer constellation: Raúl, Beckham, Casillas, Zidane, Roberto Carlos, Figo... the list is long and sexy, I would rather stop here.

Your first opportunity won't probably mean your dreamed post, but now you know how to work it out: Observe, ask, learn, connect dots, connect with people, plan, and perform as you never did before. With time, I also developed a procedure to face life-changing job interviews. From the photographer in Zaragoza to line producers, directors, agencies, multinational CEOs, entire boards, presidents, kings, and more. This is what I learnt: The employer and the creator, both of you, are in the room for the Cause of Content. That is the key. Find the shared passion, and once there, just be you. Allow your creativity, experiences, and knowledge of the craft to take over your fears and dreams. If you don't see that passion in the employer, relax, it won't be long. *Aprovecha y aprende!*

CHAPTER 3

What is Your Technology Thing?

ROADRUNNER TO SHOWRUNNER: THE MACHINES MADE IT HAPPEN

Notes

....
....
....
....
....
....
....
....
....
....
....
....
....
....
....
....
....
....
....
....
....

CHAPTER 3

Roadrunner To Showrunner: The Machines Made It Happen

I was twenty-six when I first touched a computer, and I didn't know then that machine would bring me most of the things I was dreaming about. Twenty years later, I created a Facebook account. It was 2006, and I had no idea that the *social media* thing would change the world the way it did. Today, almost 6 billion people around the globe have shifted the way they buy, eat, entertain, fall in love, have sex, gamble, score dope, and vote. Yes, technology matters, and we are looking at it during a crucial moment in human history. What is going to happen in content creation with what is coming? A bunch of good things, and some bad stuff too. Let's assume this: Technology will make the next generation of mastermind minds. The good news is that you are still in control.

So, how should you interact with technology? How can you make it do the things you want? And how can you use technology to get there faster than your competitors? Without realizing it, I had answers for these questions. I did it once: I was faster, better, and different than others. I went from apprentice to master, from fear of homelessness to consistent bank checks. Technology gave me the wings I needed, and you know what? I was blind then; I had no idea that would be the way, literally, no idea. Imagine what you will be able to accomplish knowing the power technology has to make all your dreams come true.

The digital revolution made me a showrunner. I became the mastermind mind behind a little content factory thanks to a few *hierros*. I'll be forever grateful to technology. Maybe that is another reason why I am not afraid of but excited by the upcoming horizon. I am not concerned because I already know what to do to transform machines in storytelling assets at my service. I know I will be able to create better, faster, and in a more satisfactory way. It is only a matter of learning. Machine learning and Daniel learning. It's a long trip though. There are prices to pay, efforts to make, and tons of fun and frustration in the journey.

Tech was the door to becoming a showrunner and a content house owner. It was key in every step. And when I say, 'the steps,' I mean the big ones, those that bring a bunch of 'first' big things for content creators: My first production company, my first national commercial, my first show created and sold –Yeahhhhhh!!!– It is not rocket's science. The new tech wave is going to shake the world in ways we can't imagine. The path is clear now; that's the good thing about wild transformations! Does your hero see it? Their only concern must be themselves. The only thing you can be prepare about the future is yourself. I hope your mastermind mind hero is already starting to connect dots in their brain because the outcome is huge. I became what I always dreamed in a technological revolution –with no previous education. It was hard, but it was easy *también* (at the same time.) There will be a lot of 'firsts' in the next few years –including yours and your hero's. Your successes will depend on your attitude toward tech.

Here is where the tech-opportunity resides: In the case of my hero and I, the 'firsts' came from how we used the tools that the digital uprising brought us. We did things differently and faster than others. If you feel you or your hero should've been into AI by now, and it hasn't happened yet, there's no need for shame. You both still have time. When I started researching and asking about digital video technology, I felt ashamed and lost. I had no idea what a PC exactly was. By the end of my crazy run, over a third of the European population owned a personal computer, and by then I never ever had touched one. At all. *Palabra!* I made it all the way from absolute ignorance to an entrepreneur with one of the first nonlinear editing systems in my country, and later a digitally produced on-air TV show. The run from my first contact with a PC to my first show on air was less than three years. Through some stories of success and failure, in this chapter you will learn how to overcome your tech monsters and make them work for you. You will find clues to make your hero dominate tech, even without touching it. It is already a fact: the future mastermind minds in every field, every industry, every narrative, will be those who will make the best from using their talents in conjunction with the technology available.

TECH EVOLVES AS YOU DO

How far away is your phone now? Probably. Not far. How much does it weigh? Do you know? Of course not! I'm sure some of you can compete for the 'who starts taping faster' world record. I'm not that fast, but man, I feel so light, happy, and amazed every time I record anything with my phone. I am grateful for technology every f****** day. Exercise your imagination, forget your phone for a second and picture a normal shooting day before the big tech revolution erupted. Our gear just to capture 20 minutes of video when I started was a 25-pound camera –for the archeologist among you; a Sony DXC 1610– and a 30-pound portable U-Matic videocassette recorder. Don't forget batteries, tapes, cables, audio gear, and the heaviest tripod in history –I hated that Manfrotto with every muscle of my body. To be able to edit video after that easy shooting time, you needed this: An editing system comprised of one videotape player and one video tape recorder –both big, heavy, and noisy– and a remote-control unit to make them 'insert or ensemble' in the right place, plus the audio and video monitors –not flat screens then– *Por cierto!* (btw) for simple video or/and audio cuts. No transitions, no color effects –*coño*, no effects at all– no crossfades, no graphics. Any addition meant a new specific type of equipment –that's why complex post suites were so expensive. Just the sound of the videotape machines pre-rolling for every cut will blow your mind, so, let's avoid the talk about the +55 pounds on top of you each time you want to record a video clip. Look at your side now. We all have one of those amazing pieces of technology in our hands, most of you since you were born. You have those tools we had multiplied by 2,000, and you also have not one, but multiple outlets where you can display your content. You have everything you need to tell a story in your hand, but get ready, in the next few years machine learning is going to make your device 2,000 times obsolete. You are going to experience more technological revolutions that I did. It is life, it is evolution, and it is exponential.

The 1980s brought us the very beginning of the digital age—first PCs at home, and then the expansion of video-tape camcorders. One in every household! It was an amazing time for electronic multinationals, video clubs, and family memories. The 1990s brought us MTV, digital image, computer graphics, and lighter and better equipment among some other wonders. The 2000s brought the first wave of the big digital democratization: From editing in super expensive –and complex– electronic postproduction suites to doing it digitally on our own personal computer. That was the tech-wave I caught. I paid the price of being one of the first buyers of a videoboard that allowed a PC to digitize, edit, and deliver video in broadcast quality. It was a costly investment in money, energy, and FRUSTRATION. Yes, in caps, frustration at a level anyone born after 2000 would understand. F**k, just a few highlights: No video system would work steady over Windows 3.11. The $3,000 value for nine Gigabytes hard drives –highest capacity available then– were almost the size of a current Apple Studio Max –let's avoid the conversation about its temperature. Finding the audioboard that would work with the configuration was like a peregrination. We tried half a dozen before finally making it.

Yes. It worked. I went through all of it, and the machines brought me not only temporary success, but an amazing way of life. How? With a costly investment in money, energy and frustration, that's true, but also with huge rewards. Seeing your creations evolve for the better with the help of technology is a good high. Seeing your solo initiative growing into a 19-employee company is more than a high. For me it was an undreamt dream only possible through the digital revolution and by collaborating with some other crazy seekers –and wise masterminds.

TECH, LOVE, AND VIDEO TAPES: FINDING YOUR TECH MATE

It doesn't matter if you are already a tech nerd in any area. I'm sure you also have someone who is your 'go to' when things get dirty. For those who are not tech nerds –and never will be– there is only one option to do the things you want to do: Find someone who is already in love with tech and put your energy into creating a language to communicate with your new tech-lover. When I bought a *Perception* videoboard –that was the name of the machine– in Canada and installed it in my PC in Zaragoza, I did what I could by my own, and when shit was covering me –deadlines and new tech are a risky combo– I asked, and asked, and asked, until I found another crazy tech seeker who had bought the same Canadian machine and knew more than I did. From there, work and frustration evolved into work and more work, but the results were exponentially good. Connecting with the right tech-nerd who can understand – and find– new ways that align with your content is key. If your hero is not tech-smart, if they are more focused on the story than on the means, they will need to find their tech-nerd soulmate asap. Mandatory. Especially in the times we are living. Mine was the 117 of digital video, the saver of uncountable computer-crashed-related dramas for uncountable professionals. He was the only engineer in Spain who was dedicating his life to digitally computerize video and online editing. Because of the size of my gamble, I couldn't afford to bring him from Madrid every two days; it was obvious that I needed to understand the basics, which was a scary journey when I looked at Cesar 117's vast knowledge. Communicating with him –I didn't speak tech then– brought me more effort, more time, and more energy, on top of the rest of my responsibilities and goals. Again, it was a journey that only a hunger for storytelling could support. The amazing video content I was able to create when the freaking machine worked brought me the passion I needed to spend hours in front of hundreds of Windows NT crash screens. That won't happen to your lucky hero, but there will be multiple tech challenges. Get ready.

While surviving the mandatory issues of using new technology, there's a big opportunity if you are using those tools before others. For me, that fast pace became money and success. Guaranteed. In a matter of days, when the freaking Perception was steady, I was working with 100 video layers while the rest of the industry needed $1M editing suites to edit with only 4 or 5 layers. Getting ahead of tech means overwhelming superior creative freedom than your competitors. Again, exponentially. The opportunity came immediately. The biggest production companies in town were outsourcing me for complex postproduction pieces. The use of the new technology allowed me to create content **better** than my competitors, and in a matter of months, due to that 'technology high,' I also produced a pilot and sold my first show. You pay the price of being the pioneer; bugs, crashes, money, overheated hard drives, lack of sleep, and a lot of learning, but you also get the reward: You will find gold, especially if you use that new tech to create stories in a way that no competitor is able to do.

Let's go back to your hero now. What field are they in? What do they need to tell the stories the way they want? And to do it better? And faster? From script writing, to audio, editing, producing, shooting, production design, lighting, acting, programming, selling... Everything! This new wave of technology is not a wave; it is a freaking tsunami. A good one, but the premise is totally different. My wave was about learning how to use the new tech; this one is about getting the best from what the machines can learn, which means that the AI tsunami is about understanding how far the machines can go with your help. It is not 'us' using tech. It is 'us' interacting with tech. If your protagonist understands the way of the machines and can think out of the box and connect the dots nobody else did before, your hero will be a very rich asshole on the content creation planet.

SKIING WITH MONKEYS: WHEN PASSIONS COLLIDE

Before finding the promised gold, your hero will face difficulties and small successes. Ask them to be ready. When dealing creatively with technology, hours won't matter anymore. You will lose the sense of time. You won't drink enough, eat well enough, or sleep enough. To survive you will need –more than ever!– some other passions to disconnect and recharge. A personal question for you and your hero: What is your DOC (drug of choice)? I heard that term in a rehab in Florida first, and yes, that is exactly what I am asking, but on the healthy side. Is your hero into surfing? Snowboarding? Pole dancing? What is it you do to disconnect and have fun? There is a real need to keep an eye on it. 'Unwind to succeed' is more relevant than it looks. Weird universe quantum interactions can happen when you do something entirely different than creating content.

My recharging outlets are the beach and the mountains. I learned how to ski after an ACL injury playing soccer in rehab, and I was stupid enough to trade the soccer turf for the slopes. Another 3 major injuries afterwards –but lots of fun also– and skiing is still the way to fill up my batteries and my soul. Sacred, as the Mandalorian way. A religion, almost. I'm the first to arrive, last to leave. What is your side passion, reader? What about your imaginary hero? What are their side recharging activities? What do they like? Rollerblading? Travelling? Chess? There is a golden rule for happiness: Try to get paid for what you love the most. In my case, besides storytelling and travelling, I'd say what I like the most is the mountains, specifically skiing (guys, sex is not included in this category.) The thing is that I'd never considered the possibility of having those two things together. I mean storytelling and mountains, but it came without asking –the undreamt shit again– and here is the twist: It came through technology. Yes, that's what I thought: WTF!!!!

Let your hero know that the consequences of using the new tech sooner, differently, or better are so freaking good that every effort is worth it. For your stars to measure how crazy good, here is a real-life experience about the benefits of using tech **sooner**: The person that connected me with Cesar 117 -my tech-mate- had the same technology I did –Perception videoboard– and they were producing one of the most successful shows the French media powerhouse CANAL+ ever did in Spain. Their success was also based on new technology over new technology. New software over new hardware, a critical combo. In that show, they were able to satirize politics and politicians in a way never seen before; they got with it in a very smart method: the ruthless jokes were created by composing motion graphics and real video from the public appearances of politicians, using only their rotoscoped heads. They created it with some amazing new software nobody knew about. Don't ask me how, but I got a CD with a copy of that software. It was a beta version of an unknown product, called *Dancing Monkeys,* and it had the weirdest interface I've ever seen. We did it again. We stacked our asses to our chairs and explored that thing through frustration and phone calls –no Reddit in those times. With some help, we were finally able to integrate an amazing, never-before-seen motion graphics package in our winter sports pilot. Super cool, extreme graphics for a super cool, extreme TV show. Yes, we sold the series, not only because of that, but it helped a lot. That *Dancing Monkeys* beta software was behind my marriage of two of the things I love the most, skiing and storytelling. When the monkey was baptized and came out to the market, it was called *After Effects,* one of the Adobe family crowns. I still have the CD with that hacked version.

I'm a lucky bastard, *como dicen en mi pueblo 'un capullo con suerte.'* A piece of hardware made me a showrunner with a show on air. A beta software unified my two passions and became a great source of income. But there are more cases. That's the good thing about technology; it never stops. The most important trick we all need to practice with AI is perspective. See every angle of every tool and consider every approach possible to use it at your service.

Does your hero want to know how the premise '*use the new tech sooner, differently, or better*' works? Here is a real-life sample that perfectly combines the 'sooner and differently' parts of the equation: A successful franchise with more than 20 seasons on air. Btw, during the digital revolution, the way I used one of the first digital-tape micro-cameras became a multi-awarded television format –and an outstanding business– but sadly, I wasn't involved. It all happened in front of my eyes, but I didn't see it coming. The multi-awarded/multi-seasoned franchise that became legendary didn't do it because of me nor my footage. Nope. The whole thing started with how someone else looked at that same digital micro-camera with a different perspective than I did.

I bought the mini cam overseas to use for our winter sports TV show. I stacked them to the skier's or the rider's boots or boards, fixed them on their helmets, or put them at the end of a pool. Finally, the wild stuff we were all dreaming of. I'm talking about the late 90's, no GoPro's yet guys, just 11 kilograms of machinery on our backs every time we'd get on the lift. The thing is that the small size and the –almost– broadcast quality of the camera, allowed us to shoot from unseen before angles. I never considered using the camera in any other way than the slopes, but I took my brand-new toy to my first niece's baptism. The day of the event, I drove down the mountains to see *a la familia.* It was a big moment. Despite not practicing any religion, somehow my sister –or my mum– decided to go through the whole Christian liturgy. My niece Luz was being baptized in '*La Virgen De La Luz*', a XII century church in my mum's *barrio.* Her church. I had to be there, and I was there with my super small digital toy, and of course, I used the mini-camara. While I was shooting –joking and invading everyone's space– I was talking with each person on frame, from the other side of the lens. Just my voice, and the POV of the camera I was handling while being silly. It was fun. I edited a cute video from Luz's baptism, and that was all, back to the slopes. We did a lot of cool things with that little new toy, but my sister saw something else. She saw a new language, a new way to tell stories. She made the person holding the camera the narrator of a docu-reality series she was developing, and the narrative perspective shifted, something similar to what I did documenting my niece's baptism, but with more purpose than just family memories. Those two properties that my sister Carolina created, *Mi Camara y Yo* and *Callejeros,* have been on air for +20 seasons, have +20 awards, and several spin-offs. They are forever part of the story of Spanish television. Yes, just because they used the new technology differently and faster than others.

It is clear, new technology will bring new forms of storytelling. Just be smarter than I was. Look at it from <u>every angle</u> from the very beginning. I can assure you today that your creator mind will be blown away several times with your hero's upcoming wild stuff. In my experience, despite the wave your hero catches, there are two reasons behind all those *first-time* career successes: One, I used the new technological tools before, better, or differently than the rest of the creators around me. And two, when using the new tools 'differently' I also found new market opportunities. It is evolution, no need to fear it. Technology is a matter of basic understanding, passion for your craft, and the right use of your energy.

CHAPTER 4

Do You Know How to Build a Perfect Team?

THE PEOPLE BESIDE THE MACHINES

Notes

CHAPTER 4

The People Beside The Machines

As a content lover I know you like movies about heists. Not one of us would ever miss a good story about a bunch of super-skilled misfits united under the lead of a crazy mastermind for the purpose of making money, saving the world, or taking revenge. Pick one: Ocean's Eleven, Baby Driver, Inception, Reservoir Dogs, Snatchers, The Italian Job... It's a long and sexy list. The characters surrounding the mastermind minds in heists always have amazing talents. Tech-nerds, pilots, masters of disguise, convincing liars, pocket lifters, tough guys. All of them sexy as shit, all of them the best in their businesses, all of them with the same hunger for success.

To become the mastermind mind, you need a team. If you or your hero are just starting, you may need a team better than you and as passionate as you. Not an easy task. Just like in the movies, finding your perfect gang is an art and a gamble. I'd love to see how Danny Ocean put together that team in Ocean's Eleven and how and where the members of Cruise's *Mission Impossible* got together! No mention the *Reservoir Dogs*... I'm a prequels lover by default; all those cases are quite promising. I want to see the moment of creation, when and how the mastermind met the skilled ones. In my own movie, after rehab, I realized that if I wanted to start making money from producing content, I needed skilled people alongside the technology. Good people, if possible. Those who would boost my already crazy ideas with their own. This chapter is about combining individuals with creativity, business, and performance. They are great topics separately, but quite risky when put together.

Surrounding yourself with the perfect team depends on multiple combinations, all of them starting with your ultimate goal. If your hero is creating their own ideas and setting up their own small content house, that is one way. If your hero is being called to direct or showrun an existing intellectual property for a big company, that is a totally different one. The decisions about your team are also going to depend on factors as the genre and specifications of the show and its size— in budget, challenges, and consequences. Your hero will have to consider their and their client's expectations. Ultimately, your hero must consider their mastermind mind's own strengths and weaknesses. Too many critical factors. Too many possibilities to mess it up. In my case, I needed to add another factor: I didn't know anyone in the industry in the town I was living in.

MANDATORY PRIZES TO PAY

When I told you about my digital revolution journey, I didn't mention my 're-education.' The real one, with teachers, books, and so on. By the age I should've been finishing post-graduate studies, I was still in the junkie business, living in the streets, or worse. When I came back to life, I never thought about claiming my diploma, didn't have time for that. I was too busy surviving and pursuing the 'future'. Despite the lack of money, it was mandatory that my first investment out of rehab should've been a personal computer, and there were a lot more investments afterwards: a professional camera, a linear editing system, an online editing system –the freaking Perception videoboard– and on, and on. Yes, before and during the digital revolution, this business was expensive –make a note for your hero's future tech revolutions. I had too many bills to pay and too many things to learn. I was surviving by multitasking guerrilla style. But I was very independent and happy! No bosses, no bullshit, but no help either. Alone. On my own. For a couple of years I was editing weddings, producing industrials, doing gigs as an assistant in any freaking department, offering any postproduction service, and more. On the weekends, I was shooting soccer and weddings, and on top of that, I was also covering 24/7 news for two agencies. If anything happened in the region, my phone would ring. I use another sports expression to describe that lifestyle: *agarrar todos los balones que caigan cerca.* Like on a basketball court, if the ball came close, I'd grab it if at all possible. Period.

I met some of my future team members in the most relevant gigs I was hired for. For the rest, I was mostly alone. Soon, I needed to be in two places at the same time, and the 'finding the one that can cover me' tour started. During that time, I realized I needed two important things: A 'modern' technological education and a network of creators who could either help me or hire me. Pros, amateurs, wannabes, all of them!

Take a look at your hero's situation now. What are they lacking? Do they have enough contacts? Enough education for the current times? I only needed a minute in the mirror to answer those questions— "no," and "no." So, I networked and connected with a lot of cool people. I also considered continuing my studies but putting the money I didn't have into school took many conversations with the *espejo.* Finally, I decided to sign up for a yearlong digital audio course. Weird, I know, but it worked. While learning digital audio, I realized that some of those individuals –usually the future masterminds in the room– were the perfect candidates for my 'Daniel's Eleven' mini clan. That was another reason I checked in another couple of interesting courses. *Dos pajaros de un tiro.* Skills and networking.

What abilities does your hero need to catch up with? What are the ways to get there? What are the options to learn? Who do they know in that landscape? What kind of mastermind minds are around them? The first mandatory prices to pay for anyone aspiring to mastermind the show are connections and education. It is not only the embryo of your future usual suspects team, but also a source of potential clients, a way to measure your knowledge of the business, your skills, and ultimately your content. Your hero must remember that the world of creation is always evolving. To make it and to stay ahead, they must commit to lifelong learning and lifelong dialoging. Period. Shitty prospect, I know. Probably that is why there aren't so many that make it. Force your hero to learn however they want, though it is obviously better with people around. Shared passions are a good start for future profitable connections. Make your hero understand that expanding their mastermind minds is crucial, as is staying updated with trends, technologies, people and methods in their craft.

THE BEST BY DEFINITION

Despite the type of content your hero is creating, despite owning the intellectual property or being hired, despite clients' or investors' expectations, and despite challenges or consequences of failure, they must always aspire to surround themselves with the best. After identifying the profile needed for a specific role, the size of the budget will determine what level of 'the best' your hero can approach. Here is my suggestion: Think big. Think huge. I have always thought big, –Let's blame this time my parents and my teachers. I recommend starting the list with the very best. You never know! Maybe a weird universe alignment between the type of project, the people involved, the timing, the shared passion, the shared goals, the 'I always wanted to do that,' or even weirder factors can find a perfect equilibrium, and you can have the ONE you couldn't even dream of. Just put the name on the list. From the best in the world to the best in the continent, the country, the region, your city, your *barrio*, your school, or your block. Find the best talent for that specific task. Be Danny Ocean in the time before the movie starts, when he started building his team. List your position needs and the best names. Then consider ways to make it work. I found my all-stars first team in those classrooms I went back to and in those wild shooting gigs I went through.

FEARS AND YEARS: THE SELF SWOT ANALYSIS

The time is here. Your hero got the final confirmation; the show is on. The day to start interviewing team leaders is scheduled. Now what? A mastermind mind like mine is powered by passion but also by fear. For reasons beyond my trauma and my own ignorance, every time that I am going to produce and deliver a show, my mind will go simultaneously in two directions: How to tell the best story possible and how to avoid jail. Exactly like the mastermind mind in the movie *The Hit,* Robert De Niro's character in his last big heist, with Al Pacino as the cop after him. I'm De Niro, Al Pacino is failure. And I'd do whatever it takes to avoid it. This is the process to follow: Before going through the list of candidates, analyze the riskiest elements of the project.

In my case, they are always based on fears & years of experience. What are the few things I cannot mess up this time? Make your hero go through the project with the eyes of the mirror. What is their real fear? Is it a complicated narrative structure? Is it an untested mechanic in a talent show? Is the ambitious lighting going to fracture the daily plans? Whatever it is, make them identify what they honestly fear, and start going through your team dream-list from there. There will be a lot of clarity after the exercise. *Por cierto!* I told you my mind goes towards two directions. Fear is one, the other is greatness.

MY OUTLAW RECRUITING SYSTEM

There are too many experts on recruiting and human resources already. I said before that my tips are not in the books, and what I really meant is 'my tips will add efficiency to those in the books'. Don't ignore years of studies about human behavior, please, just consider adding my recipe to your mastermind mind decision-making process. Before your hero starts focusing on the characteristics and differences between the team profiles they'd need–collaborators, employees, freelancers, partners, or whatever–before making distinctions between peers or co-workers; before being focused on titles and positions, try to make your hero think about the common factor: We are all humans. People. That's it. I've been putting teams together since I was a little kid. Street soccer, police and thieves' games, summer camp activities, school homework, and cannabis distribution. I did it based on winning, having fun, and being close to those I liked. When I started creating content as a way of living, I had to change my approach. I always consider myself very lucky with that first team in Zaragoza, the one that brought me the first show on air, then the second, then the second season of the first, and so on. We were the freaking Ocean's Eleven, twelve, and thirteen in the region, the Cubillo's nineteen at certain point. Analyzing later what we did right in those times, I put together a Cubillo's system to evaluate anyone's capability as a booster or a ballast in the pursuit of my content. Of course, I messed up a few times. But I've had issues with only a handful of the positions I've hired, and I've hired a lot. After thousands of hours on air, and some of the most relevant shows in TV history, less than half a dozen of times have I misevaluated someone. It is my fourth decade doing this, and my slip-ups weren't because of the system failures; they were because of my mistakes applying the formula. I told you I'm not a numbers person! Before going into the specifics, one more hint: There is no way to evaluate your candidate without connecting on some other levels, the human resources approach won't be enough. You share a common passion. After asking the basic questions, try to offer the candidate some of your own real passion, and see where it goes.

There are two basic filters in my recruiting technique. Anyone I am going to work with needs to be among the best, of course, but it requires a bit more than just having an amazing talent. Let me tell your hero in a very briefly way: When you work in this business, you know shit will come. Mandatory. Sooner or later, in every production or circumstance. It's life. When that happens, the pure talent of your team and collaborators is not the key anymore. You can have the most amazing DP, writer, producer, or whatever. But when the shit comes, there's no time for BS, and clients and money to lose. To avoid the ultimate failure, the first question was clear for me: Is the candidate a follower of **the showbiz golden principles**? (Always on time + Performing at their best + Making it happen regardless). That is my first filter. The second is easy to formulate but complicated to evaluate: Do they have **enough passion** for creation to be by my side –helping– when the shit comes? Once those two questions are answered positively in my mind, pure **Talent** takes over. How good are they in their craft? Let's say someone's talent serves your purpose; please consider the other factors that person can bring to your squad. When embarking yourself on real production, in weekly or daily content delivery, you really need to trust your team members. Is this person trustworthy enough in a high-pressure show delivery situation? Your mastermind mind hero needs to **know how much they can trust that team member.** The last two key elements in my recipe for hiring are **goodness** and **potential to grow**. Is this person a good human being? For me, this is key. Every time I ignored that factor, I went through pain and losses, and yes, sometimes I still ignore it because I think I'll be able to handle it. Nope. Tell your hero not to ignore it. And the last factor is about the room for growth in the future in their area of expertise, or in any other need I may have. This is as important as the rest. Ambition is in my default settings, and I tend to think everyone is as ambitious as I am, but they aren't. Not considering that factor in a new team member would be stupid. It's that simple.

Let's assume that the candidates follow the Showbiz Golden Rules. Here is the summary formula to apply afterwards –don't get used to it!– Your heroes would need to ruminate on the weight of each factor in each specific project, as they are all different. What percentage of the decision for the specific need is assigned to Passion, Talent, Trust, Goodness, and Potential? Once that is clear, make them evaluate every candidate in each of those disciplines, using values from 0 to 10, and do the numbers! The key to succeed with the system is to be brutally honest with you, your challenges, and your circumstances when deciding the weight of each factor, on each project, on each particular candidate. Learn and apply this system or make your own! But be wise when picking the humans who will share your creative journey.

THE FIRST TIMER'S CAUSE

When building a team –and spending time, energy, and resources to make it work– your hero has to pay attention to the apprentice factor. See the samples in fiction: Qui-Gon and Obi-Wan in Phantom Menace; Daniel and Mr. Miyagi in Karate Kid; Matt Damon and Robin Williams in Good Will Hunting. Apprentices who will level the master and more. In every department in the complex universes of creation, there are beginners that stand out from the rest–apprentices that sooner or later are meant to be the future mastermind minds in their craft. Before going to the specifics of the first timers –anyone new in a higher position– let me give your hero an important recommendation: Observe and spend time with the newcomers. Someone gave you your first opportunity; be the one who gives opportunities to the newbies. For me this is a principle of the spirit of creation, and probably also in any form of endeavor. Among those I have given the first opportunity in a higher role, some of them are in the top 10 professionals in Spain, Mexico, or the US Hispanic market: among the 10 best Directors, 10 best hosts, 10 best DP's, 10 best writers, 10 best content multinationals leaders, and so on! If I'd include those that told me 'No', I would've given first opportunities to almost 30% of the current top

professionals in the territories I've been working. Ask your hero to *afilar el ojo* (sharpen the eye). Creativity is a gift that very few people have. When you find someone who scores highly in at least three of the five recruiting factors (Passion, Talent, Trust, Goodness, and Potential) but is not still leading a department, push for them to step up. I have pushed a lot of first timers in my work, including positions that would mean tons of conversations and some drama with the network or the client. The reason? Not only because they deserved it –they were ready, I trusted them, and they served my purpose– but also because there was some revenge on it. Remember I said I wanted to be a top commercials director for a while? I wasn't on the A list to direct top brands/ high budget pieces. No one fought for me, so I never directed any of the big spots. Meanwhile, I was successfully directing 10 commercials per year for the same agency, same client, but the low-cost stuff. They wasted an opportunity to test new talent, and I found a new path on television thanks to that. Last recommendation for your hero: Have a mental list –usually is very short– of the best potential first timers for every department or any other need you may have.

TALENTED PEOPLE, TROUBLED PEOPLE

There are many chances that your hero will clash with their team members, despite applying the system perfectly. My goal is for your hero to minimize the chances of running into conflict. Once again, the key lies inside you. Make your hero know themselves perfectly. Make them analyze their own behaver when the shit comes. I started to know myself for real in the critical times, and it was not nice. You, as a mastermind mind, are among the first troubled people in this equation. Pretending you are not is a childish waste of energy and resources. Pretending so others will accommodate your personality is not only selfish but stupid. I've seen many times the best in their field failing dramatically after a troubled mastermind mind crisis. On set, in a writing room, and at the top offices. In my case, the issue was the ratio between how committed and demanding I was with myself and with others. The combo of **determination, dedication, and self-demand** –DDS– between myself and the rest of the team brought pain, suffering, and a waste of precious energy. I was always expecting at least a 10:9 ratio, the first number being me, the second the team member. Yeah, now it looks like a stupid expectation, but I was so focused on the results I wanted that I couldn't even consider that. For a while, I had disappointments and totally avoidable conflicts. No idea about your hero, but in my case, the problem was the combination of passion, needs, and personality. That combo made me perform higher than anyone around me, and for longer than anyone too. I give my all, and I will, always, but when it is my own show, my reputation, my money, and my future, my DDS level will be always over 10. And then I realized that the people around me, those amazing talents making my dreams possible, could never have the same amount. I couldn't expect the same DDS level with or without an extra bonus. The moment I recognized and corrected my approach; my life was better; I was able to put more energy into creation. Better content won the battle against conflicts and personalities. Creator, have you considered your hero's personal challenges dealing with others? Your mastermind mind leaders will always be among the higher DDS scores in the room. It is easy to collaborate with talented people with a similar level of determination, dedication, and self-demand, but the opposite is the norm. Make your hero conscious of this. Once they are sensible to the DDS level of the specific team member, avoiding frustration first and conflicts later is guaranteed.

Let's talk about your hero's teams. Any idea who is in your hero's Eleven? Twelve? Do they have specific names? Do they aspire to have the best in their craft? Please let them know two more important considerations about talented people. For your hero's health first, and for their success afterward, from now on, how they extract the best from their team and machines will make the difference. We all know horrible stories about endeavors failing from crises with close collaborators, partners, friends, family members, spouses, and more, whose relationships went to hell before, after, or during a challenging project. When your hero assembles their team, there will be colleagues, of course, and possibly friends, exes, and more. It doesn't matter; they are all humans. I'm not sure if they are all talented, but I know they are all troubled. Make your hero aware of one of the worst viruses for a mastermind mind: Association Induced Temporary Blindness. Very corrosive. Very dangerous. It doesn't understand, it just kills. Mastermind mind blindness with team members will slaughter everything, sooner or later, despite friendships, partnerships, marriages, successes, and debts. But the risk is worth it. Working with the best and avoiding the Association Induced Temporary Blindness virus means amazing content and a good life to enjoy it.

Last consideration. This business is an art. Most of us have *alma de artista* –meaning complicated personalities– and when a mastermind minds finds team collaborators who have even more troubled personalities than them but are so freaking good at their craft, then the only option is to make it work. If your hero wants the best in the business, dealing with complex personalities will become one of the most important tools for their success. I will tell you more later. For now, just remember this: Your content creator mastermind's hero must find ways to extract the best of the artist on time and budget. The show must go on, and now it is your responsibility.

LISTENING TO THE ROOM FOR GREATNESS

This section takes us to the movies again. Go back to your selected mainstream film in the heist, save the world, and revenge categories. Anyone with a band of talented-troubled members before the big hit. Pick your Fast, your Furious, your Ocean, your Mission, or your own, and remember the scenes where the master plan is being laid out right before striking, those scenes where each of the gifted misfits explains their part and exposes their challenges. Great storytellers have made historic passages that express talent, excitement, precision, efficacy, difficulty, hope, doubts, and fear in ways that I can't even dream of. All those scenes share a few common elements, starting with the voice. One at a time, no more. Very often, each team member's voice –one after the other– break down the plan while the mastermind mind listens, observes, and maybe adds some essential details. Take the scene to real life. Your hero not only needs to know beforehand whatever each department leader has to say, but also to look, listen, and feel the room to detect not just problems or mistakes, but any symptom of potential greatness.

Think for a second about what is happening in that space. You or your hero made it. You are the mastermind mind running the show, the one who has put together that collection of super talented misfits to finally execute a well-thought plan. Allow your hero to take care of every element of that scheme, but make them aware of something else. That same room that is going to witness –for sure!– frustration and drama, at a certain point, will also witness opportunities to improve your hero's original idea to never imagined levels. Make your stars follow whatever well-explained procedures they like to go through in the meeting –the show rundown, the script, whatever it is– but make them also aware of the unseen elements in the room. In content creation, magic rests not only in planning and execution, but also in the mastermind mind perception and openness. You must train your hero to detect the possibility of something truly extraordinary for their story. During meetings, your star is the one with the radar. Your characters must listen to the room from inside and from above. They must detect all those team members with the faster buzzing neurons in the chamber and ask them what the hell they are thinking. Your hero's first moment of creation was probably in solitude. But they are not alone anymore. They have the best team possible. It is in those rooms –with the rest of the team– where your hero's story can touch the sky. I lived it with that, a younger-than-me team that took me from sweeping stadiums to showrunner and owner of a production house in less than 3 years. It still sounds crazy to me. It also happened with my first prime time scripted drama that was developed, sold, and produced. The magic in that room brought a total of 42 episodes and several awards. It happened with a Facebook Watch live game show that I adapted and ran; 'Listening to the Room' gained 7 million followers and over 1 million players in three months. Magic is there, in that space, dormant within your own team. Your hero must seek it. It is common sense, but it requires mastermind perception.

During the meetings, make your hero knock into the team leaders' minds, make them try to understand 'how this guy thinks', and make them ask every time they perceive anything off. To be able to open the doors for magic to happen, your hero needs to detect, listen, and comprehend how their brain processes. It is an important time, within the weird quantum physics of this art. If your creator's characters are open and smart enough, if your hero's' radar works properly, when listening their team, that original idea they had can grow in directions that your hero wouldn't ever imagine. To cross the doors of glorious storytelling, all mastermind minds must follow some basic principles while in the rooms: don't take anything personal, be well prepared for the circumstances, and understand the team's peculiarities –basically, each leader's thinking process. A tip now valid for the very stressed mastermind heroes supporting tons of weight, also for young or rookie stars: make them hold onto the basics. And I mean the basics of human communication. I was very basic when writing our Star Wars sequel with my cousin after watching the first movie. While building the story and creating the sound effects –with that primitive audio tape cassette– I asked my cousin what the hell he was thinking every time I noticed any kind of change in his attitude, his energy, his eyes, or his *I-don't-fucking-know* exactly what. And I asked, and asked, again and again, until I got it. With every question, I was closer to understanding his mind. The next day, I didn't need to ask more than once. The system has worked since those days. With the basic answers, your hero will develop their own radar to detect the possibility of potential failure and potential greatness; it's a matter of practice. Glory is there, in that same room where the conflicts are. That is another side of the magic of our craft.

I hope you guys get this right–what are the two keys to becoming a successful showrunner, team leader, and content house owner? The answer is machines, and the people beside them. That's it. If I must restart again, I will apply the same formula. I would probably change the order due to the times, though, by putting the people-beside-the-machines part first –technology is going to behave based on what that group of people asks, not in simple operations anymore.

It doesn't matter what your hero is or where they come from. They will find their path. There are several ways to become a showrunner, and now they have the basics to start. I started solo, in a very humble way. I risked investing in education and technology, and during that journey, I found the perfect band of skilled misfits to become a real and successful showrunner. Your hero's path can be totally different. In the end, it doesn't really matter how you get there –some exceptions apply. Once you have arrived, once your hero is the mastermind leading a project, both elements –team and technology– in collaboration with the mirror, will dictate the journey. The next pages delve into the specifics of a recently born mastermind mind. Make your hero take notes.

CHAPTER 5

What Makes a Creative Leader?

SHOWRUNNER KEY SKILLS: MASTERMIND MIND SUPERPOWERS

Notes

CHAPTER 5

Showrunner Key Skills: Mastermind Mind Superpowers

All superheroes develop their powers after a dramatic incident. I like Deadpool's transformation –the most vulnerable-funny-loser innocents killer I've ever seen– and I also liked Jaz Sinclair as Marie Moreau in the Gen V series. Shit, what she does with her bloody superpower is mind-blowing. That first episode was crazy shocking for me; it bleeds talent every frame. The relevant thing here is that as a consequence of drama, karma, and trauma, superheroes or mutants become the extraordinary beings they are. The detonator is clear in their case–not the same for us fleshy humans! Most of us develop mastermind mind skills in a painful and long process without being aware of it. You, your hero, me, almost all of us. The difference lies in what we do when the opportunity to acquire superpowers comes. We humans learn how we learn. In my case, it's by hitting the same rock at least twice. A compilation of broken rocks and well-processed bumps will lay out the perfect mastermind mind manual. What you do after hitting a rock will either show you the right path or deflect you. Lucky superheroes, they only need to deal with shit every new movie, not as constantly as we do (your hero included). Before walking on the path to running shows, be sure your protagonist is acquiring the proper wisdom. I know now that my showrunner skills were growing inside me way before I decided to try to run any show. So, how did it happen? In my case, I felt it inside. Some of the skills came from intuition, that is a fact, while a few came from successes, and others came from failures.

This specific chapter is about the key skills that you must acquire if you are planning on staying in show business, especially if your ambition is to run shows. These are not bloody, messy superpowers, like Marie Moreau has in Gen V. Instead, they are truly the opposite. These superpowers will allow your hero to overcome messy circumstances, have fun, and stay in the business as long as they want. With just a bit of luck, maybe they will create the next great show. One of the advantages of working with some of the best in the business, those who have led shows that have changed television, is that you can observe them and see how they all share certain characteristics. You or your hero can pick the genre: Gameshows, reality, documentaries, drama, talent competition, whatever. In all cases, the mastermind minds behind those shows have the same virus –with the same symptoms– that I've broken down for your hero in my peculiar way. Those basic skills will come by contagion, by intuition, o *por el artículo 33* (by 'decree law #33' also known as *por cojones,* when there's no other way).

Would you like to help your hero find their superpowers? Then keep reading. The intuition I mentioned before is one in the list. Your star must develop it, as they will also need audacity, the capability to reinvent themselves, and the ability to live permanently on the edge –but somehow also in their childhood at the same time, as weird as it sounds. Your hero's ability to play is key. What we do is a game. To begin tapping into your hero's superpowers, you need to know what position you are the best at, what makes your hero unique in the field.

THE SECRET INGREDIENT: FIND YOUR UNIQUENESS

Superheroes and mutants make their uniqueness clear. They all know what killer ability they possess that would shatter enemies and competitors. It's not the same for us. Most of us have no idea what we are extraordinarily good at, mostly because we follow paths instead of finding them. By the time we humans finish elementary school, we all are already trapped in the matrix. It is how it is; we are going to listen, see, read, learn, and experience the stuff the system has ready for us. It's the same anywhere on the planet. We will become *ciudadanos de provecho* (useful citizens) only if we follow the paths and check the boxes properly. Forget about all the specifics of this fact –I'm talking about money, race, education, politics and shit– and stay only with the audiovisual creation part of it. We are all under the same influences, dogmas, and all-for-money rules. Different faces, but the same shit. The question is, how can you find a way to stay extraordinary in a world that promotes the ordinary? Your hero has a tough one here. If they have only had a 'mainstream approach' to their education and career, their possibility of finding uniqueness will be very limited. But it's not impossible. Now it's time for your hero to get off the freeway and drive through unknown neighborhoods. Throughout this book, there are multiple clues to navigate any unfamiliar streets for success, but first, infuse in your hero a stupid amount of curiosity. That's the first step, needed as shit.

Now, how can your hero find uniqueness? There is enough literature for you to research this topic, so I will break it down quickly. It's up to you to adapt the advice to your hero's situation: Identify your star's strengths and consider their skills, their experiences, and whatever makes them stand out. They must use the mirror and be honest –for real; don't allow them to bullshit themselves– and finally, the most difficult one: Make your protagonist ask others for input and feedback. Yeahhh... You can read it again. Painful, tricky. Especially if your hero isn't good at dealing with criticism or they live under the pressure of pleasing others. But getting feedback can be a very, very efficient tool when managed properly. I hope your hero is also wise about who to ask.

Your protagonist's uniqueness could be hiding anywhere–the way they use the camera, the precision of their dialogue, the energy they infuse in the team, how they direct talent, the accuracy in the editing suite, or those taglines that make the campaign. Uniqueness resides somehow above and below the line. It could be in the craft you master or in the way you do it. I've witnessed mastermind minds whose uniqueness dwells in how they treat their teams, what outstanding performance and behavior they will get from them in every project. I've seen others whose superpowers came from their special ability to shoot high-quality action with very limited resources and some who were able to make magic in the complicated arena of the live television, or with their wisdom in the writing room, or in the way they manage talent, the network execs, and the heavy business-affairs issues. Your hero's uniqueness will be related to their specific area of the craft, but also to the way they run their show. Every aspect of it. Btw, your star can have more than one superpower; there are no limitations in this chapter. Let your heroes change, add, or remove exceptionalities when needed. It is natural. Those superpowers will be a like a stored asset, always there when needed. Important here! Please don't allow your hero to get stuck on the one effective uniqueness that brought them success. The biggest risk is getting used to approaching any new project based on the same uniqueness. That will lead to big failure down the road: *Renovarse o morir* (renew or die).

It is important to say that your hero can be a very successful showrunner and mastermind mind without developing a superpower, but the good thing about this book's recipe is that it will be almost impossible for them not to find some uniqueness by following the formula. That's why I describe it as a secret ingredient. It will come naturally. Along with curiosity, make your hero pursue inspiration constantly. Make them watch shit, read shit, listen shit, and talk real. Make them ask questions! Force them to be in the world. And when the inspiration comes –it will come– then, it will be time for analysis, test, and evaluation. And repeat, as many times as your hero considers to be enough. It is always a good idea for uniqueness to find someone who already masters the one thing your hero is pursuing. Make them consult with and ask for help from the best –thinking big always is definitely a good shortcut for uniqueness.

IT IS A GAME: JUST PLAY!

For the next skill of a mastermind mind, we are going to give the character of Deadpool a break, but not the actor. Do you remember Ryan Reynold's character in *Free Guy*? Did you see him being killed repeatedly in horrible ways? He won't die. It's not only funny, but magical. If your hero hasn't watched *Player One* or *The Peripheral*, make them take a look. There are very good stories about real characters 'traveling' to videogames to fight and get killed with very little consequences. Nobody dies for real in a game; it is just a game.

It is exactly the same for you as a creator. Forget about your personal considerations about reality, simulations, multiverses, and stuff like that, and allow me to introduce your hero to a basic and magical concept: Your job is a game, and you are playing, always. It's that simple. You might tend to forget it when you're absorbed by the daily matrix, but it is important to remember it constantly: We creators are for sure among those whose lives are blessed *trabajando en lo que nos gusta* (working in what we love). I bet nothing can disturb you from your craft when you or your hero are in the right flow. Whatever it is! We all lose track of time when immersed in our best skills. And we all have reached occasionally that climax where you are so freaking connected that new amazing things come out with every new thought. Nonstop. That 'in the zone high' has always reminded me my childhood, when playing soccer or *policias y ladrones* with a crowd of pre-teens. Summer evenings in Madrid full of joy, pleasure, and excitement. Somehow my brain chemistry has attached the feeling of 'playing' with the feeling of 'in-the-flow-high' while working. Maybe I am not the only one. You tell me. I think it is either a consequence of suiciding my receptors early in life, or it is the magic of the human mind. The fact is that when I get in the zone, I feel like I am just playing with my mates as a kid, and pretty good stuff comes out. Somehow the sentiment of playing added to the focus on the craft opens in my brain a new flow of –what I call– 'freaking-smart-dopamine.' And boom! *Subidón.* Besides having a lot of fun, in those moments I find crazy good ideas and solutions. I have had this conversation with some other mastermind minds, friends in the industry, and they all agreed. Some of us are so conscious that playing is the best part of our craft, that when supporting a friend starting a project, we don't say 'break a leg' anymore (*mucha mierda* in Spanish), now we say *no te olvides de jugar!* (don't forget to play).

Making your living from storytelling, art, passions in general, is a freaking privilege. Even if your hero is not making enough money to survive yet, they have an endless source of energy for life. This is a real superpower when attached to strategy, discipline, and work. Make the hero of your story conscious about the 'just-a-game' side, at least in these two moments: When exploring creative ideas, and when drama arrives. In the first case it could lead to greatness and more fun. In the drama case, remember, whatever is going on is not that important; we are just playing –while being paid. Fun!! isn't it?

Do not allow shit to steal your hero's love for the game. Not a delay, nor a denial, nor a talented-troubled person. They need to find a way to go back to the player-mode; don't let anything or anyone mess up a creation day. Nonsense story notes, over-reactive executives, extra time penalties, product placement weirdness, team leaders who don't show up, fighter jets over the 'soundproof' studio. Whatever it is, there is nothing that can change the fact that we are just in a play. Literally in our case. No multiverse shit, not Nietzsche shit. We just play. We content creators live a parallel life. We are so lucky that the major risk in our peculiar videogame is to fail and learn the lessons, or not. Not too dangerous compared with other careers. When we work, there are no real risks, no real 'live or die' situations. It is just storytelling. It doesn't matter how sophisticated and expensive it is, don't tolerate your hero getting trapped in the matrix of a stressful production. No lives are at risk under our scalpels, just a team of passionate creators playing together.

LIVING ON THE EDGE: ACCOUNTABILITY

The ability to live constantly *al filo (on the edge)* is another basic skill for a showrunner. It is also a dangerous superpower in the hands of creators, artists, and seekers when not balanced properly. Dangerous enough to finish lives and careers. The 27th club is evidence of the risk. There are many clubs with creators who are victims of themselves, in every craft. All of them are testimony of how difficult is to *estar siempre en la cuerda floja* (live on the edge) and keep some kind of clear mind, not only to survive, but to thrive. No need to say how much talent, energy, and lives have been wasted because of the lack of equilibrium in the creation edge. With the goal of helping your hero practice that needed balance, here are a few. Please make your star conscious that there is no need to be that close to the 27th club circumstances, as some of us have been –more in a Kurt Kobain style in my case.– Your hero can explore, experience, and play as much –and as hard– as they want, let them have fun! Just consider a few control mechanisms: Accountability and boundaries. We'll talk about the first in this chapter, the second later.

In the *living-on-the-edge* department, running shows successfully and living a happy work life are exactly the same. A certain form of accountability is needed. I'm talking about self-accountability. The mastermind mind will always be –ruthlessly– accountable for employers, vendors, teams, ratings, clients, bosses, and more. That's not the point here. Reverse the flow. It is not accountability for others; it is for your own protagonist. It is about how your hero's energy management works, internally and externally. How are they investing their time? In what kind of actions and thoughts does your hero spend the minutes and the hours of the day? Are they conscious of this spending? If they are really aspiring to become successful mastermind minds of any kind, I'd suggest a system for self-accountability. Here is mine. Your hero can take it as a sample to develop their own personal procedure. In my case, it all started on YouTube, but the seed was planted before by a speaker in a rehab center in West Los Angeles, when they broke down how an addict's mind works in the different stages of addiction based on solid data from several research papers. If you are not scared enough, keep reading.

I developed the accountability procedure not long ago. I'm sure your hero will relate to me on this one! YouTube was the reason I started taking a system into consideration. Specifically, my YouTube history. There is no better testimony of anyone's procrastination than their social media and search sites history. When looking for a video I watched, I noticed that it wasn't only my need of escape, passions, or laziness, that kept me on the screen, it was also the content the platform offered me. The different variations of the platform's algorithm were also critically responsible for my not-that-good time management. Wondering about the YouTube algorithms –and interests behind them– I started to mentally group the different videos I watched into categories –like imaginary playlists. I divided the topics into these basic types: 1. Pure entertainment. 2. Personal escapes. 3. Knowledge & inspiration. 4. Health. Two thoughts came immediately, first; how cataleptic was I to allow the algorithm to kidnapped me the way it did? And secondly, what the fuck was YouTube offering me? I took another look at my videos history, and I started doubting where to include a bunch of them. 'Oh shit, the list of topics is not complete' were my words. And it wasn't good news. I was lacking category number 5: Pure Bullshit Content. The problem is that in terms of minutes consumed, bullshit content was fucking always in position 2 or 3. I got scared to be honest. There are Pure Bullshit videos in all the categories –entertainment, health, passions, and education. I was wasting too much time and energy *en pura basura*. That was the moment where I started taking accountability of the shit I was watching in YouTube, and from there, on the rest of the social media outlets. Ask your hero to create their imaginary lists. You don't need to be a Mandalorian to know that ignoring that data is not *the Way*.

The accountability categories created by YouTube inspiration haven't changed a bit since then, but one day, I added even more valuable data to the system. Remember my comment about the seed I got planted in my brain listening to an expert in addiction? This smart lady was explaining how the number of thoughts about '*the drug & the high*' in an addicted mind will grow in every stage, from first use to the worst stages of addiction. She broke up the size and the frequency of the 'mind time spent' in every important aspect of life. In the early stages, there is still some time for '*I have to finish the presentation*', beside '*scoring*', '*enjoying the high*', or '*catching up with friends*'. Later, the only thoughts about work –if any–will be like '*after the fix, I will deliver properly*' – which is not true. And finally, in the latest stages, the whole purpose of that mind –and the body behind it– will be '*how to find the next fix*'. Somehow, I mixed in my mind those two concepts: The *Time & topics* invested in YouTube and *how the mind-time spending* works, and the consequence was the accountability system.

Let's go with the last part of the procedure: Help your hero escalate the playlist thing from a social media platform to real life. It is a serious task. If your hero exports the accountability system to their days and weeks, is almost impossible not to act based on the statistics. Make your hero divide the day into three columns : '*stuff they watch*', '*stuff they do,*' and '*stuff they think about*'. Make them list everything that happened yesterday in those columns. Make them observe how they divide their day and take control of the energy they spend in each one of these categories. Once you are conscious of the data, it doesn't matter if you are Jedi, Mandalorian, Covenant or just a stupid human, you will see *The Way,* after you and your hero freak out.

The first step is going to be easy. I immediately decided to eliminate the bullshit category, at least from the *stuff-I-watch* column. I haven't been able to remove it completely from the *'stuff-I-think-about'* column, yet, but I'm getting there. The sordid social-media-tabloids-bullshit creators' abilities – and the narratives they promote– invade us. It is difficult not to think about them, especially if the algorithm helps them the way it does. I see the *pure bullshit* category as the consequence of a natural –and technological– evolution. We've exchanged verbal gossip for our phone screens. One day I will write about the second part; how stupid we have become as a race. In this global landscape ruled by views, likes, and shares, choosing not to watch BS is almost impossible. Shit! You see? I'm doing it again, wasting my energy on bullshit content. Let's move on.

ADAPT OR DIE I: REINVENTING YOURSELF EVERY EPISODE, EVERY SEASON, EVERY DAY.

One more mandatory skill for a mastermind mind: *Adaptation.* This is mandatory because of the nature of the beast –content is a very short-lived asset– and because of the competition in the industry. Your hero will face ferocious competition. First advice! Tell them not to take it personal, it is also the nature of the beast. I have divided the *Adapt-or-Die* superpowers in two sections. This first one helps your hero understand what to do to evolve and succeed. The second will give them tools to re-invent the wheel and die freaking rich. Let's start.

I have no idea when your hero was born, but if they joined the workforce between 2010 and 2020, the average job tenure was between 3 and 4 years. This decade ,it is already way lower. Those stats don't take the industry's volatility into consideration. Content creation forces us to always be ready for changes, and show-running forces us to identify and lead those changes. When I was a kid, most of the male adults I knew spent their entire lives working for the same company, while most of their wives stayed at home taking care of my generation. My parents were an outstanding exception. In a time in Spain when only 4 out of every 10 women worked, mum did it. She spent her entire working life as an educator. Meanwhile, ever since I can remember, dad was a photographer. His dark room was also my bedroom, and I woke up with his pictures drying around my bed until I was seven. Clearly , there was no escape for me! What I didn't know is that my dad had another job, and sometimes even more than two. I knew my dad took pictures, painted art, and fixed cars. I knew he worked as a planimetry expert for the agriculture department, but I couldn't ever imagine that I'd see him becoming an expert linear video editor, a teacher, an old school –frame by frame– cartoon animation cinematographer, an MS DOS computer programmer, and one of the coders who built the current Spanish tax system. Yes, so many cool things he did in his life, and he retired as an IRS freaking *funcionario*, subject to the absurdity of the administration. The important thing in this chapter is the number of changes he made and I witnessed. Most of the times he reinvented himself were a success. He was the exception at the time, and he planted the seed in me: You can start from 0 every time you want or you need. Period. If your hero likes something for real, make them try. Make them fucking try.

Yes, I was lucky with the seed, but when I got into show business, I realized that *Evolving* is a matter of survival. Do you and your hero want to stay in the game? Then you must adapt and change. Constantly. I'm not sure this is a superpower, a key skill, a sentence, *una maldición(a curse,)* or just the physics of show business, but I'm sure it is becoming the norm for every human on this planet, regardless of industry or career. Within the entertainment landscape there are a handful of cases of decades-long shows that allowed their teams to create a life we cannot aspire to in this business –a steady one. Let's see if your hero has an answer for this question: Why the hell are they picking a profession where every few months –if they're lucky– they will have to find a new job or renew their content? The same way that job tenure is dropping year by year, the length and size of the productions are dropping too. It doesn't matter if your hero is an independent YouTuber or a solid Daily Show showrunner. We are all condemned to recycle ourselves endlessly. It is that simple.

So far in this book, you've read more about how to guide your hero's mind than about how to run shows. There is a reason: Mastering the only real tool you have –yeah, the one in the freaking mirror– is the only way to survive a job search twice a year. After thinking carefully about that sentence, make your hero multiply the number by 3 or 4 decades of active duty. Too many of everything: jobs, bosses, co-workers, searches, negotiations, and more. That is the reality they face, but I know they are ready.

ADAPT OR DIE II: INVENTING THE NEXT WHEEL

The adapt or die skill/superpower comes with a huge bonus. Open your hero's' mind and think about the opportunities to come. Have you and your storyteller protagonist thought about how new content –the kind that nobody would bet on when it comes out– is still here after 20-plus years? Just remember the first MTV reality shows. Or the first gamers on internet. Now look at the current situation. Reality TV is one of the few totally consolidated businesses in the industry. It has generated the best pop culture icons of the last 40 years. Twitch and gaming competitions have reached numbers nobody would expect, but most of the entertainment business leaders still ignore the landscape.

Put your hero's mind on the task: What are tomorrow's cases? How many heroes will develop a new formula that will change the showbiz game forever –and make them die freaking rich simultaneously? With the advancement of technology, it is going to be a few. Make your hero go gender by gender in the audiovisual panorama. I have chills just thinking about the future landscape of game shows as a fast-paced, upcoming reality. And there will be more. In the next few years, we will be able to interact in a way that will transform storytelling and formats. Take dance competition for instance; being JLo's dance partner from your own living room is a freaking cool idea, and it's not that far out of reach. Make your hero sit down, research, and imagine. Connect the dots between the specific discipline your content is about, the story they aspire to tell, and the tech available for storytelling and related to the discipline. Another fishing ground for your hero's future is any content related to mental or physical activities. Biotech and machine learning will bring new frontiers for human health and for storytelling.

There are going to be a lot of next waves. I want your hero to catch one. Make them conscious that it is not about future job tenure, it is about The Future. The opportunity of inventing the wheel again is here. If you or your imaginary star are currently creating content in a steady initiative, you are lucky for it, but you also have work to do. As I said before, make them play even more. The old saying in our craft was 'you are as good as your last show's ratings'. Not true, but that idea forces us storytellers to complicate our lives more and more in every episode, or at least in every season. Change the reason. Don't do it only for the ratings, do it also for you. If your hero currently has a steady gig and does not need to reinvent the wheel, ask them to do it anyway as training for 'the art of catching waves.' Waves lead to the invention of new wheels. There are many new waves coming that will become part of our life, as Reality TV and game-streaming are today. All your hero needs is to practice learning how to catch the next wave. Maybe they will invent a new wheel.

There are many ways to train your hero for wave-catching and wheel-inventing. Don't miss an opportunity! With the advances in biotechnology, in the next few years, there will be shows that will make 'Alone,' 'American Ninja Warrior', or '100 Physical' look as prehistoric as bison cave paintings. Let's work out a real-life example for your hero. It was 20 years ago when I showran *Fear Factor* in Spain. I asked for many things, but I got the one I wasn't expecting at all, something almost silly –that's corporate politics, more about that later. I asked if it was somehow possible to measure and quantify the 'fear' of each participant during the challenges. The amazing producer gave me that candy –cheap for that property budget– instead of more shooting days. *Pero que listo el cabron!* (smart motherfucker mixed with love.) It was technology from the early 2000s that allowed us to see the data in real time and use it afterward in post. With the wave that is coming, and based on those shows I mentioned, *estoy salibando* (I'm drooling) just thinking in formats that would measure anything mind or body related –no wires attached nowadays.

Make your hero rehearse for the future. There are always possibilities to test stuff. A more prudent showrunner wouldn't spend any energy on any innovation during the first season. Fear Factor is a complicated show to produce, with very little room for testing and less room for failing. That team worked *como un reloj suizo* (as a Swiss watch.) Fear Factor was a failure in Spain and has never again been produced. I know one of the reasons, Tip Alert! If one day your hero runs a network programming department, ask them not to premiere a show called *Factor Miedo* while the bodies of the biggest terror attack in Madrid's history are still fragmented on the railroads. Yes, the premiere was less than 48 hours after the train bombs. It should've been postponed. Fear was the factor we all felt in Madrid, looking at those 198 dead bodies. Network nonsense. Period. The relevant thing in this chapter is that our fear level graphics were just an experiment, a little test, but it shows how the catch-the-wave training works. Real innovations in every show, that's the way your mastermind mind –and team– can rehearse for the future of job tenure, wave catching, and wheel inventing.

INSTINCTS ARE THERE TO BE FOLLOWED

This superpower is already in you. How many times in your life have you 'known' the outcome of a situation before it happened? Mentally list the most important events of your life in which you already knew what the outcome would be.. We have all experienced that *I knew it* feeling. Why not train it and use it? The reality is that practicing this superpower is becoming more and more complicated, mostly because of the current disconnection in society. Interacting with others in real life is what would give your hero the sensitivity to perceive properly, then think, ask their gut, ask their heart, and decide. It sounds crazy to consider *intuition* nowadays, in a world ruled by numbers, results, statistics, data, marketing, and fakeness. I know that, but look at those pioneers who ignored the conventionalisms of their time, the data, and the criticism, and made history with their innovations. How many world-class advances of science, content, art, literature, architecture, or business were fueled by the intuition of the showrunner? A lot, if not most. Tesla, Galileo, Pasteur, and Ford are just a few relevant examples.

Should your hero ignore the data? No. What about the analysis they made? Not at all. Any decision's mandatory starting point is data. But data is not all. A wise mastermind would reprocess the data by merging it with information from their body's organs. I am not kidding. At all. If your hero wants to develop intuition, the decision-making procedure for creative mastermind minds runs in the same way as a very old Sanskrit proverb says: **I trust my guts, listen my head, and follow my heart**. That's it. Great, now biology is among the subjects of this book, this is getting worse.

In a basic way, body parts and showrunning work like this:

- **Guts:** Your hero has a hitch inside. They know their capabilities, they've seen an opportunity, and they trust their capabilities. Guts say 'yes' to intuition.

- **Mind:** Your character has evaluated the information and seen every angle of it. They know the data, and they also have their past experiences learnings, and, importantly, they know the characters involved in the decision. In this moment the mind's answer is 'Idk'

- **Heart:** With memos from both the guts and the mind, your hero's heart will make the decision and move forward –or not– with the actions coming from that 'intuitive' moment. I'd strongly recommend finding peace and using the mirror when your hero's heart is going to finally decide.

In this chapter, I must include *intuition* as a mastermind superpower. It would be stupid not to do it, just considering the amount of genius works that came from it. I hope you are avid enough for success to try this approach: Trust your guts, listen to your head, and decide with your heart. This Sanskrit shit is somehow linked with the 'undreamt' stealth flying device. No idea how, but it is. Btw, the system doesn't work with sports betting, at least in my case. I can't ask my heart if *el Madrid va a ganar mañana. Una pena!*

ENERGY & FRUSTRATION SAVING SYSTEMS

Another mastermind mind superpower is related to the number of things that your hero will deal with. Among them there will be relevant things, less relevant things, not relevant things, stupid things, and things that neither you nor your hero can do shit about. All those *'things'* will bring energy waste and frustration, what means more energy wasting. Let's start with a question, this time it is not for your hero, it is for you. Have you ever felt the ABS system working in a car? What about a bike? I've ridden motorbikes my entire life. I got the first by fourteen in a trade in the hood –half an ounce of Moroccan hash for a Mx bike, probably stolen. Multiple mopeds later, Dad helped me to get a used Vespa 200P, and I mastered the art of getting the rear wheel to slide when needed. Fast forward a decade, already a showrunner, and you would see me in my BMW 650 GS *disfrutando como un cerdo* (literally this means 'enjoying like a pig,' that is something good in Spanish). This is not the page to start discussing bikes, but gosh, I still love that ride. If your hero is wondering how this is related to a mastermind superpower, well, remember I was talking about ABS braking systems. One rainy day getting onto the freeway, I needed to emergency break in the curved ramp accessing to the main traffic, and that thing call ABS –that I knew my bike had because only because I disactivated it for off-road– well, the thing started working when I was already calculating the area of impact, the position I should let my body go, how to let know my team know I was in the hospital, and what parts of my body would be a real mess the next few months. With all that in mind, I hit the brakes to avoid blending my head with the van in front of me, and I felt it. The brake handle and pedal both ignored me; I felt three movements on the brakes in less than a second, and that's all. Nothing happened. I mean nothing I was expecting. The bike magically applied both wheel brakes, and I was able to keep the inclination and the counter steering, avoid the van, and finish the curve, just with a little shock, dry mouth, and that 'awareness high' that you get when you are really close to a tragedy. I think they call it adrenaline. The relationship with a showrunner key skill? Your hero already knows that I like to upscale things to other aspects of life, one more for the road: Among the number of things guaranteed when masterminding in showbiz –and any other business, probably– is frustration. As sure as dead. What about a technique that would allow you to avoid frustration and save tons of energy? A special AFS (Anti-Frustration System) that would recognize what is worth spending energy on, how much, and for how long. The sensor your hero needs to wake up reacts with one single question: Is the issue under your hero's control? Or not? Binary answers only.

Make your hero consciously think about that question as often as possible. Make them observe other people's situations too. Regardless of the nature of the issue, a brief conversation with the mirror will train your hero's sensors: *Is it under my control?* There is no half and half response. Your star is an executive producer; make them decide. Yes or no. If the answer is *yes,* time to move their assess and get it solved. No more frustration, no more energy lost, it will be dedicated to the task. If the answer is *no,* your hero must let it go somehow. Jedis, Spartans, Mandalorians, Covenants, and associates don't spend their time or energy on something they cannot control. They are under enough pressure already. Ask your hero to be a Jedi and control their thoughts and actions, especially when they are showrunning hard.

MVP FOR LIFE

This last superpower wears a *'mandatory'* tag. Without it, your mastermind mind hero won't be in the business of show-running for too long. I am talking about the ability to be the key player when the game is lost and lead the *remontada* (comeback). I know about comebacks, not only because I was born a Real Madrid fan but also because of my own life and career. For those who are intrigued, yes, the Real Madrid is an expert in *remontadas.* UEFA Champions League, Benzema led the Madrid *remontada* against the Paris Saint Germain, in those times with Messi, Neymar and Kylian Mbappe in the Parisian squad. The PSG was winning by two against *los blancos,* until Karim Benzema read the battlefield and activated his superpower. In 45 minutes, he scored three times. A hat trick that eliminated the French team. Make your hero watch showrunners leading comebacks. Make them see a player call Kirk Cousins in that game against the Colts, one of the best examples ever of this superpower (Vikings losing 33-0 and winning at last). Sorry for those not into sports, they are a great source of inspiration.

Athletes, superheroes, and movie protagonists show Most Valuable Player superpowers very often. You will see how, in the middle of the chaos, a voice rises over the rest to reassess, organize, and execute, taking the losing team to ultimate success. Well, it is the same now for your showrunner hero. Welcome to the *hall-of-pain* of the entertainment industry! Did your hero consider being a quarterback in their childhood? Here it goes! There is no project that would avoid that moment of *things-not-going-as-planned*. And then there will be moments of *shit-what-a-chaos-and-now-what??* Make them aware of this truth: It will happen. Period. And your showrunner superhero will have to deal with it. There could be many reasons, as many as crafts, people, and machines are involved in the creation. An actor having a bad day, the weather, a technical limitation, never-ending paperwork, a lack of rehearsals, or whatever it is. At the end of the threat, in most cases, the '*shit-what-a-chaos-and-now-what?*' are related to not making it on time, budget, or expectations. In some others they are related to egos. Those are more complicated to deal with. We all have experienced chaos in different circumstances and setups. You and your hero have seen that explosion, the big bang of madness, I'm sure more than once. At home, at work, at school, at sports, every group effort where nothing comes together properly –and the time is running out– and then someone does/ says something, *y listo*: total chaos. Use your memories for training: Were you trapped in the madness? When did you recognize the chaos? Did you imagine a way out of the situation? A way to avoid it? The capability to detect when and how to make an intervention is key. When showrunning in the middle of the battle, the mastermind mind must see the battlefield from inside and from outside. Practice that trick. Make your hero pay attention to the content they are creating, to their craft, but also to the battlefield. They need to use their eyes, brain, and heart –again!– to oversee the whole picture. Being the one who deals with the shit and makes things happen requires your hero to really master the '*mirror*' part. The ability of isolate yourself and have whatever inner conversation you may need is crucial during crisis. The other element is '*perception*'. I am not talking about the pre-historic Perception video board that made me a showrunner, no, I am talking about you and your hero's perception. The real one. This time it is bi-directional, in and out in the same wire. What your hero perceives and how they are being perceived.

Bidirectional perception and proper isolation will make your hero a solid MVP when needed. They are not only valid for crisis, but also for greatness. When working well, your hero will also detect the possibility of when to experiment with creativity and make their content bigger and better. Directing a commercial ages ago, we were all concerned with the talent delivery; it wasn't working. After trying innumerable takes –with clients on set– I gave her some time to calm down, while the producer looked at me like the emoji with the eyes completely open. Yes, we were totally off schedule, and I was stopping again. I used my *I-got-this* smile with him, and then I left the stage alone. Two minutes later, I ran towards the director of photography, asking, 'Do you remember that thing we did yesterday while blocking?' I don't remember the exact answer, but I remember his surprised face. The previous day, while setting up lights, I saw something very interesting visually –very risky too. I called him to the monitor and asked him: 'you see where I'm going with this?' Of course he knew. He liked it, but it was a too dangerous last-minute change for a commercial with the client and agency on set. We both said together *'en este no, pero esto hay que probarlo'* (not this time, but we have to try this). Fast forward some hours and here we are, just about to mess up the whole project because the cast that I didn't pick *-low budget shit, ask your hero to get used to it-* wasn't delivering. Everyone on set was aware of the disaster. I told the important people –in a very proper way– that I was sure I would get something by changing a couple of things. They didn't believe me, but *el mero mero* –the CEO of the client company– gave me a yes with a very mild head movement and poker face. Just to add another pinch of stress to my day. I went to finish my chat with the director of photography *'let's do it, turn everything off and set up that thing we did yesterday'* and then I explained it to the team. Well, the new approach made the talent feel more comfortable and hide those moments where she wasn't great. What we did in those last 20 minutes was so good –both visually and in interpretation– that everyone was cheering, smiling, and applauding when we wrapped up. My producer came directly to me with a bottle of champagne and made me drink first. From *'shit-what-a-chaos-and-now-what?'* to *'what the fuck, this is great!!!'* in 20 minutes, after a lot of drama. A real *remontada (comeback)* only possible with perception, isolation, communication skills, y *ganas de jugar* (love for the game). *Doy por hecho* (I'm taking for granted) that your showrunner hero is already a good communicator, that they stay calm and composed during a crisis, that they know how to support and encourage their team, and they can prioritize and delegate properly. The MVP upgrade is almost there, keep moving!

CHAPTER 6

Who Are Your Friends When You Lead?

THE LONE WOLF AND THE STAIRWAY TO HEAVEN

Notes

CHAPTER 6

The Lone Wolf And The Stairway To Heaven

How is your hero doing? I hope they are practicing some of the tricks they have learned from this book already. So far, they have gone through the process of becoming a mastermind mind first and a showrunner –with a pack full of superpowers– after that. Now it is time to apply some of the learnings, time to see the challenges coming with those dreams about being a creative mastermind mind, or those about being the best in the craft, or in other words, the dreams about becoming the source, heart, mind, and soul of something that was an idea and now is a reality. The journey ahead is amazing and bumpy. Time to use all the tricks combined.

Let's go now to one of the hardest lessons to learn about your hero's new reality: They are alone. Or they will be, it is a matter of time. A mastermind mind must choose loneliness, mostly because nobody can really understand those who carry the weight of every single detail of the show, the responsibility of the budget, and the consequences of the results. There is also another type of loneliness, the one coming from the waves of any career. Sometimes you are hot, other times you are cold. Your hero's phone will be the best meter, if it is not already. How to handle those ups and downs is the next lesson for the Jedi mastermind apprentices.

This chapter comes referencing another well-known content franchise, and it is not Star Wars. I'm sure you and your hero have watched at least a piece of The Hunger Games. Despite the author of the book describing the protagonist as a '*thin young woman with dark hair, olive-toned skin, and gray eyes*', the beautiful, blue-eyed, and talented Jennifer Lawrence –Katniss Everdeen in the series– tells, in my opinion, one storyline much better than any other. Be grateful to Lawrence and the directors. Because of their work, your hero will better appreciate the journey of the mastermind mind loneliness. Forced by both her own choice and the circumstances of the show she is running, Lawrence-Katniss' journey portrays how isolation is a protective mechanism for a leader and a necessary step in the duty of leading, in her case a revolution, in your hero's case, any project.

See other examples we all like; Toretto Vin Diesel in the Fast franchise, Ender Wiggin in Ender's Game, even Dumbledore, the headmaster of Hogwarts, often isolates himself from those around him, including Harry Potter, to protect them and to bear the heavy responsibilities of fighting against Voldemort. Isolation is almost always a deliberate choice, motivated by different reasons. It reflects the loneliness of the leadership when the stakes are incredibly high. How high are your hero's stakes? How important is it to guarantee results this time? Or the next? As always, there is a prize for isolation, too. In the Game of Thrones series, the Lord of Winterfell, Ned Stark, beliefs that he must bear the burden alone to protect family and realm. Ned's isolation is driven by duty and honor, and it finishes pretty bad.

I'd like to know if your hero realizes the magnitude of the challenge. Your star, yourself, and the mastermind minds around you are all choosing a life of solitude, at least from the moment you start running shows. Forget fiction now, in the real world, responsible leaders isolate themselves from forming deep personal connections to *maintain objectivity, protect confidentiality, and avoid conflicts of interest.* Yeah, that doesn't sound like me, but it is a brief way to summarize what you can read anywhere about leaders. In the real world of the media and entertainment, if your hero won't isolate properly, they will suffer the feared Association Induced Temporary Blindness. The disease will blur the lines between the mastermind mind and the team. Then favoritism will show up, followed by lack of authority, and finally overall bad performance as the last consequence. Guaranteed. Make your protagonist aware that while behind a mastermind mind, when establishing deep ties with team members, there are always risks for conflicts of interest, and for *bronca en el gallinero* (tensions and breakdowns in team cohesion). I'm sure you and your hero agree: Too many risks for this game, that's why smart showbiz mastermind minds pick loneliness. Some of them even learn how to manage it. I'm working on it.

One of the ways to cope with showrunner loneliness is sharing the weight of the ride wisely. Do you remember my comment about the John 117 of the digital video? Cesar 117? My tech-nerd saver in the digital revolution was the first mastermind mind I started sharing the weight of the journey with. I'm not sure if it was because of the insulting number of hours we spent gutting my computers or because we both were building our showrunners' dreams at the same time. Probably this second one. *La cosa es que* (the fact is that) we became each other's ears to mastermind mind problems.

Sometimes your hero will be lucky enough to share the mastermind mind weight with someone in their own company or the company they work for. That is an exceptional blessing. Not only because of the benefit of having a trusted new voice helping in the mirror, but also because those two talents together –your hero plus their mastermind mind partner or *co-whatever*– can reach greatness easily.

That kind of magic happens when there is no fear in any one of the masterminds, when both showrunners don't feel threatened by the other. The times that I've been lucky enough to have that we have reached the sky, farther away than we both expected. Yes, I am using 'we' because it was the result of both efforts. My mastermind mind partner and me. We made that company –sales, profits, and brand value– multiply by five times its value in just two years. Part of the magic was how we both intuitively applied the tools I am sharing from the beginning. Do you want to know the funniest part of those three years of success? When I first met Lola –my mastermind mind partner in success is a she– I hated her, guys. Better said, I feared her. A lot. She was the executive producer who ran crews, facilities, and technical resources at *Estudios Picasso* –owned by the Berlusconi's empire Mediaset. She ruled the studios. Period. With five or six primetime dramas under her sight, she walked every inch of the facility mostly alone, or with one person by her side, looking at everything, and not saying a word. Lola uses one of those poker faces I can't imitate. No way to know if it is bad news or horrible news that she is bringing. You could feel in the crews the wave of respect and fear when she was seen. The very first time I felt her presence my maltreated brain started playing a melody that, little by little, took over me every time I saw her. You and your hero know the song, John Williams' *Imperial March Darth Vader's* theme. Get a second to play in your mind the first few beats. It is the perfect soundtrack for her walks in the sets. That track describes my feelings. It was my second day as a director in a prime-time drama, after shadowing the head director –another female mastermind mind I owe a lot– when the also rookie –and also female– showrunner got kind of stuck with some acting expectations, and we went overtime. We were so late that Lola Darth Vader came in person to the stage, honoring a destroyed talent and crew with her revitalizing presence. I saw from a distance how the showrunner was agitating her hands full of *separatas* (reprint scenes) while talking to Lola nonstop. Then silence. Lola said something calmly in the distance and walked towards me. Oh shit. I immediately turned away and started giving some orders to the cameras, while thinking of how to disappear. It didn't happen, I didn't disappear, and Lola approached me in silence, moved her head towards my ear, and whispered, *'in 30 minutes I'll turn the lights out and send the team home, and you are five scenes late'*. I knew she would, but I also knew that she was saying more things to me. She kind of gave me both the power and the problem. Somehow, we all helped the rookie showrunner to get three scenes of those five in 35 minutes, and Lola Moreno Vader never turned the lights off. She knew very well the art of whom, when, and how to apply pleasure. Over time, Lola become a colleague and a friend. I joined the company she was working for, and our collaboration opened a new time. Joy, success, money and appreciation. Multiplied by five. For a few years –and a lot of ups and downs– I had the privilege of sharing the mastermind mind weight with Lola. I am sure that helped us both.

Ask your isolated hero to always keep an eye on their search for someone to share the weight. Ask them also to be very prudent if the closer's friends are under their command. Most of the times you cannot share the weight you carry with your employees. If your character finds a wise mastermind mind mate, make them try to connect. They will notice soon if the candidate is good or not. When it is good, neither your hero nor the candidate will compete which each other. If your stars feel the other mastermind mind is competing directly against them, it is time to gently close the 'connection'. At the end of the day, it wasn't real.

PUÑALADAS POR LA ESPALDA STABS FROM THE BACK

Now is time to give your star the tools to overcome one of the hardest consequences of this content creation journey. Pick any character from the examples I mentioned before and call your hero's attention. All of them were betrayed, several times in some cases: Don Toretto, Ned Stark, Katniss Everdeen, and a lot more. As a mastermind mind, you must expect the consequences of ambition and betrayal from your team. It sounds hard, but it is manageable. How tough survival is in this circus makes things slightly different from other industries. If you haven't seen any episode of *House of Cards* or *Succession*, you and your hero should do it fast. While watching the ruthless manipulator protagonist of House of Cards climbing the political ladder (Kevin Spacey as Frank Underwood), I started recognizing profiles, manners, and procedures that reminded me of those around me –up and under too– who were *in-the-ladder* pursuit and not *in-the-show* interest. Same thing with *Succession*. Every dysfunctional dynamic role can be adapted to real life in our industry. It is a very interesting exercise for any content lover. *Obras de arte* (masterpieces) of storytelling have portraited ambition and betrayal in amazing ways. This one is mandatory. See how a universal truth is laid out simply. In that masterpiece of content The Godfather, Coppola shows a character (Fredo Corleone) who betrays his brother, the protagonist (Michael), and the whole Corleone family. Here are the key lines of the dialogue:

Fredo: *They've got Pentangeli. That's all I can tell you. I didn't know it was gonna be a hit, Mike. I swear to God, I didn't know it was gonna be a hit. Johnny Ola bumped into me at Beverly Hills, and he said that he wanted to talk. He said that you and - and Roth were in on a - a big deal together and that there was something in it for me if I could help 'em out. He said that - He said that you were bein' tough on the negotiations, but if they could get a little help and close the deal fast, it'd be good for the family.*

- **Michael:** *You believed that story? You believed that?*
- **Fredo:** *He said there was somethin' in it for me. On my own...*

Here we go! *'On my own'*. Fredo didn't need anything material –freaking rich mafia clan– he only needed to feel useful for the family. Let's give your hero some rest and play a different creative game with me. Imagine Fredo and Michael Corleone are not brothers. Imagine Fredo needs material shit. Imagine that Fredo also needs to find a new job every 3 months. Imagine Michae hired him for a gig, and Fredo is an ambitious guy. What do you think Fredo would do while working for Michael? Besides trying to become his friend–for future jobs or real friendship– he will try to do the *'on-my-own'* thing, as you would, and I would too. Everyone is trying to climb the ladder, that's in every industry, but in ours everyone must do it faster. It is again the laws of physics in entertainment: Like we all experience gravity in our planet, in the jungle of the showbiz, everyone has an eye on the future, but not everyone does it with ethics. Showbusiness is a landscape where *los cuchillos* (the knives) are always ready. Key positions are very hard to get and harder to keep. As a showrunner or an executive, not counting on having *puñaladas por la espalda* (stabs in the back) now and then is not realistic. Make your hero conscious of that. When I finally accepted it, pain was less severe, and my energy management improved. Your hero must take for granted that everyone has an eye on the ladder, and it is legit, but not everyone would climb the stairway to the showbiz heaven with integrity. As I am sure you and your stars have already experienced it in multiples arenas.

THE MASTERMIND MIND BEST FRIENDS

In the lone wolf journey, friendship is a hazard. It is hard to digest, but real as shit, so, this is a wakeup call for your star. Can your hero remember my words about *Temporary Association Induced Blindness*? I insisted on how dangerous and corrosive that virus is for a showrunner. The worm lives dormant inside us, waiting for the time to spell. When a team member becomes 'something else' for a showrunner, or a showrunner hires 'someone close', the virus gets immediately activated, and things will get messy. It's a fact, and nobody is safe.

Depending on the stage, the *Temporary Association Induced Blindness* will first attack the mastermind mind's basic self-regulation mechanisms. And there will be consequences. First for the show being created, and then for the joy of the creation –and the health of both the showrunner and the team. I am not saying *'don't-do-it.'* I myself have done it several times –with a lot more success than regret. I am saying *'do-it-right.'* If you hire friends or more, be ruthless in the mirror, and consider applying basic old school ethics procedures: Make sure your hero is fair and objective with the team under any circumstances. Make them give opportunities earned through performance and help them to be transparent with their team when making decisions. Do you see how easy it is to avoid the virus? It is not about defenses; it is about the mirror and activating old school ethics. It is the same technique used to reduce the likelihood of your hero being manipulated. It is also the same technique that your showrunner hero would need to create a collaborative dynamic in the team instead of a competitive one. Let's go with the last consideration for the lone wolves. This one is related to science.

TODO LO QUE SUBE, BAJA (EVERYTHING GOES UP, GOES DOWN) THE TYRANNY OF GRAVITY

I owe the law of gravity a recognition in this book. Again, the physics of the entertainment business dictates another mandatory awareness in the lone wolf journey. If you stay long enough in the craft, you will see how your own team members, interns, and old employees become *el mero mero* (the top leader) in multinational content powerhouses or worldwide show franchises. It doesn't matter whose career it is: your hero's, your peers', or the interns you raised. In the stairway to showbiz heaven, mastermind minds go up and down several times. There are three key things that differentiate those who make it to heaven: How they climbed the ladder -*with ethics or using people? -* What they did at the summit -*same note about ethics here,*- and what they did when they came back to base camp. Dear showrunners, the last section of the lone wolf chapter is dedicated to the art of being as good a mastermind mind as always, whether you're at the summit and at base camp.

I'm sure you and your hero have felt that surprising shot of energy when, on a birthday, or a special occasion, a lot of unexpected –and that is the keyword– people showed up to congratulate you, sent lovely messages, and liked whatever you posted. Let's transport that feeling to showbusiness and the showrunning life. Imagine that shot of unexpected dopamine multiplied by 100, and you and your hero will be close to what it means to be hot and recognized in this craft. The *others' appreciation* is something that every mastermind mind will experience multiple times. What is the origin and the destination of the *alagos y atenciones* (praises and attentions) is another story. The one your hero must figure out. With or without intention, every time your hero starts a project, a bunch of old mates will show up. Guaranteed. And every time your hero runs a successful one, a bunch of applicants for *future-mates* will show up too.

That's a clear symptom that you are hot as a mastermind mind—old and new mates showing up everywhere. There are more, like the sudden interest from the corporation you work for to have you at every event, or the overwhelming number of emails with amazing professionals' interesting ideas. The most important of the symptoms is not an external one. It is in your own behavior that you can notice the key sign: when you are finally showrunning, you are so focused on the product that it is inevitable to relax the mastermind's healthy habits. There are changes. Now you are almost every day in that *in-the-flow-high*, doing what you love, and busy as shit. How would you expect not to change? Almost impossible, I'm sure your hero, you, and I share that same answer. Well, surprise! *Pues resulta que no* (looks like it's not) impossible. It is possible to keep the healthy habits, and they are needed. A matter of method; in this case, I'd recommend your hero to remember the *accountability* part to better apply the concept. My recommendation is not to avoid changes, but rather to control those changes. Make your hero check in the mirror at least once every other week, with a real *showrunner-boldness* attitude, and a big

'I'm-not-bullshitting-myself' tattoo on their foreheads. The mastermind mind *adaptation* skill is needed when at the summit, but the *accountability system* must work harder to control everything up there. Maybe it's the lack of oxygen? Be aware of the high-altitude disease. To avoid it, the mirror ritual requires fine tuning regulations over the time. There are innocent variations, like the one I'm describing ahead, but even those will bring ugly consequences.

Here is a common example of the kinds of little changes you must control. We all have experienced the pain of being ignored in emails, texts, and more. No matter how busy and how up or down in the stairway to heaven we are, every one of us know there are rules that are not meant to be ignored. The demands of the mastermind mind's complicated days will extinguish the healthy habits –mirror time– gradually. You will start *delaying or/and ignoring* calls, texts, emails, conversations, word given, or worse. It is normal; it happens because of the number of fires you must put down and the little time you have to recover. Ok, allow your hero time to recover, but that *delay-or/and-ignore* policy will lead to an overwhelming snowball with major consequences for the future. No mastermind mind should change their healthy habits while climbing the leader. What would happen when shit arrives –and it will– and you see yourself at the base camp again? Now you have the time to send emails and texts! But you didn't it when you were up in the summit? C'mon guys! Unsustainable attitude.

I have assumed that your hero made the summit the first time by climbing the stairway following basic old school ethics and without cheating in any way. That would protect your star –a bit– from the high-altitude disease. A little trick now; when ascending towards creation heaven –or when at the summit– make your star stop for real every other week, only for a few hours. Exercise, walk, reconnect, and then attend to those *delayed-or/and-ignored* efforts. I'm sure some of them come from future genius masterminds or peers who can help with your next ascension. Maybe one of those emails means a fantastic undreamed dream. Do the right thing!

The high-altitude disease alters the basic DNA of the mastermind mind, and recovery is almost unknown. Of course, those with the virus can still climb and stay at the summit, but if they ramble the ladder only by *reading-and-using* people or taking advantage of being *the right profile,* then a violent fall is inevitable; it is only a matter of time. There are exceptions! As always, but this is with no doubt one of the karmic trues of the business. *Todo lo que sube, baja.* The tyranny of gravity. The problem is that in showbiz gravity is ten times stronger. My recommendation? Face the stairway ignoring that you are there, just focus on the current show. Treat everyone as you'd like to be treated, and check in with the *espejo* (mirror), especially if the ascension is fast.

The same set of remedies –ignore the stairway, focus on the show, treat others as you'd like to be treated, check with the mirror– all apply when being down in the base camp waiting for the right weather, gear, or expedition partners. It is an uncomfortable place, but we mastermind mind showrunners must accommodate the facilities at our convenience. In the down moments, your hero's efforts will be those *delayED-or/and-ignorED* by most of the *in-the-ladder* old mates and colleagues. Everyone here is fighting for survival. It is a complicated time, perfect for your hero to develop new ideas, reconnect with themselves and other honest masterminds, and allow some time to pass while training the basic skills, to strategize properly for the next attempt. The way to make it to the summit as many times as required is confined into the showbiz version of the *four agreements* –a book you should consider reading– *Cumple tu palabra* (be impeccable with your word). Don't take things personally –say less! This is showbiz. Be prepared on every occasion. Execute at your best. Basic stuff, not too difficult. Make your star try.

As you and your hero can see, every mastermind mind is a lone wolf by definition. It is a very special loneliness though. Mastermind minds are alone in the highs and in the lows, whether they realize it in the moment or later on when they're back in base camp. It's time to get your hero ready for the real adventure. The next pages are dedicated to those who are, were, or will be, showbusiness free-solo-climbers. Those who open new ascending lines and choose not to have any rope attached.

CHAPTER 7

Do You Think You Can Find What You Lack?

GUERRILLA WARFARE: IN THE FIGHT FOR ENDLESS INDEPENDENCE

Notes

CHAPTER 7

Guerrilla Warfare: In The Fight For Endless Independence

If you, reader, are pursuing creation, art, entrepreneurship, or any other *under-the-law* outlaw activity, you will be a lone wolf, whether you are trying creation alone or in a structured wolfpack. The mastermind mind needs to have skills for both traveling in wolfpacks and solo journeys. Back to your dreams again, this time with a basic question: Who hasn't considered being his-her-their own boss? Doing whatever they want? Avoiding any explanation? We all have had that shared dream. You, your hero, me, and the cyborgs of the future. This chapter is about the journey of the free. Independence in creation and life is an endless ambition, and if it is not exactly an ambition, it is something we envy when seen in others. Remind your hero that dreams won't show the other side of the coin.

The business of being your own boss is freaking complex. In the next pages, your hero will discover a formula to make it possible. Get the mirror close and ask them to find something to write with. Here is lesson one: Independence in creation is not a fair game. In 90% of the cases, it is not a game at all, it is a fight. There are a few very privileged exceptions; those who come from families with *that-kind-of* fortunes, established dynasties in the craft, or those lucky enough to be 'called' to *set up an independent initiative* with a few years of guaranteed contracts. For the rest of us pursuing creation, the 90%, there is only one way to make it. They call it now 'asymmetrical warfare.' We, the mutants, the hybrids, the mechanoids, the augmented, the rebels, the outcasts we can only make the dream possible using guerrilla tactics.

GEAR UP FOR BATTLE

You can come from the 10%, the 90%, and anywhere in the middle, but I bet you are not going to like this: In the next pages your hero will discover that the weapons are, again, in the freaking mirror. Yes. Any *under-the-law* outlaws mastermind minds, traveling solo or in packs, must be conscious of **who they truly are** and **what they truly are** before choosing a path. Is your hero able to handle both creation and administration? Do they like to knock on cold doors to sell? Are they patient enough to keep trying despite rejection? There are many questions like this. It is your hero's duty to consider them sooner than later.

Your star must also be conscious about what *they-are-not*. You are mostly aware of your personal taste and comfort zones, but it is also key to be aware about your own personality traits when trying alone. Whatever past, current, or future decisions about moving to, or initiating a solo –or a corporative– career your hero is about to make, they need to know the one in the mirror good enough to choose the right path, to change the path when needed, and to succeed in whatever path they end up on. Attention with the *mirror-self-checking* in the deciding talks! Ask your hero's image in the mirror to be ruthless. This is about making the journey to being a solo creator faster and healthier.

THE FREELANCER-SOUL TEST: THE GOOD, THE BAD, AND THE UGLY

I did it. I asked ChatGPT about the perfect profile to pursue a freelance career. And after that, I asked about what personalities shouldn't ever try. And then I read it all, and I freaking realized that I didn't fit in any of those two lists of personality traits. I am a combination of both lists. Not funny. Creator, search in your memories for a tune from an old western movie and make your hero remember the film *'The good, the bad, and the ugly,'* because those are the three pillars of the *Freelancer-Soul Test*.

After the ChatGPT shock, I decided to make three columns on my white board; the very **Good Personality Traits** for independence, the very **Bad Personality Traits**, and the third column, the **Ugly**, which was for *My Personality Traits*. The good, the bad, and the ugly. Play that old western tune in your head, and let's start with the *Good*.

I strongly recommend that your hero grab a pencil for this part. You can see my results under brackets with capital letters –*when I started in this arena*. 'A' for high score or *'yes, I have it,'* 'B' for *'kind of sometimes,'* and 'C' for *'nope, not at all.'* Do it for yourself, if not now, later.

First column: The Good Personality Traits for endless independence

These type of creators have key strengths as: Creativity (A), Self-motivation (B), Discipline (C), Adaptability (A), Confidence (B), Relationships in the craft (B), Entrepreneur spirit (C), Time management (B), Organization (C), Open mind (A), Attention to detail (B), Passion (A), Perseverance (B), Communication skills (A), Cultural awareness (B), and Sensibility (A). Your hero is probably scoring and counting results, good for them.

Of the fifteen freelancers' key strengths, when I started, I only had six A's from the *Good* column. I lacked nine strengths, totally or partially. Let's do the second column, the *Bad* treats for indie entrepreneurship.

Second column: The Bad Personality Traits for endless independence.

What kind of people should never consider freelancing? I'm going to go with ChatGPT's words for this one: *'some traits and personality types that might struggle in a freelance career in creative fields like art, entertainment, music, and dance.'* Did you see? Personalities that 'might struggle', shit, how cool is the machine. It is not *might*, it's for sure. Here we go, quick check-in with your hero's nature before you see my results. In the bad list, ask your hero to please invert the scoring system: Use C for *'yeah, that's me,'* B for *'sometimes,'* and A for *'not me.'*

Here's the list of the Bad Personality Traits to pursue a freelance career: Highly risk-averse personalities (A), People who crave constant structure and routine personalities (A), People who struggle with rejection and criticism (C), Those who dislike networking and social interaction (B), Highly dependent personalities (A), Those who are inflexible or resistant to change (A), Individuals with poor time management skills (C), People who dislike administrative tasks (A), Those needing constant feedback and validation (B), Highly impatient personalities (C).

Third column: The "Ugly" for My Personality Traits.

Stage three came because things turned nasty after seeing the results of the Good and the Bad lists. That's why the third column was named 'The Ugly.' Keep the old Western tune in your head for the final showdown. As the smart ass I am, at a certain point I decided to challenge ChatGPT with no success. I got the machine confused and I didn't get what I wanted: An explanation about how to make it work with my scores. No answers from the gods of Artificial Intelligence. The only solution I found was in a familiar place. Ask your hero to move the whiteboard to the mirror or vice versa. The last list is about YOUR own personality traits, and this one is the most relevant.

In this column your hero needs to list the traits –and their scores– from the *Good* and the *Bad* columns. Ask them to do it as they were analyzing someone else's personality, not theirs. It is just a game.

This bizarre beef with the AI started with the goal of measuring myself without judging my results. Didn't work. Judgment started –and almost forced me to quit– but after pushing myself a bit more, I noticed a warming self-esteem feeling growing inside, despite the results and the judgment. Weird. Here is how this happened. I started with the A's:

MY UGLY LIST

<u>From the Good Traits for Freelancers</u>

Creativity (A *'yes, I have it'*)

Adaptability (A *'yes, I have it'*)

Open mind (A *'yes, I have it'*)

Passion (A *'yes, I have it'*)

Communication skills (A *'yes, I have it'*)

Sensibility (A *'yes, I have it'*)

<u>From the Bad Traits for Freelancers</u>

Highly risk-averse personalities (A *'not me'*)

People who crave constant structure and routine

personalities (A *'not me'*)

Highly dependent personalities (A *'not me'*)

Those who are inflexible or resistant to change (A *'not me'*)

While writing, I realized that my best scores, the A's I have from the *Bad Traits*, came with a kind of weird hope. I paid attention to the promises hidden behind those A's I got, the things that clearly are *'not me.'* And I saw it. Shit. They can also be seen as something truly positive. Let's take one bad personality trait for freelance souls as a sample: *People who crave constant structure and routine personalities* obviously shouldn't consider independence in creation, but that is not me at all. I am the opposite. I'd do anything in my power to avoid routines. And here comes the good news: When I realized that I have that fighter spirit against structures and routines, I started seeing my trait as an asset. That's when a shadow of inner trust came to my guts. Pushed by the weird warm feeling, I went through both complete lists. The path began to show up when paying more attention to the A's, regardless of column of origin. I realized that between those A's from the *Good* and the *Bad* lists, I had a promising baseline to start working with. Solid enough to consider solutions to improve the B's and exploring how to deal with the C's when needed.

Rest of my Ugly list:

Self-motivation (B *'kind of sometimes'*)

Confidence (B *'kind of sometimes'*)

Cultural awareness (B *'kind of sometimes*)

Time management (B *'kind of sometimes'*)

Relationships in the craft *(B 'kind of sometimes')*

Attention to detail *(B 'kind of sometimes')*

Perseverance *(B 'kind of sometimes')*

Discipline *(C 'nope, not at all')*

Organization *(C 'nope, not at all')*

Entrepreneur spirit *(C 'nope, not at all')*

I still don't understand why I was so positive, but suddenly the B's were more doable, and I made plans to fix the C's too. Let's break down a C sample: I never aspired to be a traditional entrepreneur. I never liked the business part of it. Since my beginnings, I dreamt of finding that loving person who would enjoy running that part while being my soul mate. Tricky dream, let your hero know. The soul-mate part I got it. My first production company was owned by my son's mum and me. She was a very good producer for a first timer, but she never became my business soul mate, and that realization came later with new pains. Btw! Have you noticed? My plan for C failed because I got Association Induced Temporary Blindness.

How are you and your hero doing? I hope you are doing the homework. Help them with building their good, bad and ugly lists. Remind them that the most relevant thing is to go through it without bullshitting themselves. They will get to the same conclusion I did: If I am able to extract the proper energy from the A's –the things I truly am, and the things I am not– I certainly can upgrade the B's and maybe work out some of the C's too.

IMPROVING THE SCORE: FROM LACKING TO FINDING

Pues no era tan feo el muchacho (at the end the kid wasn't that ugly) is something my dad said to explain how an ugly baby would transmute into a handsome kid. Let's show your hero how to upgrade their personal traits for the indie path. If your hero has a similarly scary score as I did in the freelancer's soul test, let them know that overcoming that is a matter of a little discipline first and tons of discomfort afterwards. You got it? Discomfort. Which is better than pain, and way better than failure. Tell your hero that it is time to *meterse en faena* (get to the task).

Let me add a note about where my thoughts were when starting a solo career. Maybe your hero will get something from it. To be honest, I never paid too much attention to any failure scenarios. Never visualized them, never contemplated them, never thought about them. In my storytelling dreams, there were never doubts about making it, but a lot of anxiety about how to make it and pay the rent in the meantime. It all started with something I knew: I lacked the discipline to be my own boss.

CHAPTER 7

Discipline has been a lifelong struggle for me, a C that needed to be upgraded immediately to a B or an A. (Remind your character to use their own C's when going through these lanes.) Before rehab, I was only able to keep discipline with the things I did ENJOY. Yes, I am using caps to reinforce that word. I'd only show up for the things I enjoyed and for the time I enjoyed. No more discipline is required if I'm not enjoying it. If I like anything a lot, I'll be disciplined until the moment I don't like it. And if we are talking about something I don't like –like avoiding certain foods? Running? Doing taxes?– F**k, no! No discipline and no intention. Without discipline there are also ways to make it, through miracles and loads of money, but for the 90% of us discipline is required.

Now, how did I start to build up something I never had? After a few weeks re-inserted in society, I knew I was able to perform in the cleaning company –and keep my smart boss happy– but I wasn't sure if I would've been able to do it all by myself, with no boss and no deadlines. Here is where the *pero no había mas cojones* (there was no other way) makes the entrance again. When I quit cleaning to put all my energy into storytelling, I was so financially anxious that a doctor prescribed me benzos –fresh out of rehab, crazy! I didn't take the pills, but the panic of failure, and the fear of going back to the stadium sweeping was so high, that I started to build up a different kind of discipline since day one, Daniel's version of discipline.

Building such a wonderful personality trait starts with knowing what you must do every day, that is the route path to apply that discipline into. In my case, that was a challenging biggening. I know what I must do every day when I wake up; I don't need a list on a paper, nor anyone to remind me. I know my shit pretty well. 'Doing it' is a different conversation. Seeing all those things I needed to do listed on a piece of paper gave me nausea every time. I know it is biologic, literal: *se me remueven las tripas* (I'm legit gagging right now.)

I always hated to-do lists. I've been avoiding them since I was a little kid. In the next paragraphs you will see how I had to overcome that disease, mandatory. And this time it wasn't *por cojones*, it was *por dinero*. I ended up prioritizing the list of things for the day. The number one priority was anything related to cash. Period. I bought a couple of old school notebooks, cute markers, and I started writing those first lists of my life with a $ tattooed on my brain. From the 'only cash related' topics I moved to others, mostly related with generating more cash, which meant adding a lot of new items to the list. In the beginning, discipline was about sending invoices, writing emails, making calls and visits, and putting together offers. It all started with one, then two, then three. After the emails, the follow up, the visits, and then, whatever could came afterwards, usually another proposal to write, and some little industrial video production with it.

My discipline build up was already on the way when I had to face some other C's from my scores. Little by little, effort by effort, discomfort mutated into no discomfort, and after that, into some weird high every time I'd check a point in my to do list. F**k, that was new and felt good. Also, little by little, I started trusting myself more. The new *Daniel's kind of discipline* was working. The weirdest part is that while building discipline, some other lacked personality treats were upgrading without notice. I guess *no habia mas cojones* (there was no other way –you should know this one already.) The clients' search forced me to keep *Daniel's -kind* of organization. It still has a few of bugs in the code, but I upgraded my score from a C to a B. *Tampoco habia mas cojones* that improve relationships and continue networking. I'm still scoring a B today with that one, but I can switch to A-mode whenever I want, it is like a magic trick; if I connect with the combo *myself-project-goals*, I can deliver an A type of networking job.

With more unique wedding videos edited, more tedious industrial videos produced, more relationships in the craft, and more proposals written, the rest of the personality treats of the Ugly list were also upgraded easily with just some drops of discomfort here and there. I still do not score an A in all of them, still some B's, but Self-Motivation, Confidence, and Perseverance are solid A's -*most of the time*. This little note is important. Change the yoga sample for any other discipline: You meditate to become a Yogi Master, and you must keep meditating to keep being a Yogi Master. That simple. Tell your hero not to expect a diploma with the new score to hang on the wall forever. It doesn't work like that. There will be ups and downs, but discipline is the solution –and the key to unlocking the rest of the freelancing upgrades.

When deciding a future career –alone or in packs– based on the results of the *Freelancer-Soul Test*, it is not about the score; it is about following the paths that it will reveal. The routes that indicate your hero's strengths and weaknesses are the means to solid creation. Make your stars work in the columns to define the gaps that require filling during the solo creation journey. Each one of the points in the *Good* and *Bad* lists need to be addressed, and it will be addressed in the journey. Experiences will tackle the points of the lists with a combination of joy and pain. The *Ugly* list deserves the name but like in The Tale of the Ugly Duckling –and in my dad's expression '*Pues no era tan feo el muchacho'*– the ugly list will become beautiful once you realize the power of knowing what you are, and what you are not. Now you can plan how to get what you lack.

THE 'FOUR ELEMENTS' OF A STORYTELLING SOLO CAREER

I want to be fair to the Freelancer Soul Test, we all know –Chat GPT too– that there is no such a thing as 'perfection.' Some of the required traits for endless freedom can be very difficult to upgrade. That's why you are going to find someone who already has them. You, the visionary, the creator, the mastermind, the showrunner, the lone wolf, you are going to trust someone else. Yep. Trust is the keyword in this one. You will recruit new forces for the cause, but this time it is your hero's cause, not anyone else's. If your craft is audiovisual storytelling, you'd need a total of **Four Elements** to master the *being your own boss* life. If your hero doesn't master them, that will indicate what kind of troops they need to recruit first. The four elements start with money, sad, but real. Alongside with making more money -or any money-, the other three elements are defined in the expression: *Audio-Visual Story*telling. <u>Cash</u>, <u>images</u>, <u>sounds</u>, and a good <u>story</u> to put it all together.

First Element: Money.

If you are very creative, but you are not a freaking good communicator, you need to find someone who can sell for you. That simple. Your hero will get into the nitty gritty of the potential profiles, but for the sake of the chapter let me be clear: If you don't combine those two things, creativity and the ability to communicate your vision to make money, you need to find someone able who can do that for you. Needless to say, everything related to money counts in this element –budgets, costs, vendors, financing, banking...

Second element: Images.

I hope your hero aspires to differentiate their content from the rest. We all own cameras now. So, how are you going to do it? That is only possible through having the best **quality, vision,** and **execution in** the pack. The first one, **quality**, is a broad concept. It embraces your hero's education in visual storytelling -official and unofficial- and very important, their taste. **Vision** carries their capability to analyze what is out there and create the best visuals to serve the story. **Execution** means their ability to make that vision real. Basically, getting those amazing shoots that truly serve the story.

Third element: Sounds.

This sounds basic, but it is relevant. Don't take this one for granted, do not rely on AI, and please don't be a jerk in general. With the same goal as the second element, i.e., being the best, soundtracks are a tool that will rise your content above the rest. Just like the visuals of your story, the soundtracks must have quality, vision, and execution. This is where a big portion of the story resides. Every word, every track matters. Even if you know how to do it, be humble and get closer to a real-real pro.

Forth Element: A good story.

Give your hero another opportunity to avoid being a jerk. This one is complicated, first of all because '*we all know what a good story is*'. Really? The same way we all know how to use a camera, or we all know who should be on the World Cup team. We are mostly not qualified to evaluate a good story, even less to create it. 'Good' is another tricky word. A good story *serves the purpose, connects with the audience, entertains, and gives valuable outcomes* for both the viewer and the creator. A very good story will also transcend times and audiences.

How much does the story serve your goals? And I mean your clients' goals, if you are considering this as a career. How is your story connecting with the audience? How easy is it to watch? Meaning, is it entertaining or not? After decades analyzing and crafting stories, I have reduced all those questions to one: Does the story have soul? By that, I mean, can it connect with your audience's feelings? Does it make sense for the heart, the mind, and the eyes of viewers? Or not? That's the first question.

TROOPS RECRUITING FOR INDEPENDENT CREATORS

I hope your hero is scared by now. Yes, audiovisual storytelling feels easy, but it is not. There is way too much content out there. You want yours to be outstanding, to transcend. This is a good place to make the first cut among your heros. They need to be good with the Four Elements: Money, Visuals, Sounds, and the Story. If your hero does not master all of them, if they are not the Leonardo DaVinci of the audiovisuals, they need to find the right help, mandatory. *Por cierto!* It is almost impossible to master the Four, like there is not another DaVinci. Very few people can master all of them. Let's work out a path with the basics: If your hero is not already good, or avid to master <u>at least two of the Four Elements</u>, my recommendation is to reconsider the indie route. If your character wants to successfully dedicate a life to independent storytelling, they need to be really good in two Elements of these Four, *como minimo!* I'm sure ChatGPT would've said your hero *might struggle*, let's say it clearly: Not dominating two of the Four means that your hero won't make it long term as a freelancer. Period.

You are the only judge of your hero's capability. The ultimate decision about moving forward in the solo path resides in how much they know who they are, what they are, and what they are not. After that, the path is clear. So, what is required to master the Four Elements? Beside your hero's *cojones* and complete dedication, probably another two people to make a real difference in quality. Before making the cut into the indie creative life or exploring some other options, let me use some examples for your hero's benefit.

Let's imagine a case, someone whose gift is not the First Element. Visual talent is almost mandatory in the craft, but some creators can make it without it. That's why I am starting with this example. If your hero already masters the universe of sound because they are a producer, musician, or composer, and on top of that they have a gift for money related things -*communication skills*- move fast! You can make it faster than the average. This is what Daniel would do: I'd recommend for them to find a young, crazy film director and a young crazy writer, or a young - *they are all crazy*- comedian with shared musical passions and explore how to 'export' that passion to others with new content. Key words here are 'shared passions'. When your amazing creative vision is shared with other creators, and they connect for real, magic happens. And it will be your hero's magic, your hero's' vision, and your hero's team of *guerrilleros.*

Depending on how your protagonists would mix the Four Elements, the road would be bumpy, but that is all. If they master two, and the Four are well covered, they will rise despite the bumpy pavement. The first person I added to my *comando guerrillero* was my girlfriend -who later became *my son's mum*- she helped me with the Money element. Why? Because –I thought during my jerk phase– 'I was good enough with the other three.' Big BS. It did work for a while. I was momentarily being a jerk, but I got more time, and I used that time to create more and sell more. At a certain time, I sold so much that it was impossible to keep up without help for the Visuals and Sound, and I made my first real full-time hire as an employer. A video editor, a talented mastermind mind at least ten years younger than me. The third was a camera operator who was my assistant for wedding videos. He has a natural gift for visual storytelling. Somehow, he connected with my brain -*and with my teachings too*- and he literally got my Vision. All of it: framing, lighting, camera movements, even my editing tempo! He was the perfect mini me who allowed the real me to focus on directing and creating.

Having help after hiring those two young wonders, the time to realize that I was also being a jerk with the last of the Four arrived. So far it was easy to satisfy low budget clients with my -not that special- stories for industrials, local commercials, and so on, but when I spent more time as a director, I realized I needed to take better care of the Fourth Element, the story. I looked for a *content-related-only* guerrillero, and I found one. She was actually a *guerrillera*. With her addition, I had the Four Elements covered without my permanent presence, and things started going very well. I had time to develop new concepts, money to produce new pilots, a team to elevate them, and connections to sell them, only because of the way that *comando* covered with me the Four Elements.

OTHER *GUERRILLA* TACTICS TO CONSIDER

Maybe it is not yet the time to make a decision about your freelance future, but, if the decision is already made, take this chapter as a probed successful approach to a long, independent future in audiovisual storytelling. How can you work out and cover the 24 combinations of the Four Elements to make the dream better? Your hero could consider establishing parallel methods to raise their potential with the Four Elements.

I picked 'partnerships' after hiring the three young *guerrilleros*. I reached the top of my capability again, and partnership became the only possible route for growing. At a certain point, I met two gifted brothers who elevated my content over my own expectations, especially with the Money and Visuals factors. One was the best producer of the region, and his brother was the best cinematographer. Like me, both had already mastered at least two of the Four Elements, and they were very good people too. *Los hermanos* Torres became the brothers I never had. Later, we added a another *guerrillero* –with a promising background and speech– and here comes the lesson about partnerships in solo careers: If the candidate does not master two of the Four, I'd recommend not considering them. I did it. I ended up accepting a new senior command guerrillero against the rule of the Four (at least two!) and against my own instincts. Three years later, *los Hermanos Torres y yo,* the three of us, were facing the equivalent today to a six-figure banking debt, just because of those two decisions: Ignoring the rule, and ignoring my gut.

THE QUALITY FACTOR

Here's another creative exercise. Visualize your hero's future, when they are already on the independence path. For that time, I have a last consideration, but first please put your brain in memory search mode. Think about those fortunate artisans who are able to thrive and maintain a –freaking good– lifestyle, one that combines eternal independence with mind-blowing wealth. Yeah, I'm talking about the high class of independent creative businesses. Those that survive revolutions, trends, crises, ratings, and more. There are examples in every field, from TV franchises to fashion, design, beverages, motorbikes, magazines, suitcases, and film directors. How do they make it? What is the common factor? Yeah, obviously it is only possible through quality. Not only lifelong quality, generational quality. The kind of quality that everyone would mention as a reference.

I already knew when I started that QUALITY –yeah, caps again– was my path. The factor that will define me. Regardless of travelling solo or in packs, my decision was always to become someone who was known for giving the best possible every time. The best possible footage in every shooting, the best possible emotion in every cut, in every word, in every note.

I know your hero aspires to deliver good quality in their craft, but the Q factor is a personal commitment first. As the templars to the cross, if your hero commits to the Q Factor till the end, empires will fall under their shadow. No one can rebate quality. Despite times and trends, some clients will always prefer quality. *Asi de claro.* Your heros will find their niche. They will produce their content, and they will tell their stories. If they incorporate the Q factor, the road won't be easy, but it won't be as bumpy. *Por cierto!* Let them know that the Q factor runs both sides, in the product, and in the production. Guide them to keep high quality standards also with their troops, in their interactions, in their ethics, and in the mirror.

THE OUT OF THE BOX FACTOR

Here's another mandatory item on the path to endless independence. Guerrilla warfare is not about *the box*; it is many times against *the box*. How do you think your hero can compete against the establishment? How are you going to sell a show to a premium platform if your competitors are 1000x times bigger than you? The same way the Spanish guerrilleros defeated Napoleon and kicked him north of the Pyrenees again. How did they make it? Using out of the box methods, and a fair amount of *cojones* too.

Let me ask you, creator, if you consider yourself part of any box. You, or your hero. For good or for bad, I never did. As a kid, there was not even a toy box. Everything within my sight was considered a toy. As a teen, no box is ever considered when you hassle for dope in the big city sidewalks. When you don't belong to any box, why would you consider any limits? FYI, and with the goal of saving you some time, you probably know already! It doesn't take a lot to realize that 'the box' isn't real. It's just a story we all have been told. That simple. Society, rules, and times create the boxes. Dogmas, education, and the market economy solidify them.

You are a storyteller. You buy stories too, but please don't buy the one about the 'boxes'. Pick any field and you will notice how the names that left a mark in every area of human development are defined by society as *out-of-the-box* thinkers. What they did has an *inception* singular moment. Your hero will have their own. Either you are <u>solving a problem</u>, like lady Rhianna Fenty Beauty -*lack of diversity in the cosmetics industry*- or maybe you are <u>pursuing your unique vision</u>, like the designer Virgil Abloh –*Louis Vuitton's creative Director who turned a color, Off-White, into a movement that all the world followed,*– or perhaps the out of the box factor is coming from <u>an 'every day thing'</u> that nobody has looked at it with different eyes, something as mundane as tidying, like in Marie Kondo's case. Yes. Your hero is right; these names are not guerrilleros. They bathe in money and lead armies of employees, but they were guerrilleros once, and that's exactly the point.

The Out-Of-The-Box Factor deserves a whole book. For the moment, here is the list of *Out-Of-The-Box* recommended essentials.

- **Create Value Beyond the Obvious.** It is first in the list because it is the one I graduated with. During the first years of my little production company –I should've said 'boutique'– we made money with the content we produced in ways that nobody did before, at least not on our very small scale. I applied 'streets hassling methodology' to make Euros in any way possible. We developed an art in two areas: Content *re-packing and re-selling* and obtaining *production resources for free,* then trading them for a variety of goodies, especially presence in the stories we told.

- **Create Bridges Between Unlikely Worlds.** This one is big. In my case it has become the source of outstanding show premises but also works to develop collateral income. Push your hero with this one, *es una llave maestra*, it opens all kind of doors.

- **Break the Rules of "How It's Done".** I did it several times, from 'how' a show was shot so far to 'how' a show was sold. For other references than me, see what Steve Lacy did, when the Grammy-nominated producer started creating music on his iPhone.

- **Fill Gaps Others Ignore.** Yeah, it is a soft launch, but useful. I did it for fast income first, and then I exported the approach to some other areas of interest. It works.

- **Build Your Own Ecosystems.** What is it that you may need to not to depend on? To be free? What would work for you in every level? In every one of the Four Elements of your craft? Think about it, a lot, and build it in your mind –or do it for real– but please have your perfect ecosystem ready for when the time comes.

- **Be Strategic with Collaborations.** You already got this one, enough said in these pages about it, more to come.

- **Use Everyday Tools Creatively.** Remember the story about my pre-historic *GoPro-style* mini-camera and my sister's multi-awarded *Callejeros* docu-show? No more comments.

- **Stay Adaptable.** You, your ecosystem, your content, your everything! Life is constant change, lone wolf warriors barely forget that.

- **Owning Your Weirdness.** Prioritize Authenticity. Your work and your persona reflect *who you are*—quirky, bold, unpolished, or revolutionary. Authenticity resonates and builds trust.

- **Stay Obsessed with "What If?"** I kept this one for the last with the intent to minimize the consequences of the obsession the question brought me. You have in your hands or devices the results of one of my more recent *what if*s.

Something important to ruminate here. For the *all-the-way* weirdo and the rebel sides of your heroes. Ignore or jump box limits but remember that if you don't deliver content that fits the boxes, you won't make it. And I mean money! Clients must be satisfied. To edit more weddings, I needed to fit in the wedding videos box, but I stretched its limits. A lot. That gave me prestige, more work, and the opportunity to avoid weddings for the rest of my producing life. Let's put it this way: Tell your hero to think out of the box to find ideas, other guerrilleros, clients, production resources, and new opportunities, but regarding final creation, they must keep an eye on the box limits and force them only when they feel it is the right time.

Time to check in with your hero now, and with the mirror too! As you see, in all the personality traits described; the four elements needed for your specific craft, the commitment to quality, or the out of the box thinking, would work perfectly in both the guerrilla warfare and the corporative approach. Quick note about the personality traits: If you are not suited for a long independent life, don't waste your energy trying. Fight your way up to mastermind in a corporation, do it honorably, and keep your own creative soul in shape for when the time comes. Even if you are clear in your decision about going solo or not, it is an advantage to know what you lack and how to get it. Creator, humanoid, or rat, knowing yourself is always going to help. Adapt these words, creator. It doesn't matter if it is audiovisual storytelling, music, acting, or DJ'ing. Master at least half of the key elements of your specific craft, commit yourself to quality, think out of the box, end ENJOY the ride! It's going to be amazing. Solo, in packs, or both.

CHAPTER 8

Are You Ready For The Top Of The Creative Pyramid?

THE BIG LEAGUES AND THE OFFICES UPSTAIRS

Notes

CHAPTER 8

The Big Leagues And The Offices Upstairs

THE PLACES YOU DREAM OF BUT YOU WILL NEVER BE READY FOR

It really doesn't matter that much if you or your hero has decided to go solo, work in a pack, or do both. The only thing that matters is what is holding them back. If they follow this guide's recommendations -and if they execute the freelancer soul test properly- little by little, they will experience the consequences of the mirror accountability. Things will happen for good. Your hero is going to find a steady positive path and will start looking for the 'what's next' thing, as I did. If you are in a pack and you are looking for the 'next', you probably have ambitions for opportunities in the biggest shows, the biggest ventures, or the biggest companies. If you are solo, you will aim for the biggest productions, the biggest clients, and the biggest budgets. Yes, the entertainment business is a bit like Texas; size matters a lot.

Most of us -the 90% again- most of us creators, storytellers, and especially directors or showrunners have grown in our careers admiring and wanting to one day be in those XXL sets, managing those XXL budgets, and telling those XXL stories that at least half of the planet would recognize. Why not? This is about dream-making. Let's dream. You might make it, or maybe you already did. No matter, I have tips for both here. Let's use the mirror for just a sec: We all belong to a 'league.' I don't care what content you do or where it lives. Whether you are on Twitch, YouTube, Netflix, TikTok, NBC, or Tele-Cuenca is not relevant now. Think about these two leagues: the division you are currently playing, and the top division you'd like to play. This next soccer reference is world-wide pop culture, guys, needed even if you hate soccer! After decades of witnessing how *Real Madrid* destroyed the most important teams of the world in the Bernabeu Stadium, the Spanish press introduced the expression '*miedo escenico*' to describe how world-class players and teams would freeze when they got onto that field. These next pages are about what your hero will feel when they finally make it to their own Big League, *cuando les toque jugar en el Bernabeu.*

SIZE MATTERS: BIG EXPECTATIONS, BIG REWARDS, BIG MESS-UPS

There are XXL-sized audiovisual projects in all kinds of audiovisual content, in all languages, and in all countries. Whatever niche you tell stories about - drama, travel, dancing, health, make up, science, comedy, cycling, or horror, I don't care- There is a *top-of-the-line* budget, a real XXL size, and the rest. The following pages are about the XXL's experiences, with most of the lessons extracted from what was the Big League for me: The sacred and competitive space of the nationwide primetime broadcast. That is where the real money lies, and where bloody ratings battles leave victims every day of the week. The big leagues come with big rewards, but also the big leagues are a place where the stakes are so high, the decisions so wild, and the consequences so dramatic, that money is not the ultimate factor, which is weird, but it is true. And that is the pattern you will find in the Big Leagues of the entertainment industry, regardless of niche- insane amounts of money and an impossible understanding of its use. There is some for your hero, too. That's part of the game.

So far, the most expensive episodic story ever told is The Rings of Power from the Lord of the Rings. This Amazon series is the most expensive TV show ever made. There is no higher league if you are into scripted drama *-please ignore ratings or audience results.* I'm talking about what it means to 'play' in that league. Can your hero imagine? It's a weekly show with eight episodes. Do the math! Can you imagine being part of that? There are more Big Leagues cases in serial scripted drama, but no one has exceeded the Rings of Power budget of $58.1 million per episode. Those numbers are sick. Imagine now a daily broadcast of a gameshow like *The Price Is Right* with a budget of $600k per episode. As a daily show, that's a lot of money in a year. And it has been on air for decades. That is the real business in the TV landscape: A daily show in the Big Leagues, whatever it is, means good money. With the globalization of content over the last 30 years, a few groups have acquired the companies behind the most successful shows on earth, and they have also colonized territories with the most well-known franchises. Today, you can watch The Price Is Right in 40 countries. I'm talking about 40 languages, guys! Forty different versions in a single day. Do the math! Even if the production budget is only a third of the CBS version, it is insane what that Intellectual Property has done for the owners. All that business can only come hand in hand with big corporations. The Big League means Big Corporative shit. That's how it is. Only the worldwide content and distribution powerhouses play up there, so tell your hero they might need every drop of energy to understand that environment. And remind them this: money is not the thing up there, despite the crazy numbers in every genre: The production cost of an NFL Super Bowl game is around $30 million (no rights included). In news, a daily prime time national broadcast can be around $500k per bulletin (every day!) The cooking competition Hell's Kitchen is $2 million per episode. *Survivor* is $4 million, and *The Bachelor* is $2 million *-pause here! Let me give you a little taste of what is coming in this chapter.* That show, *The Bachelor* in Spain, was my first prime time as a showrunner in the Big Leagues, my painful baptism in the Big League's absurdity, and my first big mess-up, too. All together.

I saw it coming, it was so obvious! But my excitement for the opportunity was so high that I ignored my skills, avoided the mirror, and decided to go with the impossible. What would you do? What do you think your hero would do? F**k! I was running one of the first adaptations of *The Bachelor*, a show that premiered on ABC the previous season with freaking good results. My very first big show as a showrunner for a big network, in a big international intellectual property! The freaking Big Leagues, a lifetime opportunity. So, I canceled all my storyteller survival mechanisms and decided to ignore a basic rule in storytelling: You cannot properly build up a romantic storyline if you can't figure out how it ends. That rule is one of the foundations in a show like *The Bachelor*: You tape everything, from the first rose ceremony to the last one, and then you build the episodes to get the best from those dramatic and romantic days. Sounds like common sense, no? Well, one of the first international versions of *The Bachelor* was adapted in Spain, but we decided to do it 'live' *-to tell the story in freaking real time!-* and to include audience voting in the weekly rose elimination ceremonies. Surreal, impossible, but we did our best to make it work, and, of course, it didn't. On top of that, we had three bachelors, not just one *-The Bachelor* Spain was called 'Xti' in Antena3. We lasted on air for less than 3 weeks. Yes, absurd, stupid, pretentious, and more. We all ignored the storytelling laws, including my bosses at Endemol and at the network. After spending a few years around them, I bet today that those executives on both sides of the table were sharing that crazy idea. It wasn't my decision. I did my best, but I was blinded by my first game in the Big Leagues. I suffered the *miedo escenico* of the Bernabeu Stadium, and more. The people upstairs -my bosses- were blinded by the success of a show called *Big Brother, which was* produced live by another network and the same production company. Some TV history for your hero: In the pre-smartphone era, almost all talent and reality competitions in Europe were live TV, not pre-recorded. Among other reasons, this was because of the insane amount of money that the parties were making from phone voting. This story is for your hero to realize the absurdity of the Big Leagues. Some of the most brilliant minds in Spanish storytelling decided to murder themselves, kill their clients, and burn out all that XXL money, while ignoring a basic premise we all knew as professional storytellers.

I hope the lesson for your hero is clear: In the Big Leagues, everyone loses their common sense. When you are a rookie, you lack common sense because you're so excited to have made it. Later, when you are a veteran, you lose common sense because of how things work up there. The Big Leagues and the big corporations are driven by egos and hidden agendas. Let your hero know that surviving that environment deserves this effort. I've seen crazier things than *The Bachelor* live version in the showbiz Big Leagues; that was just the first. And the fact is, they all will come from the most unexpected and surreal reasons. You cannot prepare for that. It is that simple. No matter the number of years of experience or the master's degree you obtain. No mastermind mind can ever be ready for the higher divisions because of one single reason: They all come with what I call '*The Uncertainty Factor*', which is caused by the lethal combination of egos and hidden agendas. In my first experience with *The Bachelor*, the only uncertainty was which day the network would cancel the show. The mistake was obvious, and motivated by blind ambition, but that one wasn't the worst I've experienced. The truth of the Big Leagues is that something will happen 'upstairs' that will mess up everything. Sooner or later. Guaranteed. And I am talking about crazy, impossible things. The kinds of decisions that ignore the basic laws of physics in our universe -*Kafka se queda corto*- It is like depending on god's will, but twice. God, and the offices upstairs.

This new deity you are serving will decide your hero's destiny up there. Most of the time, it has the shape of a smartphone -sometimes it is just an email. The funny thing is that the deity doesn't give a shit about your performance, your show results, your audience, or the profits made. And speaking of results, remind your hero that the Big Leagues in entertainment come with some harsh realities. When playing in the Bernabeu stadium of content, results are the most important thing, but it's not the same as in normal life. By normal, I mean compared with any other industry. Pharma's executives scoreboard updates **once or twice a year**—or even less— Marathon vibes kind of race, easy. They think about big pressure, but in slow motion. The tech big shots do monthly or quarterly check-ins, but the big shit happens when those **quarterly** results drop. Their race pacing is quarterly sprints. Intense, but they get at least a few months to see if the new app works. In Banking, execs are measured by **annual** performance reports, plus a bonus season if you're on Wall Street. That's like a walk in the park on a sunny day. How is it in our beloved entertainment landscape? **Every. Single. Day.**

While a banking or pharma big shot sweats under that quarterly or annual spotlight, the showbiz Big Leagues competitors are sprinting in a daily race—no commercial breaks allowed. It feels like you are alone running 100 races, against 100 clones of Usain Bolt, with Dr Martins on your feet. Stupid, and stressful: Daily ratings, view counts, streaming numbers, social media chatter, interactions—every show, every slot, every single day. If last night's episode tanked, you'll be hearing about it early in the morning. It's like a 24/7 sentence designed by Kafka.

That is a normal day in the top leagues, with no major issues; when there are issues, it is chaos. One flop and it is happening. The world's talking about your show on Twitter, or in Parliament, so imagine what's going on in the offices upstairs. *The Uncertainty Factor* becomes certain: That upstairs number will show up on your screen. Even if you are the CEO of a multinational content outlet, there will be an upstairs number. We all have a direct report line to yield to, no matter how high the position is.

Do you see yourself navigating those waters? I did, and I was wrong. I believed that giving my 150% in the project -as I did to get to the Big Leagues- would've been enough to make it, but no. In the Big Leagues, you cannot spend all your gas on the show. You need to keep enough gas for yourself and for corporate politics, at least if you want to endure up there as a mastermind mind. And tell your hero this: the more shit there is under their lead, the more they are exposed to the upstairs gods. I think it is clear enough, no? These are the Big Leagues, the places you dream of, but you will never be ready for.

THE GOOD AMBITION

I don't need to know the specifics of your star's Big Leagues; whatever type of content they create, your hero's 'next thing' will be fueled by ambition, which is needed, but it will only become real through collaboration. Ambition is another keyword of the chapter. It is part of the mastermind mind DNA, but it needs to be used for good. These two ingredients are delicate; sometimes 'ambition' doesn't mix well with 'collaboration', and it has horrible consequences. We all want to grow in our careers; it is legit to aspire to the highest league, but you cannot get there over the dead bodies of co-workers, employees, partners, bosses, or exes. When a talented mastermind mind's ambition glands get corrupted, things get messy fast, bringing pain and suffering to everyone involved in the project. The higher a mastermind mind hikes the stairway to heaven, the worse the consequences of mismanaged ambition. On the other side, when ambition is mixed with an immaculate work ethic, things go far. The perfect recipe has these ingredients: healthy ambition, immaculate work ethic, and quality in your delivery. If you can get this right, I can guarantee you will go farther and faster.

A Mastermind mind's ambition must be properly regulated, and to do that, it is important to know where it is coming from. Ambition for bigger, better, and more lucrative storytelling was my engine. Whatever your hero's ambition, a leading position, more money, stability, fame, or just a job, the 'storytelling' part is what makes all that possible. I always put 'storytelling' first. I want to tell more relevant stories in a more relevant manner in a more relevant outlet. That's first in my case, and then -if possible- with more money, more stability, and better positions -I never consider fame. When I was already satisfying my ambition and moving to higher leagues, I heard these words for the first time. I'm sure you have heard them too: 'Don't think about the money when pursuing your dreams'. I've heard it from professors in business schools, world-class athletes, spiritual gurus, successful artists, priests, therapists, and yoga masters. No idea what your hero thinks about it, but I can only say that in my case, it worked, and it still works. I'm not good with faith in general, 'leaps of faith' even less, but it was already happening. The money factor wasn't the most relevant topic when I was ambitioning, and the money was coming without asking. Weird. Today, I still don't think about the money, nor the fame, nor the position when I aspire to the next thing. What else is left to think about? Yes: Storytelling. In my case, 'better and bigger audiovisual storytelling'. In yours, whatever your creative shit is.

My ambition to escape from wedding videos and small industrial productions was pure, uncorrupted, and mandatory. My leagues so far were local TV commercials, small-sized industrial videos, and the most relevant, in terms of $, was the BBC. Not the Brit one! *BBC* is a Spaniard funny acronym used for *Bodas, Bautizos y Comuniones,* also defined as *'Reportaje Social'-* You can visualize that easily, creators! Imagine 200 churches with 200 brides walking down 200 aisles, and 200 ceremonies with the whole *antes-durante-despues.* Yes, I was sick of it. After a couple of years, the most exciting thing about my league was the fact that I was able to live from it. This is a good moment to observe one of the multiple contradictions of our craft: After a difficult journey to make it possible, we all will hate –sooner or later- the storytelling we are living from. There's no 'big' or 'small' league in this fact. It is real despite a project's size, league, budget, viewership, platform, and benefits. But also, despite the type of content you do. Romantic comedies, weddings videos, podcast, news, infomercials, tutorials, late nights shows, conferences, surgeries, real housewives, church services, make up tips or porn. You will get sick of it. When that happens, there are only two options: Fix it, or leave it.

THE DUALITY OF THE INDUSTRY

To better navigate the universal laws of the entertainment industry, especially in the big leagues, you should accept fast -and don't forget ever- that show business is like no other business, also in this sense: The extreme duality you face in every aspect of it. This premise is embedded in the foundations of the industry, but it is not limited to showbiz. See the pillars that sustain the duality: There are two social classes -*High and low*; two types of professionals: *Those that do the work, and those that take advantage of others*; two sides in the table: *Buyers and sellers*; and two positions in the marketplace: You -*your show-* are either *hot, or cold.* Yes, all of that also happens in other industries, but not in such a rough way. Advice for your heroes: The higher the league, the more radical the duality. To steer the showbiz Big Leagues without getting too lost, you need to always remember those 'two sides'.

TRANSITIONING TO HIGHER LEAGUES

Tell your hero they cannot jump from the bottom league to the top one. It won't work. It is mandatory for a mastermind mind to stop by in some intermediate leagues to have enough time to get used to it. They must build some tolerance in their system before going big for real. The risks of a Big League overdose are serious. It usually means no coming back.

My first interaction with a league bigger than mine was a real drama. My early showrunner ambition got me into a wrecking partnership -and a never-dreamt-of content landscape: The Pyrenees mountains. I was trying not to go back to the BBC -Bodas, Bautizos y Comuniones- the news, and the low-budget industrials when the opportunity to grow, a big one, the most important Four Elements for a storytelling career, came. A new partner would improve the Money Factor. The Euros came in the shape of a winter sports show contract with a regional network. If, and only if, we impressed the network CEO with a killer pilot. The opportunity to scale from local to regional was huge for me. So big that I ignored the basic premise about the Four Elements: Don't add people to your team who don't master at least two of the Four. And I did. We were three partners with a team of eight behind us (side note, most of them paid by me). I told you about my partners before, the $100k debt case. Among the partners, Carlos T and I mastered two of the Four Elements. The third partner, Pepe G, only mastered the Money factor. I owe Pepe G an early lesson about the industry duality thing: I learned that there are people who do the job, and people that don't do shit and take advantage of it. Pepe G had the relationships and hundreds of hours of good footage in the snow, but he couldn't do anything with what he captured on tape–not one of the other three basic elements – visuals, sound, story. Wrong decision from my side. We did the pilot, and we rocked it –yeah, the After Effects beta version pilot, that one. Back to the drama: The CEO of the regional network was happy with the pilot, and he committed to a season. We would be on air soon. Just to make things funnier, let me tell you that the network CEO's name was also Pepe. Pepe Quilez -Pepe Q from now on.

Well, it was done! I made it! I was directing and producing an access prime-time show on a regional network. A league bigger than mine, and a good opportunity to shine and learn. And I did shine, and I did learn, this last one with a lot of pain involved. I'll give you now two scenes to visualize: The editing suite in our little production house, and the network CEO's office afterwards. Same main characters: My partners Carlos T and Pepe G, the network boss Pepe Q, and myself.

The day of the premiere arrived; the delivery was just a few hours before airtime because the show included a last-minute mountain weather report. We were finishing composing the segment when the network CEO, Pepe Q, called my partner Pepe G asking for the status of the master tape, and Pepe G started lying about it. With no need. For no reason. Ask your heroe to remember the 'no need, no reason'; it will be a constant in the Big Leagues. On the call my partner Pepe G told the network that the final render was done, and we were mastering to tape already -yes kids, we delivered tapes by hand in those times- but in fact, we were finishing the weather segment in a 1999 Windows NT computer that at that very moment crashed. That was normal, but this time I felt something unusual.

There were only three video editing suites running on computers in town, and we had two of them with us. Yes, that piece of tech, that Perception video board, was my blessing and my curse. The same technology that gave us the creative space to commission the show was f***ing up the whole thing. Think about Murphy's Law and imagine the rest. I'll save you the details of the technological drama, but two hours later, in the moment when my partner Pepe G told the network CEO ~Pepe Q~ that he was *'leaving our site with the tape in his hand'*, we were actually rendering the show. The lies continued for another three or four calls. In theory, my partner, Pepe G, needed almost four hours to cross town with the tape. Zaragoza is similar to Phoenix in size and population, but smaller in area. Can you imagine Pepe Q's face when Pepe G showed up 20 minutes before airtime? I wish I had seen that look. I don't know what Pepe Q had in mind when the tape arrived, but I was about to learn it with key lessons for the Big Leagues.

Waiting, exhausted, for the cancellation of our show before the premiere wasn't easy. We were still dealing with Windows NT crashes when my phone rang. It was my partner Pepe G in the line: *'Que dice Pepe ~Pepe Q, of course~ que os vengais Carlos y tu para aca.'* Exactly, Pepe Q, the network CEO wanted to see us three. Shit. Not good. When we all got into the CEO's office, I was embarrassed, paralyzed, and afraid of losing the best project of my life. There was more weight on my shoulders; an exhausted team waiting to be paid, and an insane amount of money we owed to the banks. When Pepe Q finished his incredulity-based speech ~he was also playing a major game with advertisers and his bosses in Madrid~ there was silence. Long and tense silence. Pepe G said nothing. Carlos T said nothing. I decided to stay put. If Pepe Q were to do what he should do after discovering his new vendor was dishonest and delivered late, we were all fucked. Well, I was more fucked than my partners, a matter of paying employees and bank loans. After a few seconds to get his shit together ~I mean exactly his hear and his glasses~ Pepe Q looked at me and asked: *'can I trust you?'*

I don't know if I was the only one looking at Pepe Q's eyes. I'm sure Pepe G wasn't; he usually only looked at the floor, but I know the network CEO was looking straight into my eyes, and in that moment, my life changed forever. I felt it. I became the de facto new Mastermind Mind of the show that my partner Pepe G had sold him. The actual showrunner of Dentro Nieve, named right there, through the killer look of a very pissed off regional network CEO. I never looked at my partners before answering, there was no need, they were there when I got the freaking new title! I said *'yes, completely'*. Pepe Q paused for some seconds looking through his office window, then he turned towards us, but only looked at me again, to say something like *'next Thursday the show will be here by 1:30 for quality control. Or you can say goodbye to your careers. All of you'*.

I said something on the realm of *'Gracias Pepe por mantenernos en el aire, y por confiar en que vamos a hacer algo muy especial. No te vas a arrepentir'.* And it was exactly like that. We delivered an amazing season. He never regretted it, and I'm sure Pepe Q is still as proud as I am of that show.

That first test in a higher league came with valuable learnings and a painful debt. We finished the season, and Pepe G left us *con un pufo del quince* (slang for big debt) in a shiny Mercedes 500 that he bought during the pilot production. Seeing him buy that car should've been a big enough red flag, but Carlos and I decided to also ignore it. I was driving a Hyundai Accent in those times, *si, a veces soy asi de gilipollas* (yep, sometimes I'm just that big of a dumbass).

The transition to a higher league gave me a taste of the big game, but I wasn't ready for the Bernabeu yet. I mastered the concept of 'industry duality' in several departments: Two types of professionals: workers and parasites; and two sides of the table: power and servers. The power side of the table made me a showrunner with a show on air, and my partners never spoke about it. Is it clear enough for your hero? *Lo que dice la cadena va a misa. Punto.* (What the network says is mandatory. Period.)

The regional network round also taught me that the cutting-edge technology that will make your hero rich will make them suffer first. They need to be prepared for that. I also learned that the quality I aimed for was, most of the time, not compatible with my deadlines and resources. I had to lower my expectations a bit. I also learned how to always *'Over Deliver - On Time'*, which is an art. You know why? Because in the creative field, properly mixing ambition, quality, resources, and deadlines is more complicated than Goya's painting palette. But the most important things I got from the transition to a higher league were how to ski properly with 50lb of production gear on me and a lifelong love for Benasque, the mountain village where we set our field team— and where I bought a house after I made it into the Big-big Leagues.

ARRIVING IN THE BIG LEAGUES: NAVIGATING THE CORPORATIVE NONSENSE

I've compared the **Uncertainty Factor** *-corporative decisions coming from egos and hidden agendas-* to a deity for a reason: You can't prevent it, but you can train for it. Ready? Let's go. Let your hero know how the first contact with the summits of storytelling goes: Inexplicable processes, endless bureaucracy, overwhelming internal communications *-600 emails is my record in a day, held in NBCUniversal.* The most painful time-wasting feeling your hero will ever experience, leaving no time for real work. If your hero asks their new mastermind mind co-workers, they will complain about the same, but nobody does shit. It's like the corporation is this *no-men-behind-the-wheel* entity that can eat your ass if you don't keep up. That is the welcome package to the Big

Leagues, but nobody will tell you about it, and if they do, your hero will think, *'I'll deal with that later'*, as I did. Why? Because the Big Leagues also come with big treats, that's why. When you make it to the offices upstairs in a giant content corporation, your lifestyle –and your ego– will get a sapphire upgrade; forget the platinum concept. This is the Big Leagues. It's not only what seats you fly on, or the kind of hotel you have in Cannes, or the drivers, or the VIP events, nope, it is the people around you. In the showbiz circus, your hero will be flattered in ways they couldn't ever imagine.

Yes. I'm guilty. I have succumbed to flattery. A few times. But the pleasure never came from 'outside' the corporation. With 'outside' I mean I was able to handle pretty well *los alagos* of vendors, agents, talent, clients, old friends, and more. That kind of shit I was used to in the streets, and in the lower leagues, the kind of unhealthy flattery you see coming. But we are going to ignore that kind of flattery –I trust your hero's ethics. The next lines to focus on are *los alagos* from the closest people they are going to meet, their co-workers in the *Entity*. Same level executives, a few more from upstairs and downstairs, and a court of personal assistants, direct report lines, and the whole floating ecosystem of projects and departments. People who, in theory, are pursuing the same goals as your hero, but in reality are an oversized army of servers that pay tribute and obedience to a master *-who knows which one?-* while pursuing their own personal agendas.

THE EGO GAME AND THE HIDDEN AGENDAS

If there is a place where your hero must remember the tips from *The Lone Wolf and the Stairway to Heaven* chapter, it is the Big Leagues. Don't blame your heroes if they need some time to realize it. We all do; no mastermind mind ego can afford the level of adulation experienced in a content giant without gaining a few pounds. — It's that simple. In a few days, your hero will notice that almost everyone up there has size XXL egos. I think it's part of the strategy of the *Entity*, feeding the mastermind mind's ego for the sake of chaos. Another weapon of the *Entity* is the hidden agenda, which is absolutely lethal when it's used in combination with an extra-large ego. Those kinds of leaders will ignore the people around them who are doing the job, the clients they serve, and the company they belong to.

Those two elements, agendas and egos, are the second and third most important allocation of your hero's energy upstairs. The number one energy destination should still be whatever show they are running. In the Big Leagues, your hero will realize that they need to spend energy being aware of their environment, not only in the pursuit of a common goal, but also to avoid being stabbed in the back. That's lesson 101 in the Big Leagues journey, and of course, I learned it the hard way. If your hero puts their everything into the project, by the end of the first one *-even with good results-* they will become easy prey for the predators around, below, and upstairs.

Tell your hero that it is important to consider not only the *Entity* –that strange being that has no heart, no soul, but is alive and eating– but also the humans that –they believe– are in charge of the *Entity*. Knowing the different 'types' of mastermind minds around your hero –especially in the offices upstairs– will help them to co-exist with the *Uncertainty Factor*. If they can detect and differentiate the modus operandi of the upstairs fauna, they will be able to keep more energy in the show and less in the BS. The humans around your hero come and go. You will find them eventually in the smallest endeavors, but in a big corporation, your star will meet all these archetypes I'm describing as soon as they arrive. I'd like to encourage your hero to be humble. If they see themselves in the following descriptions, it's time to go back to the mirror and re-adjust. Your hero doesn't want to be tagged under any of these mastermind mind profiles:

The -not that well- Hidden Agenda type:

They are the "Yes, BUT..." kind of crowd: They smile and nod in meetings, but they'll pivot the plan or take credit when you're not around.

Among the hidden agenda type are also the Scorekeepers, those who always want the upper hand. Even if you're technically on the same team, they see you as competition; they will try to outscore your hero always, but the worst part is that they will keep mental tallies of who "owes" them, to use when needed. Projects become more about personal wins than collective success, and your hero will lose interest fast.

The Power Trip type:

- **The Micromanagers:** These people want a say in literally everything, from the ironing of the backdrop curtains in the backstage area for a silly 15" headshot tease– to the color of the pages on the printed scripts. Very relevant stuff, five minutes away from a live national premiere. The weirdest thing is that, usually, they won't give a shit about the stuff that really matters. More accurately, they don't know shit about the stuff that really matters, and they fear you, your talent, and your success. If you've had that kind of *jefe* around, you know what I mean.

- **The Title Tossers:** These kind of people love flaunting their positions and their sapphire status everywhere. What's the point of having a VIP pass to Coachella if no one knows about it? From trendy festivals to the 4th-floor cafeteria, they'll expect you to treat them like creative corporate royalty. In some exceptions, these individuals know their shit –your hero will learn from them– but in general, it is not like that. More likely, they will bury your hero's ideas because they are stifled by their inflated egos.

The Office Politics type:

- **The Clan member:** Clans, cartels, gangs, alliances, commandos, the tag is not relevant. In big corporations, there are squads, associations, and ride-or-die buddy systems. The upstairs power struggles are at stake, the big battles of the Big Leagues. In my experience, after a couple of successful seasons, the people behind the project can become a new clan, and that is not convenient. Since the very beginning, those mastermind minds behind a project that can not only make the cut, but thrive, will become victims of the cartels' recruiting agents –better with me than against me– and let me tell your hero, it is going to be scary when the moment arrives. Depending on the circumstances, the recruiting agent could also be the leader of the clan. Those are the scariest minutes. One time, I was running programming and development for unscripted content when I received a call from an SVP who wasn't at all involved in my report line, nor in my performance, nor even in unscripted content. Let your hero know that if in the first five minutes of the conversation that person drops a line like '*you have a great future in this company Daniel*', they have three options: Be ready to move on, dedicate more energy to politics, or bow to the *mero mero* *immediately.*

Another subtype of the Office Politics people are <u>the Gossip Cuffs</u>, those who are constantly hustling information, rumors, hypotheses, and lies. One slip, and your hero's words might get twisted into a poisoned rumor. Being on the wrong side of a gossip can derail not only your hero's reputation, but their performance and their soul.

The "Too Good to Be True" type:

- **The Social Butterflies:** Some of the first to arrive. They'll connect with everyone in the building, from the intern to the CEO. It's great until you realize it's mostly surface-level, probably to pad their contact list.

- **The Transactional Connectors:** They'll be your "best friend" if you can offer something: introductions, resources, or clout. Once that's gone, so are they. As the mastermind mind lone wolves already know, your friends are not your friends, especially within the *Entity* borders. Your hero might mistake a purely strategic relationship for genuine mentorship or friendship. When the hype dies down, say goodbye to any real support system.

Los notas- The Performative type:

Los Notas. Punto. There is no translation in English for that, but if you hear the expression in Madrid, you will get the meaning, even coming from Mars.

- **The Buzzword Kings/Queens:** They'll drop terms like "synergy," "disrupt," and "innovate" in every sentence. But ask for an actual strategy, and you get nothing.

- **There are also 'All Talk, No Walk' Execs:** They give TED Talk-worthy speeches on company culture and vision, but vanish when it's time to do the real lifting. While asking themselves why their leaders aren't walking the talk, ask your hero to not waste too much time chasing their confusing orders or vague promises, because that's what comes from this kind of leader–if anything arises after the bubbly keynote. I know you get it. These leaders create a fake culture where saying the right things matters more than actual results. Very unhealthy for a real creative mastermind mind.

The Gatekeeping type:

I'm tempted to use another Spanish expression, *'los porteros'*, and I am not referring to soccer goalkeepers. Nope, I'm talking about the doormen.

- **The Information Hoarders:** Certain leaders act like secret knowledge is their personal currency. They keep data, contacts, conversations, or strategies locked up to control as much as they can. A subtype of *porteros* are the <u>Access Controllers</u>: Whether it's the ear of the CEO or an invite to a meeting, they only share resources with their "in" crowd. I've found both types, but usually they come in a single pack. You hero will feel isolated and undervalued, and that will kill their motivation over time. If they decide to go on with it, I hope the treats and perks are really worth it. An important note here: The senior exec's cousin's best friend's kid might magically appear in a senior role. Not only can the gatekeeper leaders be blamed for nepotism and favoritism, but in the gatekeepers' case, a surprising hire-*or promotion*- will be the first consequence of the hidden strategy.

- **Teacher's Pet:** Sometimes, it's less about what you know and more about how close you are to certain decision-makers. Some of the people upstairs bow to every powerful figure with the sole interest of 'being there when it happens'. Hard work will be overlooked in favor of personal-strategic relationships. Not a good climate for creative mastermind minds.

The Heirs type:

They act as if they were to inherit the corporation, or they want to impress their bosses. Good luck with both. They are the Seven Eleven of the upstairs offices. 'Always On', as are their expectations: Emails at midnight, weekend messages, mandatory "urgent" calls—the Big Leagues corporations blur boundaries hard. No Boundaries: No Breaks. Vacations become mythical creatures for *The Heirs*; they never see them. Weekends are when this type actually work. Recharge? Self-care? Good luck, too. Besides causing the damage around them, this type of mastermind minds are destroying themselves. No title is worth your well-being. Tell your hero to be careful with this type; they can find themselves stuck in a cycle of overwork with minimal actual reward.

I hope your star has realized that talent alone won't get them to the top in the Big Leagues. That is how things are up there. Let them know that the offices upstairs *-right on your hero's floor, up and below-* are actually an advanced VR experience. If they remove their 3D glasses, they will see that within those walls is a wild hunting ground and a fight for hierarchy in the wolf pack. Only the strongest will make it.

CHAPTER 9

Is Creation Possible In Corporate Environments?

THE CREATIVE SEED IN THE BIG LEAGUES

Notes

CHAPTER 9

The Creative Seed In The Big Leagues

I have no doubt your hero will make it if they learn and persevere. They will taste the rewarding nectar of their own big league and survive the stinky predators around. Let them know that all of that comes with some side effects, a painful down payment that can empty their creative arc, which is not covered for creative souls.

So far, your hero has learnt the basics of the big leagues: duality, uncertainty, ambition, egos, agendas, pressure, and predators. All of that in XXL size. Now, it's time for the main course, with an important piece of advice: Every one of us will experience our own customized version of the big-league basics –*Predators, pressure, agendas, egos, ambition, uncertainty, and duality.* You can only train for it; avoidance is impossible. The previous chapter summarized the reality of the Big Leagues–like the intro in a videogame the intro in a videogame. The following pages are dedicated to Big Leagues survival skills–the real struggles, with real examples. Your hero will learn the recipe for success and for failure. Because that is how it is up there. It is all or nothing. Remind your star that no player can stay at the intermediate level if they want to debut in the Bernabeu Stadium.

THE CORPORATION, THE BOSS, AND THE CREATIVE SEED

Here's a fact that's true in every industry: The top floors of a corporation –any kind– are always challenging for creative minds. Even more so in a content or media *Entity.* It's crazy, when the core of the industry is supposedly creativity! In the current times in the top-top game, 'content is King', distribution is the Emperor, and Wall Street is God. So yes, the King is fucked up. Creativity in the big media corps is in deficit. Not good times *para la lirica* for creative mastermind minds. The corporation needs our creativity, but the people running the corporation are in survival mode; they won't see it. The *Entities'* big shots are investing their energy in winning subscriber races, surviving stock shifts, begging for consolidations, and fighting to get those IP creators they once owned and let go. Yeah, a real mess, but at the same time, audiences are seriously demanding more and better content, and the powerhouses must deliver or move on.

Now ask your hero to imagine how things are upstairs, *como esta el patio* (like in a bad day in San Quentin) For us creative souls, breaking into a corporation through creativity as our only weapon won't work. Imagine how dry the soil would be for any creative seed joining the entity with that mess upstairs. Your hero must have –at least!– an intermediate level in the *Upstairs Offices VR Experience* game to make it for a long time. If surviving is not enough for your hero, if they have big ambitions, they must be freaking experts in the upstairs game. This is for two reasons: to thrive within the wolf pack, and to keep their creative ideas flourishing in that wild environment.

If all the above is not enough, we can add another layer of misery for creative souls in the showbiz top leagues: The corporations need us, sometimes depend on us, and most of the time hate us. Does your hero want to know why? Because too many times, those in control –*los meros meros*– won't ever have the creative talent we do. A creator's life usually depends on a non-creator's whim. These big bosses' wisdom and egos will control your hero's future in the entity. But there is some good news! At the same time, the opportunity is <u>always</u> there. There will be a new, amazing record-breaking shows; not just one, but hundreds of new shows. Remind your star: The next *big-big thing* everyone will be watching and talking about can be your hero's thing.

THE BIG PRIZE IN THE BIG LEAGUES: THE GOOD MASTER GARDENER

Let your hero know that, on top of the circumstances coming from the context of the moment, each player in the upstairs offices' *VR experience* has a customized level of difficulty, depending on their personality traits. For those who clearly lean on the content/storytelling side, the upstairs game is more complicated. Accept this fact fast, guys. There are some exceptions, and those exceptions truly feel like winning the Lotto. Yes, the big one . If your heroes' boss is a good gardener, it could be the most amazing ride in your hero's career. A never-dreamed-of mind-blowing kind of success. It all depends on the real connection between your protagonists and their bosses. Oh shit.

In the case of pure creative or artistic masterminds, winning in the big game of the Big Leagues starts with a few answers in the mirror: 1. Who hired you? 2. Who is actually in control? 3. What is that person's real agenda? 4. How clear are the reasons why they are hiring you for both parts? We will revisit the answers later –yes, in the mirror.– Let's keep the focus now on the one in control. When the *mero mero* gives your hero the resources and pushes them to fly high, Nirvana is right around the corner –call it Paradise, Wakanda, Utopia, Asgard or Shangri-La, whatever you want, the real good shit. Ask your hero to pray for that winning Lotto ticket when they are in the Big Leagues. If they don't get it, the journey will be long and hard.

Time for another showbiz universal law: If your hero has a storyteller soul, they will only flourish if the real boss waters those creative seeds. If the *mero mero* loves plants, your hero can see themselves in the freaking penthouse of the *entity* building –in less time that they would've ever imagined. I've had that experience, a total communion between the content side and the real boss in terms of targets, strategy, resources, and content weapons. It is a very good ride when you *supermatch* with the mastermind mind in total control. A freaking good one. The first time I experienced that was in a couple of 'births' in the industry *-new TV channels in the lower leagues*. That communion gave me a unique and exciting trip. The high of *creating everything from cero* is great, but man, it is way better to be part of small changes in a big-Big League project. The high is similar, but the rewards are way better. Yes, it is a matter of size, again. If the gods of the showbiz put your hero in an XXL project in the Big Leagues, and they are lucky enough to have the boss I once had, enjoy the ride and ask them to spend their money wisely. The sky is the limit as long as the *mero mero* waters those content flowers.

I've been lucky in that department. I don't know why I landed in the right place, at the right time, with the right gardener. I guess the universe's timing was especially generous. I met bosses who gave me wings and successes, and bosses who gave me overwork, failure, and disease. The good ones were extremely different characters who knew what *tecla tenian que tocar* (what *-piano-* key they must touch) to get the best from my creativity and performance. You already know about the industry's extreme duality and its XXL sizes. Here's another truth for your hero: The entertainment Big Leagues don't know the term *ni tanto, ni tan corto* (not too long, not that short). It is an expression that Spaniard mums have used for centuries, demanding measurement and balance while avoiding difficult topics and embarrassing specifications. In the Big Leagues, nobody knows that concept. Drinking a cocktail made with XXL sizes and XXL egos *o te pasas, o te quedas corto* (either you get dramatically drunk, or you won't feel shit). After being lucky with the master gardeners a couple of times, with outstanding results, here is my outtake for your heroes: We succeeded because my CEO/president/whatever understood the *ni tanto ni tan corto* concept better than the average CEO/president/whatever. I think it is because they didn't come from the entertainment industry. Oh shit, again. From the three bosses who oversaw my biggest hits, only one was a real showbiz pro. The other two were formerly running banks, air companies, law firms, or seafood distribution. Yes, weird. In 66% of the cases, the biggest successes of my career –those shows that have lasted for years, the record breaking numbers IPs, the '*for the first time ever*', and most important, the big-big profits– they all grew in a flowerpot whose gardeners had very little idea about storytelling. They were humble, they allowed me to work, and they supported me even in the XXL mess-ups. When the deities of *The Uncertainty Factor* came to visit, they helped, too. They also understood the term my mum used with a chilling tone: '*Daniel, ni tanto ni tan corto.*' A concept my bosses also applied when dealing with me.

AMERICAN XXL SIZES: WHAT TO EXPECT WHEN IN TEXAS

Size matters, that's a fact: The size of your hero's commitment, ambition, talent, and more. Also, the size of the content they are creating, their league, their platform, their audience, and, of course, their location. The Mecca of entertainment is north Rio Grande, and magically, everything north of that river is extra-large, especially in our industry. When I came to the USA, I didn't know what it meant to work for an American entertainment corporation. Even though I've worked for/with most of the world's content giants -they were Dutch, British, German, or French - I quickly noticed that the *Offices Upstairs VR Game* interface in the land of the free is totally different. America *es otra peli* (yes, it's a different movie). Not only because American XXL sizes are bigger than in the rest of the world. If everything is bigger in Texas, that would also include duality, uncertainty, ambition, egos, agendas, pressure, and predators. The Hollywood interface is way more sophisticated –and populated. The interesting thing is that the players north of the Rio Grande have exactly the same rules, weapons, armors, and challenges as the rest of the players around the globe. So, tell your hero not to be afraid; the game is the same in America, Europe, Africa, or Mars. In the USA, the universe is bigger, the graphics are better, and the creations are global franchises, but the fight is the freaking same. For those out of the Homeland Security lines, allow me to explain to your heros the kind of shock that even a first-class migrant will have breaking into the Big Leagues in the land of the free. I knew the big game in my EU version. I was an *upstairs offices* player for more than a decade, with experience in every genre and every kind of content there was. But my American baptism was truly shocking. I was expecting bigger sizes, and I got the biggest sizes, and also the biggest lesson ever, the one your hero is going to learn, and they cannot forget.

When the offer to showrun a Big League talent show in the USA came, I wasn't expecting anything other than big sizes, a lot of work, some money, some learnings, and as much fun as possible. At the end of the day, production was in Miami! Fun. With time, there was more than XXL shit, hard work, and a Miami lifestyle. Something I wasn't expecting at all. Probably this is one of the biggest reasons I decided to stay around and keep dreaming. I found the perfect boss in a gigantic content powerhouse –big in a way that I couldn't ever imagine being part of– I found this *mero mero* --technically they found me– that was recently hired to lead this enormous *Entity*. I was then running shows for their competitors, but I was already part of a bigger plan. Their plan, not mine. The new leader of the competitor entity wanted to transform the creature from within. Long story short, I moved from one Big-League team to another, and they were, are, and will be forever rivals. It's like a Real Madrid vs Barcelona thing. Super-teams don't like their players moving to their opponents. The *Entity* I was running shows for took it like I was Ronaldo, Figo, Schuster, or Laudrup –yes, all of them left Barcelona to play with *la blanca*– and I wasn't, of course. I could consider myself the Laudrup of content development, but that's all. Let's setup the scene, a mastermind mind moving to a rival team because of a beautiful promise. The promise came with a contract and a surreal situation: In the absence of an SVP of Programming –he was coming in 'a few' months– my direct report was the CEO/President/whatever. Yes, the *mero mero* in charge.

I have to say that their plan to transform the entity was ambitious, sexy, doable, and fun as shit. I wanted to be part of that under any circumstances. I am using 'their plan' because the *mero mero* had help from outside of the entity. Time to introduce the characters: At the wheel of the corporation was a Mexican gentleman whose demeanor, intelligence, elegance, and business skills felt like the best emperor in the time of the best Romans. From now on, let's call the CEO/President that way, E for emperor, R for Roman. Mr. ER had no background in entertainment, but he was a solid business leader and a veteran in the top offices. His *out-of-the-entity* consultant was an expert in guerrilla content warfare and think-big strategies. He still is the one David of the small creators who beat Goliath several times. From now on, Mr. DG, D for David, G for Goliath. Well, I would love to know the story behind Mr. ER and Mr. DG's collaboration, but just the fact that both shared Jewish roots –despite being from different hemispheres– was enough. That was also a big lesson for me! Unlike in Hollywood, at home it doesn't matter if you are Jewish or not. There were no Jewish people where I was born. None. Since the XV century. Blame the 'convert, leave, or die' policy of the Catholic church and the Spaniard royal family. Back to Mr. ER and Mr. DG. The two mastermind minds' plan was to transform the old school network –basically news, telenovelas, and 'Caso Cerrado' (a court show)– into an XXI century modern TV outlet with talent shows, reality competitions, narco-series, music events, gossip talk shows, and all the rest of the menu.

From the day I signed in, my life took place in two worlds: The *offices upstairs,* and the one office on the top-top floor: the *penthouse.* The headquarters of the *mero mero.* A privileged situation that almost gets me crazy. Tell your hero I am using Kafka again. The few steps that separated the penthouse –with the 'ambitious, sexy, doable, and fun ass shit' plans– from the *caspa* of the rest of the offices was more Kafkaesque than the original Kafka. *Caspa* in Spanish means literally dandruff, but in Madrid, it is also a mix of trash, cheesy, cheap, low, and worse. *Pues eso,* the *caspa* of the *upstairs offices* mixed with the *penthouse-high.* Enough to get crazy.

Just a few steps away from the amazingly good ideas and plans came the painful realization: The inhabitants of the *offices upstairs* weren't ready to execute those plans. Almost none of those professionals upstairs had any experience with all that new content they wanted to implement. No one knew how to adapt, produce, and succeed with worldwide formats and extra-demanding weekly prime times. Until that moment, the best rating in a talent show in the Hispanic market was... In my show. The one I came to run a year before. The US Hispanic industry had been shyly trying talent-reality content for a while with no real success. Why? Because they were 'emulating' what they saw in the big American shows. Not asking for the rights and the show bible, not copying, nor adapting, but emulating. Nothing was real, nothing was *unscripted*, but rather *imitated*. A real shock, but a wake-up call. If a big-Big League entity –one of the top TV outlets in the nation– is faking a whole show, what are those in charge faking? How much do they really know about what they are doing?

At the end, the big surprise in America wasn't the extra-large sizes, nope. It was the realization of the power that 'emulate' or 'imitate' has, particularly up in the summits. The biggest surprise was the 'fake it until you make it' thing. Tell your hero it is embedded in the system, in the people, and especially in the showbiz industry. Let them know they must also look at the upstairs fauna also from that perspective. How many of those in the top leagues are 'faking it'? Because those are the most dangerous predators around. As a last note about the 'fake it until you make it': I'm grateful to the old Endemol Latino execs for many reasons, but the Dutch entity guys in Miami convinced the network –and proved to them– that producing a 'real' talent-reality was better than emulating it. And thanks to that, and to those executives, I made it to the land of the free.

THE BIG SHIT IN THE BIG LEAGUES: REALITY CHECK SAPPHIRE LEVEL

Once I had digested the surprising lesson of my arrival –I had to fake my reactions until I made it– I paid attention once more to the XXL sizes. Everything is bigger in Texas, including the things you can do with your super-match *mero mero*, and the things that can happen due to the *Uncertainty Factor*. Let me explain your hero; some dishes on the Big League's menu are perfectly cooked– tasty, with amazing presentations. Remember the sapphire upgrade? Michelin star kind of shit: The extra privileged *-and always named-* parking spots, the all-access badges, the perks, the flattering, the impacts of your posts in social media. In general, the quality of your hero's lifestyle will improve – Btw! Tell them to be careful about overspending. Yes, they made it there, but they are not part of the sapphire elite.– Ask your stars to *mantener los pies en el suelo* (keep their feet on the ground) while enjoying the good life. That's all I'm asking for. Back to the menu: The rest of the dishes of the Big Leagues are not Michelin star kind of shit. No sapphire treatment. The kind of food your hero will need to put in their mouths is going to be nasty, but the real problem is that they must swallow everything –like the contestants in Fear Factor. To thrive in the offices upstairs, your hero will have to eat every bite –until the last drop– of the freaking menu. Mandatory.

Down below are some basic survival tricks for your heroes to use while they are up there. Some 'must do' strategies for creative mastermind minds, garnished with real-life Big League examples. The amount of shit your hero will swallow depends on their ability to navigate the game. The variety of predators and prey –and the peculiarity of their modus operandi– requires a special suit. Very special. Spartan stuff. A Masterchief 117 kind of armor. The perfect balance between protection, mobility, and performance. The fabric of the suit is the learnings your hero is extracting from these pages, and they already have experience with most of them.

Learning while Performing

I am going to include this reference for performance in two different aspects: Your hero's <u>show results</u> –whatever project they lead– and your hero's <u>gaming score</u> in the *Upstairs Offices VR Experience* game. Continuous learning in both areas is required. The best shield in the Big Leagues is competence in both your hero's projects and the upstairs game. Everything your hero needs to do has been described already in these pages. If they use the mirror, stay updated on industry trends, sharpen their skills, and keep their six covered, they will be hard to sideline.

Observe First, Act Second

By this time, your showrunner hero is already an expert at reading rooms. This is the big game; ask them to be focused and wise. If your star is like me, <u>keep them quiet.</u> Use your nails if needed. Creative and artistic-passioned individuals –*como yo*– tend to say things out loud as they come straight from the brain spark, without thinking about the consequences. Calculating risks and being strategic is key.

Find Knowledge Around

Seek out people you trust –both mentors for wisdom and peers *para las cañas de despues.* Yes, for the after-work happy hour.– When you are having drinks with your peers, always remember that you are a mastermind mind – which means you are a lone wolf by your own decision. Keep it together.

Stay Adaptable

Different archetypes require different approaches. Your hero must adapt and flex their style accordingly. The key is to keep moving towards the goal without losing your core values.

Lean into Authenticity

Despite what they show, people appreciate realness. Even in a cutthroat environment, authenticity stands out like a beacon. That is true, but in my experience in the Big Leagues, that is not relevant for corporations. The *Entity* doesn't give a shit. Authenticity benefits are for your hero's mental health savings account, not for the corporation. It's good enough for your hero's soul, and their future, *palabra*.

Those are the ingredients. Only your protagonist can control the amounts. Now I'd like to give your hero a taste of the kind of challenges they will face, with potential solutions. I practiced all those strategies and have a few lessons for your hero; they are coming from mess-ups and successes in the top offices. Especially the mess-ups. I'm including my grades at the time. Ask your hero to be compassionate.

The Learning while Performing practice:

I got a **C**. I performed very well, but I didn't learn shit. My bad. I guess I didn't show up in class the day they explained 'how to practice the upstairs game while trying to change 50 years of Hispanic television'. I only paid attention to the *upstairs offices game* to get what my bosses –Mr. ER, Mr. DG– and *servidor* needed. I did all the homework. I practiced all my tricks! I read rooms, checked the mirror, did the whole thing to learn how to get the best from those *offices upstairs* professionals. Wait! Stop for a second. Did your hero see it? No? I said: 'to get the best from'. I didn't say 'to win the upstairs game'. I spent all my mastermind mind skills on the company, on the common goals, and on my *mero mero* vision. That was my mistake. I should've also read those rooms -and its predators- to improve my score in the game and to freaking protect my six. I finally got those learnings, forced, of course. Suddenly, the gods of Uncertainty decided to change my Roman emperor boss, and the creative plants were never watered again. **C** is a fair score in this practice.

The Observe First, Act Second practice:

Another **C** in this subject. Mr. ER left –Mr. DG some months later– and a Madison Avenue kind of television executive came to town. The new *mero mero* was an Italian-American who relocated from New Jersey to Miami to assume the role of the new emperor. I don't know if he drove a Ferrari in New Jersey, but he did when he cames to work in Miami. From now on, he is *el señor* New Jersey -Mr. NJ. He has a Spanish last name, but no Hispanic background at all. After Mr. NJ's arrival, my creative brain processed a few relevant things, but somehow it decided to play blind with others. I was seeing but not paying attention, and, more specifically, not doing shit for my six. Masterchief John 117 wouldn't have been proud of me. While I was focused –and super excited–

developing ambitious content deals with people like Pitbull, Ricky Martin, Zoe Saldana, or Eva Longoria, I decided to ignore the new *mero mero* game and keep my energy on the cool tasks. Wrong. That master gardener didn't like plants, and he didn't like how the plants looked or smelled. At least not this creative plant. My nurturing creative soil in the entity penthouse got dry. My leaves started to fade. I saw it coming –like in my early mess up with The Bachelor Spaniard version– but I didn't act. I ignored the game. Twice!! **C** is a fair grade for this one.

The Find Knowledge Around practice:

This is a subject where I got an **A** that could've been an **A+**. I've been blessed with wise and generous mentors at a few crucial times. They helped me understand the unwritten rules of the specific mission and how to look at the broader mission picture from wider and new angles. If your hero is authentically passionate, smart, and proactive, wise people will approach them. Guaranteed. Mastermind minds recognize each other despite age, genre, race, or other shit. In a Big League entity, those potential mentors who are committed to the higher cause of content will show up to meet your hero. Even if those mentors also have their own ego and hidden agendas, please ask your star to be wise and listen. There are three relevant things to take into consideration when finding knowledge within the offices upstairs: The cause of content ––to connect. The learnings your heroes can get –to grow. And the ability to keep an eye on the upstairs game and their six covered.

One of the main characters in my mentee times in the top offices was the *out-of-the-entity* consultant of our good Roman emperor –Yes, Mr. DG, the guerrilla warfare expert on US soil. Well, I was already very successful with the content I was doing in America. I could've passed on Mr. DG's advice, but I didn't. If your hero is rocking it with their content, now is the perfect time to learn about some other things. For me, the 'other thing' besides content was knowing the American industry landscape. Mr. DG was key in my adaptation to the US; he helped me to understand some of the XXL size 'Hollywood ways.' Totally different from the rest of the world, guys!

The reason why I can't score an **A+** in this matter is that I wasn't smart enough to understand Mr. DG's long-term strategy. That mistake didn't affect the Big League scores, but it hurt my pride. No + here.

The **Stay Adaptable** *practice:*

This one is tricky; I got a B in my Big Leagues journey. Sometimes I did, and sometimes I didn't. To put it better, I can be flexible with some things but not with others. Your hero can blame my freaking high obsession with the Q Factor –yes, quality in the product and the procedures would limit my flexibility– but you can also blame my old school ethics and my obsession with keeping my word.

'Staying adaptable' is nice advice that ignores an important factor: How adaptable your hero is. What is their flexibility, and where are their limits? In the upstairs offices your star's elasticity will be tested several times. Besides more yoga, the most important thing for your hero is their boundaries. They need to set the limits of their adaptability, which is a difficult task when they are fighting for success–or survival–on– on the predator's upper floors. Your star will need to make painful decisions that will affect the content they are working on and their relationships. Including the mirror.

Yeah! Back to the mirror thing. Would your hero be ready to reconsider their ethics and values? Would they be able to betray their own standards? To ignore their own words? Because that is where the real limits are. The upstairs game is a bold, bloody race. The XXL sizes, the egos, the dollars, the agendas, the power, and the sapphire treatment are so tempting that anyone could submit to the Big League's spell and forget about ethics and values. Only the mirror will save your hero. They need to be adaptable, but they also need to be brutally honest with their limits.

Integrity and ethics cost me my first position as a young Head of Content in Fremantle Media Spain –Yes! Good memory, guys. That's the entity that owns The Price Is Right, American Idol, and a lot more. As the new Head of Content in Madrid, I was reporting simultaneously to the Spanish Fremantle CEO and the global Head of Content in London, exactly what I call an XXL company. We were adapting the first show I pitched and sold, a version of the British chef Jamie Oliver's docu-show called *Jamie's Kitchen* for Spain. There was a major format rule to follow in any adaptation of the show, enforced with a fine of a couple of million pounds –yes, to Chef Jamie– if we didn't respect it. Nothing concerning, the format was OK and clear in my mind, but my *mero mero*, the CEO of the big entity, got herself in big trouble because of her big mouth in a big meeting with a big network boss. Do you remember my comment about the '*no need, no reason*' thing? It happened again. A very expensive mess-up. A two-million-pound not-needed comment when the show was already sold. Long story short, she asked me to edit two different versions of the show: The 'official' version for the network to air –with her never needed format change suggestion– and an altered tape for the London HQ. Yeah, I quit after London told me I should continue reporting to her. You read it right, the global HQ didn't care that much. The top league's entity attitude was impossible for me to understand. I can only blame the XXL sizes shit.

The important thing for your hero is to realize that those two factors –quality of the content and ethical limits– must rule over their adaptability boundaries. They can be flexible when navigating the upstairs waters, but if they betray themselves, the long-term side effects are lethal for both your hero's career and their soul. I'd recommend setting your hero's boundaries within the limits of pursuing excellence AND good ethics. In the big-Big Leagues, quality and ethical boundaries will bring internal and external conflicts, but they will survive balancing adaptability with integrity. That's why I scored a **B** in this subject; I stayed adaptable up to an ethical limit, but then I had to leave. And if your hero is curious, you can tell them: Yes, my friends that are family called me crazy when I left the XXL multinational that made me Head of Content for the first time.

The Lean into Authenticity practice:

This is the last one for a reason, guys! Not for the score, which is a **B**, but for the learnings. Authenticity got me success, but also troubles. Your star will need to be themself. There's no need to become anyone else or hide under some character. In the top offices in the Big Leagues, the slogan is not '*embrace your weirdness*' as much as it is '*know your weirdness and be wise.*' But the first one is recommended for the rest of the leagues and for your hero's mental health.

My first big challenge with authenticity in the Big Leagues came in the third season of that monster TV show called Big Brother. It was the most watched show on air at the time. The Big Brother experience was a great ride! It was wild, it was live, and it was exhausting, but it was also successful as shit. The entity had three showrunners and a fourth top figure, only for the participants. Let your hero know that there are some *extra-extra* XXL shows that are like intergalactic space super-cruises; very difficult to maneuver in tight spaces with gravity. One of the most skilled mastermind minds I've ever met reigned over all of us –the four showrunners– over our teams, over our delivery, and over our lives. She was then the Head of Content of the entity, and the person whom I learnt the most from in my whole career. Period.

The scene is set up for your hero: Writers room in Guadalix de la Sierra –the location of the Big Brother house– where the master of masters – the entity Head of Content,– the showrunners, and the most relevant writers and producers were trying to figure out a live Christmas Eve special in prime time that the network asked for within two weeks' time. Yes, the *Uncertainly Factor* deities had a face this time–the smiling network execs. For your hero to understand the challenge: *La cena de Nochebuena, en directo desde Gran Hermano-* (Christmas Eve dinner, live from the Big Brother house). By the way, in our culture, Christmas Eve is the biggest event, bigger than Christmas Day. Back to the room with the top office people; I was still *un novato* (a rookie) in the upstairs game during the crisis committee meeting. We, the top commanders of the cruise, were the lowest-ranking people in the room. The most important specimens of the entity's top floors game were also there, trying to figure out what to do with those new three hours of very expensive TV –that also meant big money for the entity. In the room, I was authentic, calm, quiet, observing, and practicing all my creative mastermind skills with patience and assurance. I shine when out-of-the-box, urgent solutions, and doable ideas are needed.

I'm good at it, and I knew it. So, I was listening to and looking at my co-showrunners' expressions, waiting for the right time to lay out a couple of solutions, when someone said, 'what about bringing a homeless person to the Big Brother Christmas dinner?' Yes. Live on national prime time.

Oh shit, all my mastermind mind self-control mechanisms failed simultaneously. For a few seconds, I considered the proposal seriously, until I recalled all those Christmas movies with happy endings for the homeless, and I noticed how impossible a real happy ending was for the homeless, and for us. From the moment of the realization, 'authentic' Daniel took over. I didn't freaking care about the ranking and position of the people in the room. Not about the upstairs office game, not about anything else except common sense. At that time, there was a lot of pressure from the media against the show. We had ugly headlines twice a week –extra Uncertainty Factor stuff, your hero will learn how to live with that too. The Spanish press used an uncomfortable expression to describe the Reality TV phenomenon: Tele-basura. Yeah, 'tele-trash' in direct translation. And we were the most watched tele-basura ever invented. Only the Real Madrid games in the Champions would beat our show ratings. In my opinion, that is not tele-basura; that is 'we were killing it with our work.' No doubt it was my inner authenticity that put the words I said on my lips. It wasn't the ambitious showrunner pursuing a long career, I promise. While the big boys and big girls of the Big League, big shows, big shit were throwing ideas to make the 'homeless at the BB dinner' possible, my authentic-self upraised like a wolf from within with a voice that silenced the whole room: "Are we really considering this? Do we really want to do 'tele basura' for real? A real person? In real need? As an entertainment asset on live TV? On Christmas night?" F**k no. I didn't say 'f**k no," but I said the rest. The real authentic me also suggested developing surprises with the family, which ended up being a better solution and a very emotional Christmas special, where every set of eyes could find relatable elements.

Make your hero conscious that there are two engines behind being your true self and playing the upstairs game correctly at the same time. One engine is passion for the content task –to create more, better, and faster– and the other is knowing themselves. I already told you, remember this part: It is not 'embrace your weirdness' as much as it is 'know your weirdness and be wise.' I've been a bit weird my entire life, and it has been impossible to hide. That means I always need to be somehow authentic to not scare people too much. I don't know how much I scared those big players from the entity's top offices in the Big Brother Christmas crisis room, but since that time, I connected easily with them. They saw me, and I think they liked me.

Another Lean into Authenticity practice for your hero is to learn how to strategize 'authenticity', and where and how to stop it. I know they will do better than I did. Fast forward a few years, back to the good master gardener times in the NBCUniversal powerhouse. The Roman emperor –Mr. ER– left with his job unfinished, after we made modern Hispanic television history with shows like *El Señor de los Cielos*, *La Voz Kids*, or *Suelta La Sopa*. It was a good ride, a privileged one. When the upper floors predators were pursuing their egos and agendas making my work impossible, when the corporative shit was in the very limit, a call to the *mero mero* Mr. ER would solve everything. Like getting the young talent I needed and wanted –but the rest of the upstairs predators didn't– to sending a yellow convertible to gift a capricious talent, because she was still hesitant to sign the contract after a painful negotiation. Both things on the same day. That's Big League shit! I'm telling you, a freaking good ride for adrenaline junkies mastermind minds.

It is easy to be authentic when you have a direct line to God. But God left without finishing the task, and from that moment my 'authenticity' was under threat. I survived my good master gardener for a while due to two reasons: One, the results were outstanding. Two: The rest of the predators upstairs still didn't know how to do the shit I was doing, but it was a matter of time. Questions for your hero: Should I be authentic and teach them? Which would be my default mode. Or should I be *listo* (smart) and mislead them? What would your hero do? Of course, I ended up helping the entity and the predators after my position; that's why I only got a **B**.

Can your hero see the patterns after my 'in the upstairs' game? Despite the mediocre grades I got, there's a clear path for your star to follow, here we go: **Know the game** but don't let it devour your hero's integrity. No sapphire lifestyle is worth losing yourself. **Use authenticity strategically!** Being yourself will win trust and loyalty, but timing and tone matter. If you're good at what you do, speaking up for what's right or what's best creatively will pay off—even if it's risky. Audiences and peers often favor realness and honesty, but corporate structures resist it. Tell your hero to choose their battles wisely while staying genuine. **Never stop learning**—mastering content, tech, and corporate signals is a long process, if your hero wants to grow big in the Big Leagues, speed it up! Now, the most important: **Set clear boundaries** so that compromise doesn't turn into self-betrayal. Your hero will do it by **balancing ethics, adaptability, and self-preservation**. Betraying personal values for short-term gains will damage their career and soul in the long run. Ethics and quality standards might cost opportunities in the short term, but they protect your hero's reputation and feed their creative soul. And the last one, if your hero is an adrenaline junkies storyteller, help them to **find the good master gardener** or to **become the one!** That's where the real fun is.

CHAPTER 10

The Holly Trinity: Product-Client-Profits

THE HOLLY
TRINITY:
PRODUCT-
CLIENT-PROFITS

Notes

....
....
....
....
....
....
....
....
....
....
....
....
....
....
....
....
....
....
....
....
....
....
....

CHAPTER 10

The Holly Trinity:
Product - Client - Profits

There is a clear path for your hero to thrive in any league, any creation, and any platform, but it requires faith. Big amounts of faith. Do you, reader, remember what I said about my lack of it? I have changed. Years in this shitty industry had made me a believer. Yes. I do have faith in what I call *La Sagrada Trinidad*, and I'd recommend your hero start believing and practicing it too. In the next pages, your protagonist will learn the magic formula to keep success, reputation, ethics, and karma.

A few things to consider before going through the definitions of my peculiar faith.: First, there's no need to convert as there's no need for dogma. No rituals, no worship. It is compatible with any other religion -including *money* - or lack of it. Your star is going to learn how to navigate any creative business path without a GPS. Yes! Faith is that powerful. Let's set the scene: It's a dystopian thriller. Imagine your hero driving in the middle of nowhere, with no signal, and no map. One of those scenes you've seen in movies thousands of times. Pick whatever remote location you like. Nothing around, and the big threat is stepping on your protagonist's heels. Imagine your hero is lost and being chased by mutant predators. A very stressful ride from nowhere to no idea; but it looks like maybe they can make it to civilization. With the threat behind and around them, running out of gas, and after a curve, with only an unknown city and unknown freeways ahead, there is still no signal on their phones. What direction should they take? Should they continue? Towards where? Should they hide? Should they try to fill the tank? And still no signal, and still no maps.

In tough times, that is pretty much the feeling the lead creative mastermind mind will have when making decisions under stress. Here is where faith comes in: Imagine having a voice inside that tells your hero what direction to take at every crossroad of your creative or storytelling career or business. No implants, no devices, no need of that shit. This is pure magic. In every crucial decision, the voice will tell your hero the direction to go. That's the power of faith in the *Holy Trinity*. Let your hero know that it works within the whole creative spectrum—any stage, any league, any setting. Without the Holy Trinity's guidance, your hero will succumb to the circumstances of the moment.

Their decisions will come from whatever they are dealing with, whether it's mutant predators or very difficult talent. Usually, those decisions are made from urgent need, pain, fear, flattering, or egos. None of those prospects is a good starting point. Time for another special superpower! If your hero has faith in the Holy Trinity, they won't be able to rewind time, but they will slow it dramatically and have a 'higher' vision of the circumstances. Like in an out-of-body experience, it will allow your hero to look at the room from above before any decision is made. I named it *La Santisima Trinidad* to honor my parents' old Catholic *dichos* (idioms), and it is not a magic voice in your hero's head; like in any other religion, it is a real system of beliefs. Only in this case, it won't clean your hero's sins, but it will unveil their path to success in any league.

CONTENT: ONE GOD AND THREE PERSONS WITHIN

In religion, a 'system of beliefs' provides meaning, purpose, and structure to human life. In show business, a system of beliefs will provide meaning, purpose, structure, and health to your hero's career and business. Our god is Creation. That is our supreme being or ultimate reality. The divine force, the cosmic order that rules our universe. Whatever show your hero is running is their current God. Whatever piece of content your hero is involved in is the supreme deity. That's where everything starts and finishes. Like in Catholicism - where the Holy Trinity is described as one God in three persons - in content creation, your hero's piece of content is the one God with the three persons within. Your hero's piece of content is also the Father, the Son, and the Holy Spirit.

THE SHOWRUNNER SYSTEM OF BELIEFS

"One God in three persons"— '*Distinct yet of the same divine essence, coexisting in eternal unity*'.

My Catholic childhood has helped me to Please separate 'In' from 'religious' structure the creator's religious foundation. Let's go with it. In the Catholic doctrine, God is three figures at the same time. *Pues eso, lo mismo para nosotros* creators. The same rule applies to you in this craft.

The Father is The PRODUCT -The Show-

In religious dogma, The Father figure embodies the Creator, the source of all existence, and represents divine authority. In your craft, The Father is your current show. The one you were hired to create, lead, or be part of. The source of your hero's existence, laughs, and headaches. It is the one and only deity you must serve. Everything must be done in the interest of Father Product. Every decision must first consider The Product. That makes things easier during challenging times. If it serves the product, it is good; that's the direction to take. If it doesn't, tell your hero to avoid that route. Simple and easy so far.

The Son is The CLIENT

For Catholics, The Son –Jesus Christ– *is the incarnate Word of God, both fully divine and fully human, who redeems humanity.* For you, it is the audiovisual creation that becomes fully human, and not that divine, when someone watches it. That is the moment when your hero will be redeemed or condemned by The Client. This whole storytelling/content/art/communication universe only makes sense when the clients /audience are happy and enjoy the show. What's the point of creating if your hero won't consider their clients' needs? The second person of the trinity –the incarnate figure of your hero's God– is their audience when watching the content. But it is more complex than that; sometimes God will double your hero's incarnations. Your hero will face clients and audience who can both redeem or condemn, and sometimes they don't agree at all. Your hero will have to face painful decisions in those cases, and use all their communication skills to convince the client to buy their idea. They won't convince the audience, that's a fact.

The Holy Spirit is The PROFITS

The Catholic System of Beliefs gets even more complicated with the last of the three persons. This third one is an 'intangible' thing, a spirit. When you think of spirits, you might think of 'forces', but for Catholics, the Holy Spirit is not a force or energy, but *a living, conscious, and active divine being who speaks, teaches, and guides. The Holy Spirit is the breath, power, or presence of God. The divine force that empowers believers, guides the Church, and transforms lives.* We need to stop here. Have you guys noticed it? The Holy Spirit behaves exactly like Money. Make your hero re-read the paragraph, trading the subject '*Holy Spirit*' for 'Money', *believers* for 'industry peers', and *Church* for 'corporation'. They will get how the 'intangible' spirit becomes completely real. *Por cierto!* Tell your hero that Profits are not only measured in their show's financial revenues but also by its prestige, notoriety, awards, and so on. Entities also consider those as Profits because they lead to new creations and more clients.

HOLY TRINITY QUICK START SETUP

This one God –creation– and three persons mystery –Product-Client-Profits– is summarized as *La Sagrada Trinidad* for another reason. The *sagrada* part of it. If size matters in our business, priorities matter too. For your hero's *decision-making GPS* to work perfectly, they need to apply the system in this <u>sacred</u> specific order: First is Product, second is Client, and third is Profits. That's how a complex decision-making process will become easy and will serve God –the creation– in a much better way. The reason behind the belief system hierarchy is important; it is your hero's boarding card for a lifelong career in creation. Let's explore the main *Sagrada Trinidad GPS* settings when making key decisions:

- **Possibility One:** When your hero takes good care of the Product in every choice, the Product will be great, Clients will be satisfied, and Profits will grow. Bingo.

- **Possibility Two:** If your hero makes decisions that prioritize the the Client, the Product can suffer the consequences and end up being not as good as your hero would like. Remind your hero that in this arena, they are only as good as their last show! The third person of the *Sagrada Trinidad* (Profits) will also be damaged in the long term if your hero chooses directions that prioritize the Client instead of serving the story, the Product.

- **Possibility Three:** Your hero prioritizes Profits; well, both the Product and the Client will pay the consequences. I don't need any spirit coming to make me see your hero's future: Failure. Money is important, it is sacred, it needs to be controlled, but it is the last priority to consider in your hero's decision-making process. The nature of your job is to tell the best story possible with the resources you have. Once those boundaries are established, the rest of the journey is *Sagrada Trinidad* shit, in that order: First the show, then the audience, and finally the company.

REAL LIFE APPLICATIONS

In real life, any decision in content creation should be guided by the *Creator's Beliefs System*, but this is is not the case. The higher the league, the less the top players practice with the tool. Looks like *nadie va a misa* in the offices upstairs! Shocking, but real. Let's classify it as another showbiz big-sized coding issue. Top league players magically forget about their service to Creation, Clients, and Profits. It's either *Entity* coding bugs or the egos-agendas thing.

In real life, the elements of the trinity 'product-client-profits' are interconnected like our neurons. Especially *The Father Product* and *The Son Client*. Storytelling decisions that serve the story without considering the audience make no sense. Yet that type of thing happens a lot. You have your perfect story, and then some visionary will come along with the latest data about audience preferences, and the same visionary –or a group of them– will try to make you change your story. Now, I have admired the Data Research people since I was a kid. They know their shit. The problem isn't the data; real problem comes from the interpretation of that data. That's why I used the term *visionary*. Give me the data, and I will figure out a way to satisfy audiences in a manner that will improve the story. *Estamos?* Please don't just tell me the data mixed with your *mero mero* visions. Those visionaries will give a couple of storylines 'suggestions' that are not at all your hero's story. They haven't created the product, nor written it, nor adapted it, nor produced it, but they had their vision. And they have power too! So, make your hero re-read the big leagues handbook. They will need to find a way to convince that visionary. It is fair to point out here that I've experienced those circumstances for good. Visionaries who have improved *The Father Product* after an audience analysis report. They just approached the product creators at the right time and in the right way. *Por cierto!* Advice for your heroes when the visionaries come: Immediately after the surreal narrative suggestions, they will also have talent suggestions. It is how it goes.

Let me bring a new angle now. Remember the duality of the industry? Does your hero think the *Sagrada Trinidad* works the same, depending on what side of the table they are on? And I mean, for the *exhibitors* –the big outlets, networks, platforms, or whatever– and the *authors* –creators, production companies, showrunners, others. Does the *Holy Trinity* work the same? What does your hero think?

Let's try to break it down with real-life examples for your star to see the different angles. When one of the parts involved in *The Creation* –God– does not practice the Holy Trinity in that order –product-client-benefits– the end of that *God* is a matter of time. Finito. Done. Remind your hero that in showbiz, just seeing your creation on a screen is a complicated journey, seeing it for more than one season *es un milagro* (yes, *a* miracle). Less than 15% of the content out there makes it to a second round. Multiple rounds of the same *Creation* is a one-digit percentage. That's the nature of the beast. Your protagonist cannot forget this fact. Another *Show-business Universal Law*: After winning the lottery of seeing your creation on the screen, only less than one in every ten creations will remain on the screen the following season. Welcome to the jungle!

Taking that *less than 1%* fact into consideration, let's dissect whether the *Holy Trinity* works the same on both sides of the table, for authors and exhibitors. In theory, it should. Same God –The Product– which is your hero's piece of content. Both parts venerating together the same God, with the same ceremonials, with shared faith. All good until the cold numbers arrive. *El demonio* Nielsen will give the ratings verdict the following morning, and those small numbers on your screen will affect the *Holy Trinity*, regardless. For good, or for bad. And I mean, both sides will have different interpretations of the dogma after the results. The *Sagrada Trinidad* will be under inquiry by inquisitors. It doesn't matter if your hero's content did good or bad. Data is first, then the visionaries will arrive, remember that?

Two sides, two interpretations of the *Sagrada Trinidad*. For your hero, God is The Product –the show– but the platform where your hero's Clients watch that content, that Product is just a small piece in a big puzzle. Let's go back to the Catholic faith to understand the system's bug. Remember the "*One God in three persons"* thing: For your hero, that figure is *The Creation.* For the exhibitors, that figure is not. The mastermind minds from the platform will make your hero feel they believe in the same *God* –your hero's show– and they do, no doubt about that, but only as a 'part' of their own system of beliefs. In the platform dogma, *The Product* is not your hero's show; it is The Platform itself, and it is the one they serve. They have their own "*One God in three persons*" and that God is called 'The Platform'. Your hero's *One God* will be relegated to *'one of the three persons within'* the exhibitors' God. That's how it goes.

Good news now: Your hero's counterpart has the same goal as your star: The content's success! Most of the time, both sides of the table –authors and platform– practice the same religion, which is none other than your hero's dogma. But occasionally, their priorities do not align properly. Let's start with a real case. A reality show that was –and still is– so successful that the platform, in this case the leading network in the country, decided to saturate the daily grid with extra content from that successful show. Nothing bad in this! I practice, worship, and preach this technique; when well done, it creates a beautiful snowball that will benefit your hero's show's finale –and the renewal for further seasons if it hasn't happened yet. Back to the case. The content was so good, so successful, that both authors and exhibitors where literally ascending to heaven with every new Nielsen data report. The nation was on its knees waiting for the weekly drama to unfold in our prime-time show. The network was also spreading out extra content in their daily late-night show, with such a good result that our Product became the main source of content for the leading late-night show nationwide. Tell your hero it is crazy to see your shit as the main topic every morning in every office, coffee shop, bar, school, or business in the country. Time to be humble. The ride was good while we – authors– controlled the content they –exhibitors– were using. But that changed. Probably the showrunners of the late-night show worshiped only their own divinity, the Probably the showrunners of the late-night show worshiped only their own divinity, ignoring the real God behind their success, our Product. At a certain point, someone got greedy and started to use content we didn't allow. That meant chaos for us. Storylines were constantly questioned and re-oriented, participants were publicly humiliated, and more. How do you guys think the *Holy Trinity* operates here? That is the context your hero's need for the next scene. Enjoy it!

CASE ONE: CUT TO THE FISH BOWL

I've been at a few tables where the priorities didn't align properly. I've also been in a few control rooms where the drama between the two sides about the *Santisima Trinidad* was happening live on air. Yeah! Welcome back, adrenaline junkies! This is a double black diamond kind of ride. My first encounter with drama was in the network's studio, while I was running the show live. It was Big Leagues shit. Top of the game times. I was part of Big Brother at a time when the show was breaking rating records. And in the Big Brother house, there was always a fish bowl. My direct *mero mero* –co-owner of the production company I worked for– showed up unexpectedly in the control room, and a few minutes later, the network's programming SVP arrived with a '*what are you doing here*' kind of facial expression. The conversation started in the hallway, but during the on-air countdown, they made their way into the control room. Half way into the first segment, the conversation between *los jefazos* (big bosses) got more agitated, up to a point where their voices raised not only over my own voice –while I was trying to tell the whole team that we were ignoring the next two video packages– but also over the director's voice cutting cameras, over the team leaders giving orders from their intercoms, and over the head writer's voice giving me options for changes in the outro. In that craziness, suddenly, the only two voices heard were the two *jefes* screaming at each other. When everyone in the control room was looking at them in silence, they finally moved out to the hallway. I would've loved to hear the rest, but it became a silent movie. What does your hero think were their *Holly Trinity* priorities? Father *Product*? Son *Client*? Or *Holy Spirit Profits*? I was as lost as your hero when I asked myself the same question. This little incident could've come from anywhere, including a silly small thing, but no. It grew. Wild. Up to a degree where both sides of the table –the big network and the producers of the most watched show in the country– made decisions *meandose en la santisima trinidad* (yeah, good Spanish guys! It means pissing off). Both sides made choices that clearly damaged their product, clients, and profits. The universe's timing gave me a role in that weird suicidal war. I was the executioner of those decisions from the production company side. A blessing –I was learning a lot about the Big Leagues– and a curse: the execution was set up to be on-air. On prime time. Live. On my baby, on my show.

A few days after the incident, there was one of those big 'reality TV elimination nights.' We were live on primetime, and, as nighttime television leaders, we had a whole country watching. Right before the show, my boss called me aside with this message: '*The moment I let you know, you cut to the camera inside the fish-bowl, and you stay there until you get a new order.* ' Have your hero imagine the consequences of the command. Imagine it – it's the moment when the Big Brother villain is going to try to eliminate someone. After amazing storytelling leading up to this intense moment, just as he starts to speak, the camera cuts to the fish bowl. With this single act, the work of 300 people and the distraction of 10 million more would be more than *meado* (yes, pissed off). The biggest sin ever imagined towards the *Holly Trinity*. A well-crafted story (*The Product*), a very interested audience (*The Client*), and an epic headache for the network sales team (*The Profits*). The three persons of the *Santisima Trinidad* f***ed up in a suicidal decision. Why would any creative mastermind mind do that? Where did my bosses get that crazy idea? Cutting to the fish bowl for several minutes while 10 million people were watching live? I was freaking out. Would your hero execute their *mero mero*'s command, shooting their own baby on the head? Their other option is to ignore it and continue the show; it's live, and they are running it. What would your hero do? Those bosses I had then were dangerous. You wouldn't want to play with them. They were also wise, smart, and generous. They taught me a lot about storytelling and show business. They respected my creative work, and they gave me big opportunities, so I don't know what your hero would do, but I executed the order. It was surreal.

My bosses waited until the third segment of the show to call the fish bowl for the first time, with all the storylines built up towards the conclusion. Smart move *para joder* (literally, to fuck) even more la *Santisima Trinidad*. Another smart move from my bosses: It was a live show, so they called the fish bowl while their competitors –the rest of the networks– were in commercial breaks. I couldn't look at anyone during the first fish bowl minute in the control room. I kept my head down, my mouth closed, my eyes on the fish, my finger in the intercom, and my brain saying, '*you are making television history asshole!*' It was a weird feeling. Disturbing. I was stabbing my own baby in the heart. It was freaking painful, but somehow, I also felt proud. Yes. Proud of being part of such a badass group of creators despite *la meada* over our God Creation and the whole holy *Product-Client-Profits* trinity. It took me a while to understand the reasons behind my bosses' sacrilege, and after understanding the strategy, it ended up not being a sacrilege at all, actually the opposite; Martyrdom. The ultimate sacrifice for our common God: The Creation.

Here is the rationale of the Case for your hero: Let's start with the exhibitor's faith. If I am one of the network mastermind minds, and I see the ratings growing as a consequence of spreading out extra content for one of our shows, I want that show everywhere too! It is legit, but do it properly. They didn't. How do you think the network executives used their GPS? Did it work? Did the Holy Trinity speak to them? Were the voices in their heads? I don't think so. If you don't practice the *Product-Client-Profits* dogma in that order, the GPS won't work. In the exhibitors' system of beliefs, *Father Platform* should be first for them. Do you think it was? The lines between *Father Platform* and *Holy Spirit Profits* got blurred for the network execs. They didn't have enough with a few picks in the daily ratings curves coming from our reality competition. They wanted more. They wanted to raise those numbers. They got greedy. They decide to pursue *Profits* without considering the consequences. Due to the show's success, the network's decision-makers didn't stop the late-night producers from stealing our content in their quest for higher ratings. That shoplifted footage was used only for controversy and notoriety, in dangerous ways for not only the storylines, but also for the participants involved. It was disgusting. My bosses in the production company tried to stop it, but they couldn't until the fish bowl drama started. The network kept using the 'illegal' footage, and we continued cutting to the fish bowl with 10 million people watching for a while. Very painful for me as a storyteller and showrunner, but I learned quickly how to use the fishbowl airtime to fine-tune the rest of the show run-down. Adaptation!

Does your hero understand the sin against the Trinity? The network execs' offense was modifying the order of the three-person dogma, putting profits first, then the rest. But it is more, *se mearon en The Son: The Client.* They ignored their audience, several times, for minutes. They didn't care about a few tenths of a share lost during our galas –ignoring 10 million clients– because they were growing during other time slots. Shows that barely will make 200,000 eyeballs. I still don't get why they did it, but it was related to Saint Nielsen rating data delivery.

Let's analyze the show creators' decision. Have you considered being in such a conflict with the other side of the table? Whoever sits there, the other part is 'using' your creation without your approval and out of the limits established. How do you manage that? What happens if it is your first and only show? I can't imagine my bosses' stress level, but I can imagine the scenarios they explored; the legal path means total war between the 'parents' of very successful content, which is not good for the *Product.* I'm sure they also considered *comerselo y callarse* (ignoring the situation) to avoid further issues, but I know at least three of them were against that; you can call it just *orgullo* (proud). I have no idea who came up with the solution, but I would've paid a fortune for being a fly on the wall the day they decided to *cut to the fish-ball.* In that meeting, the creators found a way to protect the show and their position in a silent and risky move. They resolved the issue of stolen Big Brother footage, and they renewed with the network under very favorable conditions. I'm sure there were very valuable creative business lessons in that decision-making meeting. *Cutting to the fish-ball* means *mearse en tu audiencia* (you got it, pee on your audience) and testing unexplored waters with the platform –would they escalate?– Risky, but they had to do something to pressure the network, and to protect the show and the participants.

Your hero's task during stressful decision-making times is to protect the *Product,* yes, but it is also to analyze how each side of the table is worshiping the *Holy Trinity.* Your star will have a certain type of vision and knowledge that will be very useful when making decisions, searching for alliances, or negotiating solutions. My bosses somehow inferred that the network wouldn't counter-attack the *cut to the fish ball* in a violent way. My bosses knew the network liked the Holy Spirit Profits too much to escalate the conflict. The *cut to the fish-ball* measure was enough to agitate audiences, press, and the rest of the media just a bit. It is a public shame to broadcast a fish-ball from inside for minutes in the most watched show of the night. Network execs had to give up. My bosses succeeded.

Make your hero use the *Product - Client - Profits* prism when evaluating the predators around them. Ask them to practice the Holy Trinity game just to kill time; who is that decision serving? *Father Product? Son Client?* Or the *Holy*

Spirit Profits? My bosses and the network execs showed such a lack of respect for the client/audience that I was completely in shock. That was what struck me the most at the time, and it was a very good lesson.

Like in the Catholic faith, I understand now that my *jefes* were sacrificing *The Son Client* –audience– to keep *The Father Product* –our show– alive, but I'm not sure I'd have the balls. Hostilities ended in two weeks, when they started negotiating the following season. Ceasefire first, and then some new arrangements. The sensationalist late-night show kept doing their thing but with very limited footage. This war happened in season three of the reality competition. This year, the reality show will air for the 21st time. *Un pastón!* Yes, a big chunk of money for *los dos padres de la criatura*. Looks like both sides of the table have finally proved solid faith in their common God Creation, and the *Santisima Trinidad*.

CASE TWO: INFLUENCERS WITH INFLUENZA

This case is a real exception. Let's allow your heroes to draw their conclusions about this case; mine are at the end of the section. Let's set up the scene. I was consulting for the biggest social media content publisher in Spanish. One of the biggest publishers in the world regardless of language. I am talking about a company that put together 100 million followers between the big three –YouTube-Facebook-Instagram.– A company that at the time was producing over 20 shows for Facebook Watch and YouTube. With monthly, weekly and daily episodes. A real giant. The big-big leagues in social media content creation.

I know your hero is going to freak out when I tell you where this company is located. And nope, it is not in Los Angeles. Nor in San Francisco, Barcelona, Madrid, Mexico City, Bogota, or New York. Nope! It is in the city of Tijuana, a company formed by a group of cousins and a few friends. Yes. Right in the backyard of the border wall and in ground cero of the war on drugs, close to the beach. Your hero would never think they would learn about modern storytelling in a place like Tijuana. That was my case, *soy un incredulo*, I must confess. I did learn a lot. I'm not going to tell you what I was expecting, but this is what I saw: I got into a building with armed security –of course!– and a guard and a gun, both, escorted me through security and into the lift. When we got out of the elevator, I saw +400 passionate young content creators between 18 to 29 working in the biggest independent content factory I've ever seen. Young creators functioning together in a way my experienced producer eyes had never seen before. And the best part of it? The vast majority of them weren't 'educated storytellers', not at all. Young Mexicans –mostly– from a variety of backgrounds. Maybe 10% came from media or entertainment backgrounds, no more.

In that weird place, I experienced the weirdest situation ever related to decision-making in the content landscape. A situation where a group of mastermind minds with an amazing business decided not to increase their profits –$75,000– doing nothing more than signing a paper. A one-minute time investment that meant $75K, but they decided not to do it. This is the exercise for your hero: We are not in those bosses' minds; they are the only ones that can answer the question *'Why did you refuse $75K after saying 'yes' to the business multiple times?'* I tried to ask, with no answer. That is going to be the norm. Your hero probably will never know the origin of the final decision-making, and the ultimate reasons behind it, but they can figure it out, as I did. Your hero, you, and I, we all need to use our mastermind mind superpowers. Let's go with the case:

I met the TJ company *mero mero* time before. They were collaborating in *Confetti Mexico*, a show I adapted and ran for Facebook Watch. A huge success. When the pandemic hit, the show was already over. I put together a couple of concepts and visited our Tijuana collaborators. By the end of the meeting, I was already consulting about content with their influencers and doing business development for them. All in a two-hour span, looking at the border wall through the window. Surreal.

One of the Tijuana company's biggest successes was a show they had stopped producing recently. That idea made them famous on social media. The concept is simple and powerful: the sidewalk of any Mexican city. A female host gets into a coffee shop looking for established couples. She approaches the first one and offers them money if they both allow her to check their phone messages and pictures and answer her questions. Who else are they both messaging with? And, for what? Your hero can imagine the rest. Fake or real, they produced over 160 episodes, and let me tell you, they felt real. The show was called "*Exponiendo Infieles*". Yes, *Cheaters* revisited for Gen Z. The 25 most watched episodes of the show have –all of them– have over 23 million views on YouTube. Crazy successful.

I told you I was doing business development for the Mexican content powerhouse, and I saw an opportunity in that show. For me, those over 160 episodes were the perfect package to offer to a medium or small size outlet. A platform in Spanish with needs in their content grid. An opportunity to get fresh dollars with something that was already produced, already paid, and already resting in a hard drive after years of profits. The Tijuana friends would receive a gift from the gods of content if I could re-package and sell it. And I did. They invested a few resources in producing a reel. We re-edited a few episodes, and I sold it to the first platform I visited. I knew it. Let's skip the details and go straight to the numbers. I pitched the Tijuana friends' show –as a finished product– to a niche streaming platform with content in both English and Spanish. The platform loved it as I did. Negotiations were fast, and the cut for the Tijuana owners was $75k, in a single check, with nothing else to do but sign the paperwork. I already had the hard drive in my desktop, and I was supposed to re-edit the episodes, but it never happened.

What does your hero think stopped the TJ influencers from grabbing that money? What kind of virus did they have? *Que bicho les pico a los de Tijuana para rechazar $75k???* Who would've expected that outcome from anyone born and raised in Tijuana? I didn't. My bad again. Let's analyze the facts with your hero: The Mexican Influencers were top league players. They were used to signing big contracts with big companies as YouTube, Facebook, and others, so I don't think it was *miedo escenico*. They had been playing in the Bernabeu Stadium of social media content for a while. There also weren't any risks about their intellectual property. It was a *lata* (can) –finished program– that the outlet would program for a limited time. No rights, no edits, no format alterations, no adaptations, no other risk than more exposure! Especially if the show is broadcast on an American platform dedicated to queer content in two languages. Not the Tijuana team's regular audience, that's for sure, but a very interesting niche of new viewers and an entrance to the huge American market. Any idea, guys? Not *miedo escenico*, not IP risks, not responsibility at all, good perspectives, and a clean check of $75k, but they didn't take it. What does your hero have in mind?

I have three theories about why one of the biggest influencer platforms got that weird virus and refused easy money. Let's see if your stars would agree: The first one is about 'Hispanic machismo'. I think they may not like the idea of anyone associating their IPs with a gay platform. This theory comes from the fact that from the five owners of the monster company, only one is a woman; the rest are Mexican alpha-males, with all that is attached to the concept in the border town of Tijuana. It would be surprising for me because of how young they are, how cool they look, and how open the creative industry they are part of is, but maybe that was the reason behind their decision. They don't look as old school Spanish macho, but who knows? It could be the Mexican version of the 'fake it until you make it' in the *inclusion, equity, and diversity* times?

My second theory is the 'they didn't like me' one. It could be a very destructive thought –please ask your hero not to stay too long with that kind of hypothesis– even though your star needs to consider it too. Maybe the Tijuana mastermind minds decided not to move forward to strangle any possible future collaboration with me? I don't think so, but it also could be. My third theory is directly related to the Holy Trinity system of beliefs. What if they were protecting their supreme God? The big One with the three persons within? In their case, their God Product –their content and their brand.– What about that? Has your hero considered it? Let's break down that thought.

The system of beliefs only works in one direction: Pushing your creation up. Not down, not steady. If the motivations behind the decision-makers are not driven by healthy ambition, but by fear, the system won't work. Back to the influencers with influenza to prove it. What if at the end they were just afraid of growing more? Afraid of getting into an unknown content landscape? They were only creating social media content, a lot of it, but nothing else. My third theory is that at a certain point, they were thinking big, but then they acted small. They got scared of jumping to a new world, streaming platforms in this case. My recommendation for your hero: You cannot think big and then get tight and scared. If you say you go, you must go. Period. Why would you hire people, invest resources, or strategize in the name of only God Creation, if at the end of the day you behave small? If you stop just a few yards from the dreamed finish line, why spend the energy and money? In the holy trinity system of beliefs, it is not enough to think about the product; it is about praising it. Every decision we make has one goal: Make the God Creation bigger and better. If the product is not growing with the decision, there is no need for a decision.

The Tijuana mastermind minds are the only ones who can answer, so let's talk about my role now. If I would've practiced properly the holy trinity system, I wouldn't have ended up *en lios* (in troubles) with the acquiring platform. The buyers of the show, the platform mastermind minds, trusted me, and I failed. I was too focused on the money-shot during the operation, so much that I didn't see the Tijuana influencers' struggles, and I promise, the symptoms of struggles were there. My '*sight on the prize*' attitude at the time not only blinded my perception but also made me forget my faith. I went straight to Profits mode, and I lost my GPS.

CASE THREE: SOCIAL PLATFORMS WITH COMMUNITY ISSUES

This last case has ties to the Tijuana influencers. Another real-life situation where the decision makers' faith failed, and mine too. This time for lack of *cojones* in my case. Let's set the scene for your hero: A couple of years before that first trip to Tijuana, I received a call from an unknown number. Thanks to that call, I got two things I won't ever forget. One I am proud of, the other I am ashamed of. Thanks to that call, I was invited to be responsible for the biggest success in Facebook Watch history at the time. My second try in the Social Media content landscape became not only the biggest success I've had in America so far, but also my rematch with two genres where I had failed in the past: Comedy and Quiz Shows. This is the part I am most proud of from that call. The dark side of the invitation, the shaming part, is that to be in the Facebook project, I left a friend –also a partner– two weeks after starting our production of an investigative docu series

that I helped to format and sell. Tell your hero to not leave the boat during the journey, and if they need to do it, ask them to do it right. I did it right, but in these cases 'right' is never enough. Especially when friends are involved. I am realizing now that I've done that twice in my life, and those two people are close friends to each other. Feels like a curse! I can be their common example of 'what not to do'. Shameful, I'm telling you.

Back to the call for your hero to understand. On the other end of the line, there was a very solid American production company, founded by two mastermind minds who made TV history with the MTV hit show *The Real World*. Both owners of this company were part of the team behind that piece of television I love, which, for me, was enough to be curious and excited about the meeting. Scene two: Mar Vista, Los Angeles, meeting room of the production company –very cool offices, btw. It was easy to connect with both owners. We spoke the same language; we shared creative DNA and production experiences. They sought me out for some thoughts on how to adapt a Facebook Watch Intellectual Property to the Mexican market. I felt proud, and I am not sorry for my feelings, Catholic friends! I know I am one of the best at 'translating' – adapting and interconnecting cultures with stories. Not only because I've been the cultural alien in the room my entire life –decoding and rendering nonstop– but also because I have spent more than a decade acquiring, adapting, selling, and producing content from unexpected overseas markets. Does your hero know that the big content fairs like Cannes have also *planta de oprtunidades*? Like the Macy's final sales stuff in the dirty corner of the top-top floor. In those messy places, your hero will find Japanese, Korean, Israeli, Polish, or Turkish content jewels that can make them rich and famous, if they adapt them well. Of course, your hero doesn't need to go to Cannes anymore; have them scroll on the right screens and inspiration will come. Back to Case Three, I'm good at adapting. That was the point and the reason for the call.

By the end of the meeting, I had a mission. Two missions, to be precise; first, outline the key elements for the adaptation to succeed, and, second, make a list of potential showrunners. And I did both things. Something important for your hero to consider here! Very important. Having faith in *la Santisima Trinidad* means your hero will write in that list the names of the BEST possible mastermind minds they know about for the task. It doesn't matter if they are your hero's competitors, rivals, enemies, or best *panas*. I don't care. God Content doesn't care. Your hero must give their best in the mission, even if that means swallowing some pride and past shit. That's what I did. I called each one of those names to check their interest and availability and went to the production house with my two lists.

Two or three weeks later, I was on the Mediterranean shores, not only enjoying life at its best, but also co-running that investigative series when my phone rang again. This time, the number was in my contacts: Mr. Ex-Real-World, the mastermind mind who hired me to consult, offered me to run the Facebook project. Holy shit! I accepted, of course. Does your hero remember I used the word 'karma' at the beginning of the chapter? This is how things are. It looks like I swallowed a lot of old garbage in that list of potential showrunners. That's holy trinity magic shit, no doubt. I was honored and excited. My partner and friend would understand. He already had 3 Emmys under his belt, too many hours of showbiz shit not to be happy for me!

The second act of Case Three is set in Playa Vista, Los Angeles. Our studio was a few yards away from Facebook's headquarters in Silicon Beach. In that facility, the company that hired me was producing three versions of the same Facebook Watch show. Yes, three. They set up a production hub that allowed them to deliver three daily shows –USA, Canada, and Mexico– Monday through Friday, from the same facilities, with the same technical crew, and with three different content teams and hosts. A very good set up, I have to say. I like production hubs. Your hero needs to learn how to take advantage of that. My first hub experience was on Fear Factor, in Buenos Aires. Only the US version of the show was filmed in the US; the rest of the world –over 10 countries–- did it under the humid Argentinian summer. Then the *Blind Faith* hub (*Love Island*'s ancestors), and a few more. Content globalization, again. Back to Playa Vista. When I arrived for pre-production, the US version was already on air, the Canadian was next to premiere, and Mexico was coming afterward. For me, the time in Confetti –that was the name of the show– was another undreamed dream that came true. Very happy times for many reasons: my bosses, their managing style, the product, the crew, my new peers –showrunners of the other versions– my writers room –one of the best in my whole freaking life– our host, and the lifelong friends I made.

The scene is set for the third act: The unexpected success we had. By 'we,' I mean the Mexican version of the show. Does your hero remember that app on your phone where you would play a game –answering a few questions– and get money if you got all the answers right? It was called 'HQ', and it was an interactive quiz-show game that ran through an app you downloaded on your phone. It was very trendy for a while. Well, the Facebook Watch IP *Confetti* was exactly like that, but it would run over your hero's Facebook. It was an interactive quiz show where you would get money for correctly answering 10 questions, while laughing your ass off listening to the jokes of a very attractive –and a bit crazy– host. Because of the holy trinity, or because of our talent, or because of the novelty for the Mexican market, our version had 7 million followers in three months and around one million players playing live –daily– for several weeks. If your hero is asking if that is a lot or a little, here is one more number: Neither the American nor the Canadian versions had more than 35k players ever. Of course, not six-figure numbers of followers. We did seven times seven figures of followers just in a few weeks. Crazy successful.

Here is the relevant twist of the Case: The two mastermind minds who taught me EVERYTHING about the Facebook show were the American showrunner and his head writer. They did the same with the Canadian team. Two of the most talented people I've ever met. Craig and Aaron were very generous with me. They took me under their wing until I understood all the – complicated and exciting– secrets of an interactive game show. Thanks to them, we succeeded. Obviously, they knew their shit pretty well. What happened then? Why did neither the Canadian nor the American version ever take off? What does your hero think?

Here is where 'community issues' affect the holy trinity and the decision makers, at every table! Let your star know this is important. Let's start with my table. For *Father Product* –the quiz-show in Mexico– I put together a very diverse team of Hispanic writers. All backgrounds, From Bilbao to Caracas, to CDMX –of course– to Los Angeles, but all working for Mexican audiences. I put in place two extra filters for final script approvals, with the goal to 'Mexicanize for Gen Z' *Father Product* as best as possible. We also hired a Mexican female host, and she got the role impeccably. All good, it went perfectly. God Content was happy and delivered. I did all of that as part of the road map I brought to my boss in the first consulting gig. It wasn't new for him, and he encouraged me to do it. Both of us were thinking about *Father Product* then. Interestingly, my boss didn't apply the same philosophy to the American and Canadian versions. Mexican host, Mexican writers, make sense. Afro-American host, all white writers, doesn't make sense. Is it that simple? I don't know! Maybe! But for me, that was the main reason: the other North American versions had a lack of connection between the words said and the person delivering them. They felt like two different things. And here is where I stop to recognize my capital sin. Let your hero know that it doesn't matter what the rest of the people do. Despite our gigantic success, neither my boss, nor the American showrunner, nor the Canadian, nor the extra-talented American head writer, ever asked me '*what do you think Daniel? What would you do?*'. They never asked, but that is not what I regret. I regret not telling them what I thought without asking. I was tempted, *pero no hubo cojones.*

Does your hero think the Facebook execs and the ex *Real World* owners ever consider the 'community issue' reason as an option? Did the thought cross their minds? Hard to say. I like them all, they are all extraordinarily –and I mean extraordinarily– nice people and freaking good pros. I will jump into the next project with them without question, but I think they were so caught up in the 'systemic' part of the 'community' issue that they didn't see it. Sad if that's the case.

Case Three ended after the Mexican version was doubled due to its success –yes, instead of 5 shows per week, 10 of them– which meant around 400 episodes before Facebook decided to cancel the interactive experiment. And for your hero's question, the answer is 'yes'. The *Sagrada Trinidad* is pro-diversity, pro-equity, pro-inclusion, but especially! Pro being consistent with *Father Product*. A last note from the holy trinity: Writers' rooms and on-screen talent are the same figure in our altar; they are not on two different altars. Please make your hero conscious of that before jumping into the next chapter. Now, it's time to talk about on-screen talent.

CHAPTER 11

What About Those In Front Of The Camera?

ON SCREEN TALENT: SIDE EFFECTS AND HOME REMEDIES

Notes

CHAPTER 11

On Screen Talent: Side Effects And Home Remedies

Once your hero has total control of the creation and themselves, on-screen talent is probably the most sensitive topic they are going to face. In audiovisual storytelling –despite genres and formats– creators always depend on on-screen talent to ultimately deliver what they have imagined. That is a very serious fact that affects the two sides –creators and talent– in ways that transcend the specifics of the project: contract negotiations, creative control, and conflict resolution. Nope. It's even worse than all of that. The bridge between your hero's creation and the audience is that person in front of the lens. The physical reincarnation of the once dreamed vision depends on another human being –oh shit! once again. This human being is probably going to have a whole different view of the world, so, please make your hero conscious; the association between those pieces –mastermind minds and camera talent– could mean the weakest or the strongest link ever for the creator's visions and the team's efforts. A very complicated tie that affects the mind, the heart, and the soul of the three parts involved: the creation, the visionary, and the performer. This communication line is not easy to handle under any circumstances, but it is way worse when talented and troubled people are the main characters. But there is good news again! Your hero has already practiced all the techniques needed to handle this matter. The good thing about on-screen talent being the last link of the process? Your hero have used their super-powers a lot already. Now, it is a matter of how to apply them to the topic of on-screen talent. *Empezamos!*

THE BRIDGE BETWEEN VISION AND PERFORMANCE: LOS MUÑECOS (The Toy Dolls)

Here's an important fact. The unseen bond between your hero's first vision and the final performance of their executed creation, that invisible bridge, always starts in your hero's mind and finishes in the on-screen talent's body. Each time. The final connection from the creative mastermind imagination to a screen depends on *los muñecos* (the toy-dolls). Time now for another Spanish lesson for you and your hero. Also, time for an apology for all the talented on-screen people I have known, and those I haven't. I'm guilty of using the word *muñecos* (toy-dolls) to describe you all when you are not present on set. Sorry!

In my defense, I have to say that I haven't created the term, even though I love it and I use it. It is a crew thing. Ruminations of my blue-collar soul. I heard it decades ago, when I was still young, and it took over me. It was pure Spaniard crew slang. I was –as always– observing how a team did their thing during a shooting. Gaffer and a director of photography were discussing sun, shadows, scene movements and so on. In a surreal conversation, one of them couldn't explain his hypothesis, and ended up frustrated saying *'si me ponen ahi a los muñecos me dejas vendido con el cinco mil'* (If they put the talent there, I'm screwed with the 5K). I don't see any wrong on the term, I'm not –we are not– despising anyone, that's not the point. The opposite, *es una palabra cariñosa* (as a term of endearment). We use it for all talent; models, news anchors, actors, contributors, contestants, dancers, hosts, experts... whatever it is! Your hero's audiovisual creation, my own creation, cannot happen without the *muñecos*, so let's work this out properly.

That invisible bridge between vision and performance –your hero and their *muñecos*– means an opportunity to raise up or to drop off the content ball. It is like that every time, every project, every show: Adding value to your creation thorough that special bond, or the opposite. It is also a great opportunity for your star to learn a lot about storytelling. The bridge between creators and on-screen talent is one of the better sources of wisdom in this craft.

What does your hero think that invisible bridge is built with? What are the specifics of the connection? And more important, what is at stake on each side of the bridge? Understanding the answer to the last question is your hero's first assignment. Both sides are deeply invested in the project's success, and both feel personally exposed. Actors, hosts, panelists, contributors, contestants, or whoever you put in from of the camera, put themselves on display. Make your hero aware of the concept of 'putting themselves on display.' It is physical; they 'are' the audiovisual creation. Their faces, voices, and bodies are the canvas for the story your hero is telling. They become the story, and the story will represent them in the future. Your creation is their body in action. Major stuff, no doubt. In the other corner, the side of the creative mastermind, what is at stake are months or years of work, reputation, money, friends, employees, and collaborators. The results of uncountable hours of effort, joy, pain, fear, and fun. Major stuff too. Does your hero see it? Is it another *'all of nothing'* situation for both parts? Of course it is. The key word here is **vulnerability**. Recognizing this shared exposure is your hero's first step. Ask them to never approach camera talent dismissing this fact: They expose themselves directly. Ignoring it is the worst mistake an audiovisual storyteller can commit.

That shared link –the creation– and that shared co-dependency on each other make me see this *'bridge between talent and creators'* as the bridge between marriages. And it is like that. In order to produce beautiful babies – your hero's new show– your protagonists will romance and marry as many on screen talent as new shows they will premiere. A lot of fun! But uncountable hours of couples therapy will be required. Recognized and shared vulnerability builds empathy and mutual respect. What to do with that respect afterwards is the second lesson for your hero to learn.

IT IS A MARRIAGE: KEY ELEMENTS FOR SUCCESS

As surreal as it sounds, I am asking your hero to marry their toy-dolls and to keep that marriage healthy until their baby is at least a toddler. If needed, I am asking them to keep also a perfect relationship with their *muñecos* even during divorces. I know I am asking a lot, but there is no other way. When approaching talent, whether on or off screen, your hero will need to remember the *rules of engagement* already described in this book. That will give them the key elements for success.

Now I am going to build with you the *Previously On* for this chapter about on-screen talent. Each cut has been selected from the previous pages of this book and hides a key element for your future hero's interactions with on screen talent.

The *Previously On* starts with something your hero will remember from Chapter Two -*How to Become the Mastermind Mind*- from the section titled 'The First Call and the Magic Around It'; the selected lines are about what your hero shares with the person interviewing them for that first dreamed position. Do you guys recall that? In my case it was a wedding photographer; does your hero remember the common thing we shared? The common element between my potential employer and me? It was Passion. SHARED passion. Yes, with caps, shared passion for storytelling. That's why the *Previously On* of this chapter about talent starts with that concept. Extrapolate it to the *on-screen* people. That is the first key to a successful marriage between a creator and an on-screen talent. In any interaction they may have, make your hero remember that is the baseline. **Shared Passion** is the foundation of the couple's love nest.

The second pod of lines for the *Previously On* comes from chapter four. Your hero will immediately remember the lessons: I asked them to be the *Danny Ocean* of showbiz, finding the perfect *Ocean's Eleven* for their creation. This time, they will apply the formula to on-screen talent. Think of the best candidates, put those best names at the top of your list, and start moving your ass. Let's continue; from the same chapter, the *Previously On* includes lines from the section 'My Outlaw Recruiting System': Is the candidate a follower of **the showbiz golden principles**? (Always on time + Performing at their best + Making it happen regardless). Can your hero **trust** that person? Is she/he/it a **good** person? And the last element to consider, what is that talented person's **potential to grow** along with your hero's creation?

I think it is done. With those lines I got my chapter's *Previously On,* and your stars got the key elements for their next marriage with their *muñecos* (on-screen talent). It doesn't matter the specifics –Actors? Hosts? Reality stars?– I don't care. Does not apply yet. Despite genre, format, or the type of product, the described approach will give your hero all they need. The specifics of each gender and format bring their own challenges with their own side effects. The way to prevent those diseases and to get the best for the creation is applying the explained home remedies since the beginning of the marriage, before the challenges arrive.

Something else important to consider here. Sometimes, your on-screen spouse it is also your business partner. In those cases, there is a key addition to the *Previously On.* If your hero is planning to get involved with on-screen talent during the development stages, if they are considering somehow partnering with talent, I have to add some lines for your stars coming from chapter seven *-Guerrilla Warfare: In the Search of Endless Independence-* Those mentioned in the section 'The Four Elements for a storytelling solo career'. You are going to recall this: The Elements are **Funding - Video- Audio - Story**. Remember now? If your hero wants to successfully dedicate their life to storytelling, they need to be really good in two of these *Four Elements*, and more important, if your hero is partnering with anyone –especially on-screen talent– that partner should master at least two of the *Four Elements.* This book is about success, not only about survival. If your hero wants success, make them raise their bars.

Regarding your star's future on-screen marriages, please ask them not to be scared, expecting the worst, or naïve, presuming the best. A successful marriage between creator and *muñeco* will become easy and beneficial for both spouses only by keeping these few rules of engagement: Shared passion, proven devotion to the *Showbiz Golden Principals*, real talent for storytelling, goodness, and mutual trust. It is not that difficult, and that is good, because, like in a marriage, shit will happen sooner or later –mandatory– but if the foundations are good, some hours of couples therapy later, the marriage will overcome the issues and continue the creative journey together.

DOUBLE TALENTED PEOPLE: THE SHOWBUSINESS LEONARDO DAVINCI

I haven't mentioned exceptions yet, the mastermind minds that can perform at the higher level on both sides of the screen. The Reese Witherspoons, George Clooneys, Tyler Perrys, Jordan Peeles, or Oprah Winfreys *de la vida.* Pick yours, there are a few more. The exceptionally double talented people who are lucky enough to avoid 'building' the freaking invisible bridge that connects their imagination with the face on the screen. Have you guys thought about it? Do it for a second. It is better than telepathy. When I think about it, I just can feel the relief of not having to say a single word to your on-screen talent. That must be nice. And weird.

If your hero's ambition is leading the creative process on both sides, the on-camera delivery and the content itself, if they are a Leonardo Davinci kind of ambitious, make them read the chapter twice. Sorry. Ambition costs extra, guys! First pass read the lines as a showrunner. Then, read them as a talent for hire. That would be the first step. The second tip for your double talented stars is 'run for help'. Fast. The day I taped the first episode of my podcast I understood how difficult that double task is. My soul is not focused enough to lead and perform in both sides with my high-quality requirements. If one day I can make them both right, I'll write about it. *Prometido!*

ON SCREEN TALENT AND GENRE EXPECTATIONS

As mentioned before, each genre requires a different approach to talent. In this section, your hero will think about each genre / format talent-related issues they may face. What should they take into consideration when dealing with the real housewives? And with legacy actresses? Comedians? News anchors? Professional athletes? Bullfighters? Pop Stars? Within on-screen relationships, the specifics of the talent don't matter. What is guaranteed is that issues will show up with time, and your hero's readiness will make the difference. As is well known by now, the way I'm going to tell your hero what I learnt about on-screen faces is going to be through my own successes and my own mess-ups. Of course. When you f*****d up things, the least you can do is get the lessons, so, here are mine.

From 'No Listers' to 'A Listers'

If your star has started in their craft from the very-very bottom, while they were growing with their creations, they naturally have learned how on-screen talent behaves. There are some differences from having totally unknown faces in front of the camera to working with worldwide celebrities. With your hero's career, the 'size' of the personality in front of the lens will grow. I hope along with their wisdom. In my case, the biggest lessons from the early times came from working in low budget commercials with first time models, kids, and animals. Let's skip this last one, we will get into the other two soon enough. In my first stages in the craft, I also got lessons from working with professional athletes, pop stars, and kings. And I am not kidding. Kings of pop like Michael Jackson, and the king of my own country. And I do not believe in monarchy, *cosas de la vida!*

It doesn't matter who is in front of the lens, whether it is a well-trained actor with a scary deep voice for your horror short film, or a talented host with magical energy, or a Mexican American Chef –who doesn't speak Spanish– hosting a cooking competition show in Spanish. Yes, those things happen. Does your hero remember *The Uncertainty Factor*? In the third case –The Mexican Chef who does not speak Spanish– the moment the big boss allowed us –writers and me– to meet the talent and learn about the dramatic language barrier was just 24 hours before the shooting started. A big 'oh shit' this time. Make your hero aware of the physics of show business. Its universal laws tell us that '*The Uncertainty Factor*' and the 'on-camera talent' are related in ways that we still don't understand. Let's hope for quantum computing to solve the mystery.

Maybe you are already aware of this: The ultimate reason why you are reading these pages is for your hero to be – somehow – ready for '*The Uncertainty Factor*'. Do you remember the movie Forrest Gump? '*La vida es como una caja de bombones, hasta que no lo abres, no sabes que te va a tocar*' ('Life was like a box of chocolates. You never know what you're gonna get'). That's how things work with the faces that will tell your hero's stories. The personality, background, and education of the on-screen talent is like Forrest Gump said, a box of chocolates, but there are two elements that will give your hero enough wisdom to be ready for any chocolate from the box. Element one: the real professions of the on-camera person –actor? Pop star? Scientific? NBA player? Gamer? Chef? – and element 2; what is the position of this person in the celebrity scale?

From A listers to no listers, your hero must consider what that person does and how much experience they have in front of the camera. Which is the same as saying how many videos, photos, articles, or memes that person has on the internet. The more they have, the more difficult is going to be for the creators to engage with the talent in a creative romance. The higher on the list, the more your hero will need to remember the lessons from the previous pages. Creative nuptials with A listers are almost always complicated, but they don't have the exclusive. No listers can also be problematic. As my auntie said '*hay de todo en todas partes*' (there is everything everywhere). Regardless of profession, experience, or position in the lists, your hero will find all kinds of personalities, and they must be ready to evaluate, adapt, and keep the romance alive fast. Their creation is on stake.

Pro-Athletes and Camera Lenses

The key with pro-athletes is to find a way for them to be themselves. That's it. Ask your hero not to waste efforts trying to do anything in any other way than the talented pro athletes' own way. That is an important rule to apply to anyone who is not already an on-screen professional, but with athletes, it is more important.

If your creator's protagonists –or their bosses– are asking the athletes to do something that is not 'them', or to say something they wouldn't say, or saying things in ways that it is not them, it won't work. When asking anyone who is not an 'on-camera pro' to say words from a script, chances are it's not going to go well. Time for your hero to find a way to connect with the 'persona' underneath the athlete – shared passions? Shared origins? Shared favorite food? Shared whatever? Find it! – Make your hero win a little bit of the pro-athlete's trust, make them relax, and explore how they can deliver the message while being themselves. If it doesn't work, ask your hero to start considering changing either talent or content.

If the situation is the opposite, and your hero is capturing the athlete in their own world, the plan is different. If your hero's talent plays for Real Madrid, and it is his last game in the Estadio Bernabeu, your hero can relax and enjoy shooting day. That was exactly my case. I spent time with Emilio Butrageño –a Real Madrid soccer legend – during his last hours of his last day in his last game in the Bernabeu stadium, shooting for a long-form documentary. That day, the only thing I needed to tell Emilio was *'what's next?'*. It was a matter of visual storytelling for me. Butrageño was the story, and he took care of the content just by being himself and doing his thing. It was an easy assignment to document those hours of the soccer superstar. 'A lister' advantages.

I had the same kind of assignment some time before and it wasn't as easy. Probably because instead of the last day as a pro-soccer in the Real Madrid, this still teenager pro-athlete was having his first season in the top leagues of the bull fighting scene. He was also an 'A lister' in the small *mundo de los toros*. I spent 24 hours with El Juli –an outstanding matador– during his first times in the craft. It was the same mission as with the Real Madrid soccer star, following him thorough his day 'at the office'. But it didn't work as well or as easily as with the soccer legend. When your hero's' on-camera talent's actions and words don't feel natural, regardless of the reasons behind, your star must get into emergency mode. Whoever runs that shooting, the first thing to think about is how to give the talent more space and consider either giving the talent less direction, or maybe some direction, but that only can happen when they re-stablish the connection with the on-screen athlete. They may need to reset and reboot their romance Bluetooth devices. With the matador, I think the kid was scared enough with the size of the event, the media around, and the two *Núñez del Cuvillo's* –1,600 lb. bulls– he was facing in an hour. I don't think I would like to have extra visitors with cameras and demands if I was in his place. I immediately decided to clean up the room. I sent away part of the crew. Everyone who was left walked backwards a few steps, acting as flies on the wall, except for a couple of words here and there to ask El Juli to dress up slowly, or to breathe deeply with his eyes closed. Something magical happened that day, because after all those nerves, by the end of the *corrida*, El Juli was leaving the *plaza por la puerta grande, con dos orejas y un rabo*. Which means they opened the bullring-cathedral doors for the laureled hero to leave, lifted by his squad, acclaimed by the crowd, with bull's bloody parts amputated in his hands. Yeah, a bit like *Gladiator*, but in unscripted mode. All real. Weird Mediterranean stuff.

Make your star aware that any person who dedicates *absolutamente todo* (everything they are) to an activity has a lot in common with us creators. We both pursue dreams, we share that. I am ambitious, but still not 'pro-athlete ambitious'. I am not *dándolo todo* (giving my all) to be among the 0.1% of humans as a pro-athlete is, but I am doing my best for being at least in the 1% of the humans that tell stories in an outstanding way.

Have your hero ruminate on this for a second: What if in the pursuit of their dream, they must risk their own lives? As a natural part of the activity, I mean. As a bullfighter, an MMA fighter, a 14,000-foot mountaineer, a Formula 1 driver, or a solo sailor, all those who risk their lives pursuing success and following their passions have seen the face of death and felt the fear of the end. They all are connected with something deep we humans all share and most of us avoid. This is very important. If your hero is dealing with professionals who are risking their physical integrity, the better way to connect with them is through that fact. It took me one bullfighter, one K2 mountaineer, and one boxing fighter to understand the whole thing properly. If your hero's on-camera talent belongs to that very exclusive club, the first thing I'd recommend is '*somehow let your talent know that you know*'. I've been too close to death a handful of times in my life. It is painful and tough to remember those moments, but I just need to reconnect with one of those experiences to find a natural way to express to the talent my deepest respect, admiration, and probably envy too. And then the romance starts, your hero will see. *Por cierto* (btw) guys, I am not saying '*tell the talent your close- to-death experiences*', nope. I am saying '*connect with the experience to find a way to connect with the talent*'.

'A-Listers' Only: The Real Deal

I am responsible for a few celebrity talent competition shows. I've been dancing with stars, cooking with stars, defying fear and eating cucarachas with stars, and so on. You are right, there are not so many A listers on those shows, only a few, but I have romanced *listers* from every single letter in the alphabet. But now we are going to talk only about royalty. Only regal shit. Kings of Pop, kings of Spain, and other royal on-screen faces. When your hero is dealing with *la nobleza* (the nobles) there are three clear advantages: One; they usually know their shit pretty well, they are good and efficient. Two; there is a protocol when working with *la realeza*, and their court –their entourage– is going to be sure everyone follows it –no pics, no one talks to the king or the queen directly, and many others.– And three; their time is very limited, what means your star *tienen que mover el culo* (you got it! They must move their asses) and be efficient as never before.

These three A-listers characteristics make things easier, despite what your hero will feel when they read the royal email with the royal conditions of the royal visit to the not-so-royal set. Allow them to lose their shit a bit, scream their indignation to the gods, and then calm down; it is all normal. Your hero is going to be amazed and in shock for a while. Only in terms of resources; making the royal visit possible is going to devour a big part of the episode budget. And guys, I am not talking about whatever the crazy fee for the A lister is, nope. I am talking about the direct production cost of the royal procedures. Your hero could have five B listers with the amount of assets that the royal protocol demands. But that is how it works, and your hero won't need to overthink it. Ask them to put the energy into getting the best from the A-lister.

Another advantage of the top stars in the galaxy, particularly among pop music royalty, is that they are surrounded by talent. Within the king's or the queen's entourage, there is going to be a key person who will make your hero's life better. They must pay attention! Twice in my career, I owe the artist's entourage a big on-screen success. Not due to the artist, not to me, not to the director, but due to that talented member of the royal court who made the show better. Way better. In those two cases, the A-lister's choreographers were responsible for telling the story of the musical number better and faster. I'm sure one of them was a camera director too, shit, it was mind-blowing how they did it. When the princess of pop and her court arrived, we never saw her royal highness until the number, but the entourage came to our set first. In the first stage walk through, I saw her highness's choreographer checking camera positions, how they were mounted, lights, etc. After just one pass rehearsal with the dance crew, where the choreographer was doing the A lister queen part, he asked to see the complete take in the control room with us. It was an amazing experience. Not only because the showrunner, camera director, and pop star choreographer's creative visions were completely in sync, but also because the A lister court member saved us a lot of time -and money- while getting outstanding results. Yes, the lesson is clear, with A listers, most of the times the romance between the creative mind and the face in the screen is thru a proxy. And sometimes the most important proxy is not the one you are communicating with -manager, agent, assistant- sometimes it is, but sometimes it is not, so yes, your heroes will need all their detective skills. Who is that person that can make the king/queen listen for real if needed? Who in the court has that power?

As your hero can see, once again, the creative mastermind mind responsibility is the show –how it looks and preforms– but it is also the people that make the show. Everyone on set has a valid opinion, that's why they are there. When having A listers on set, the artist's entourage becomes both, your heroes *pesadilla* (nightmare), and your heroes opportunity *de petarla* (Spaniard slang for 'to shine big'). The key? The people, regardless roles.

Fish out of Water A-Listers

Here's some important advice for your hero: When the A-listers are not 'doing their thing' –performing a song, performing a role, driving a Formula 1 Ferrari, or cooking a 3 Michelin stars meal– the procedures are totally different, especially for the showrunners. Any A-lister out of their environment or attending the cameras for reasons that are not part of their craft, is a *bomba de relojeria;* it is only a matter of time *que explote.* It also could be a matter of what the A-lister is asked to do or to say, it depends, but what is for sure for your hero is that the superstar mood will always be a matter of how their public image is at that specific moment. It's challenging, I'm telling you. There is only one way to get what you need from the few minutes you can spend with the A-lister, and it is all about *tacto, intuicion, y huevos* (tact, intuition, and *cojones*).

For the intuition part your hero has a few tools. They must know what level of pressure from public scrutiny their superstars are under. Knowing a bit about what they are dealing with, and observing their body language when entering in set, would be enough for your hero's first creative romantic approach. Your star must present themselves with self-confidence, charisma, and perfect control of what is about to happen. All of that wrapped up in real story-teller passion and immaculate ethics. If they still have resources available, your hero can try to look cool in front of the superstar, but that is last. Clear? Now make your hero try to do all of that when the A-lister is completely ignoring them –and everyone else– on set. You are all transparent, everything is transparent on the A-lister's eyes, but the entourage-court or their own devices. It is surreal. I've been in front of an A-lister for minutes, waiting for their regal attention or a simple gesture. Nothing came. Here is where the tact and the *cojones* make their entrance. The story to illustrate the statement is the story of my interactions with the one and only King of Pop, Mr. Michael Jackson. Oh shit. Let's set up the scene, this time with a bite of pop culture history.

It was during the '*History World Tour*' that Michael did in the late 90's, when he stopped in Zaragoza for three days. It was his first tour after the child abuse accusations and four years without seeing a stage. A big moment for Michael, and a very good story for the newsrooms of the known universe. It was before I even dreamed of working with Camilla, JLo, Banderas, Paulina Rubio, Prince Royce or Eva Longoria, way before that. It was in the time where I was taking every gig under the sun to keep my *culo* out of the wedding videos, and it was working. In those times there were only six or seven broadcast camcorders in town, and I owned one, which meant I was doing a lot of coverages for sports –mostly La Liga stuff– and news. And because of the interest in Michael's visit, I received two calls from two media outlets in two different days to cover Michael Jackson's time in town. The calls ended up with *servidor* following Michael's visit from landing at the airport to his live performance three days later. Before continuing, I must confess that Michael's accusations affected me deeply enough to not to be excited about his visit to town. To be honest, deeply enough to be against the genius artist in general, despite how much I value his art, and it is a lot. But I am a pro, and I had a story to tell. One of my clients took the *King of Pop* visit seriously, and they wanted to produce a long piece about him. Somehow, they got a one-on-one interview with Mr. Michael Jackson when the rest of the media did it all at once in the press room. I was the lucky guy who was in both his hotel suite and the press room. And that hotel room was the place where I found the very much needed *cojones* to ask Michael Jackson what my client wanted me to ask, and the question was about the child abuse allegations. Oh shit!! This time *elevado a la enésima potencia* (raised to the n-th power).

By the time I made it to Michael's hotel suite, I already had footage of his gigantic private Russian plane landing, the 300 people entourage with kids among them, something outstanding to me – the royal limousine procession, and Michael greeting fans while protecting himself with a mask and an umbrella. Enough footage to tell the story of an artist that is idolatrized, isolated, fragile, sick, *y solo Dios sabe que mas* (only God knows what else Michael is carrying). Since the network's news SVP called me, the fear of asking Michael the question grew in my mind every second. I needed more stuff from him; that specific question would be the last thing to ask for. So, what would be the first thing to do when getting into Michael Jackson's hotel suite, located in one of his private three floors of the Boston hotel? The first thing would be being seen, and we weren't.

I was ready to kneel in front of the *King of Pop*, to kiss the ring, and to do whatever was needed, but once in the room, nobody talked to us. They continued doing their thing as if we were invisible. Surrounded by two security guys, but still invisible. Holy shit. Michael was in an armchair about 20 feet away, and I knew he checked on us while we weren't looking. I knew it because I'm very good at finding reflections when I'm in a space I am about to shoot, and I saw him in a reflection when his assistant was explaining him who the hell we were. The weird thing is that there was no reaction at all. Nobody talked to us for a few more eternal minutes. There were a lot of people moving around –kids included– and everyone ignored us. The absurdity of the situation was stressing me. Big time. I was seriously considering that the same person who brought us here and disappeared would come back and escort us out when the time was over, with or without an interview. What would I say to the news SVP? I found myself in flight or fight mode, showrunner style. I convinced myself to get into action and thought, let's get at least some B-roll and see if anybody reacts. Well, we had two security people in our sides, and there's no way you can hit the record button in Michael Jackson's hotel suite without permission, so, the *cojones* came, along with a blessing of inspiration, and I said these words out loud, directed to anyone and everyone, including Michael and security: 'Guys, if you don't mind, I'd like to get some B-roll of the crowd in the sidewalks from the suite window while Michael is getting ready, may I?' And we took the camera to the window and hit the button. Of course, what I was doing was telling Michael –and the court– what we wanted. The direct translation of my words was: 'We are here to tell the story of an icon, the passions he awakes, and how his work is touching so many lives in places as remote as this old European town.' And he got it! In less than a minute, he stood up from the armchair and came to the window to greet his fans a few floors underneath. Holy shit, happened! That's where I saw the star for real. We shared the proposed narrative, we were connected. He was helping me to tell a story he loved and started trusting me. Of course we didn't stop at the window. We did our B-roll, the assistant came back –nobody could talk straight to Michael until he was seated for the interview– and I built up my 'tormented talented idol narrative' with every question to Michael, until the last one, which I laid out from the fans perspective, saying: *'What do you have to say to the fans that are listening to all those accusations and coming tomorrow to the show?'* I 'adapted' the news SVP question to the circumstances. Michael answered, we packed our shit, and left the hotel. Some minutes later, tired of just being able of use his hand thru the suite window, Michael sat over the hotel's rooftop ledge to interact with the fans. Clearly, he shared the narrative we used.

Yes, your hero is in part right. Are we considering that Michael was in an *'out of the fishbowl'* situation in his own suite? Yes, we are. He wasn't performing, rehearsing, or recording music, A-listers usually are among the 0.1% of humans who are very good in an activity –with some respectfully Kardashian saga style exceptions. In my experience, anything out of the superstar's main activity is going to make the king or queen very nervous, and your hero's creative romance with the on-screen royalty is on risk. The showrunner survival toolkit for the A-list royalty is made with your protagonist's wisdom, tact, intuition and balls, so, keep practicing!

The Legacy Stars

This section is about actors, actress, and acting performances. Better said, it is about those actors and actresses that have changed lives and won every award possible with their performances. Your hero will also work with actresses and actors as hosts, panelists, judges, or competitors, but these lines are purely about scripted content and legacy names. The reason for this is simple: If your hero is lucky enough to work with one of those, it is like a condensed master's degree while being paid.

I haven't worked with the selected club of American *grandes damas de la escena* (the grand dames of the stage). Artists I admire, such as Meryl Streep, Glen Close, Angela Bassett, Julian Moore, Susan Sarandon, Jessica Lange, Diane Keyton, or Viola Davies. I'd love to do it! And who knows, maybe one day the universe will align perfectly, and I can at least try to creatively enamor one of those talented names. Let's hope for it! What I have done, a few times, is work with some of the *grandes damas de la escena* in the Spanish language. I am selecting for your hero the learnings from a creative romance with Concha Velasco, an iconic Spanish artist. I am choosing that experience because in her case, the romance started at the very beginning of the development stages. Without the Legacy Star on board, the show we were working on so hard would not have had any opportunity. As a side note: Yes, attaching legacy stars to your hero's projects is a well-known formula that helps get your creation on screen, but the journey has so many tricky turns that despite telling your hero more later in this chapter, there will be a whole book coming out just about content development and its secrets. I'll keep you all posted.

Back to the legacy thing. Concha Velasco was as an artist, a combination of Barbra Streisand and Meryl Streep. All three of them share versatility and impact first, then time in the craft. Streisand has reigned over six decades in multiple entertainment fields, exactly as Concha, another triple threat talent. Theater, movies, recorded albums, television, and more. Comedy, drama, musicals, and more. The three talented women also share strong stage presence and voice, a similar artistic legacy, and the fact that they became national icons. Enough for me. That's why we call them Grandes Damas.

What comes to your creative hero's mind when I use the term "grand dame of the stage?" There are a few common characteristics we all think about when considering legacy actresses. Very often, the term *gran dama* is associated with terms like fragile personality, emotional volatility, easily manipulated by men –husbands, managers, or studio bosses– past trauma, self-esteem issues, fear of aging, desperate comebacks, diva attitudes, and a life of regrets or mental disease. Wow, sounds difficult! Doesn't it? Your hero can blame Hollywood narratives, the gossip industry, and audience fascination for the screen superstars. That is the public perception –quite negative– the question is, is it all that true? And if it is, how the hell is your showrunner hero going to enamor *a una vieja imposible*? Back to basics guys, we've been here before. They will connect with the superstar through shared passion for storytelling. And those ladies have had a lot of that passion to make it where they are, especially with all those struggles along the journey. Would your hero still be there? Still fighting? On top of that, they have been the lead faces and voices of very relevant stories, even before your hero arrived on earth, so **Respect** is the first keyword for your star to romance with legacy talent.

The second keyword for Your heroes is **prove it**. Your heroes needs to prove their passion as a storyteller and their outstanding ability to tell stories to the superstar, and they need to prove it fast. Make your heroes show the legacy talent how good they are and how much they've invested in the project but ask them also to do it from a humble position. Showbiz legacy people have seen it all. Make your hero remember that. My romance with the Spanish *Barbra Streisand mixed with Meryl Streep* started in a hotel lobby in Madrid at a time when she was mentioned two or three times per week in the *TMZ-tyle* tv shows due to her nasty divorce. Tough times for her. Our ambitioned *Gran Dama* was out of the screens for a while, financially broken because of her husband/manager, and living in a hotel room. Shit. It totally felt like a 'Sunset Boulevard' remake, exactly what we all have in mind when we hear the term 'grand dame of the stages', but I had no time for that. I knew she was the very best option to sell the project and the best actress for our story's lead character. Convincing her was more important than any upcoming side effects. Let your hero know that it is key to focus on the tasks one after the other. In the beginning –especially if they are trying to attach the talent to their project– it is all about connecting and making the creative romance possible. The rest will come later.

And the side effects of the romance with the Spaniard *gran dama* came later, of course, little by little, alongside with some of the best experiences of my career. Your hero's first encounter with legacy talent is key. That first meeting we had in a hotel lobby was the incarnation of **vulnerability** and **creative vision**, both directions –from and towards– on both sides of the table. That evening in Madrid, the parts told each other the harsh reality of their situations. We were first to talk. We started with the keyword *respect*, then we moved to proving to her that we knew our shit –she already knew my EP partner, you do too, Lola aka *Darth Vader*– and then we laid out our own challenges and needs before pitching her the show's concept and her character. The needs: In our case, in a market with 5 buyers –our media outlet clients– and over 200 providers –our competitors, all solid production companies– it was almost a dream to think that a newbie with no background in scripted drama would be commissioned to produce a drama series. No network executive would ever trust us without a very-very-very good idea, and the presence and support of someone big-big-big, as big as our Spanish Barbra Streisand mixed with Maryl Streep. *'Te necesitamos, eres la mejor, si te gusta, es tuyo'* (we need you, you are the best, if you like the role, it is yours). Those were the words we said before pitching the show we wrote for her. Those were the words, but my thoughts were *'Let's see now what she thinks of our crazy idea'* and I started pitching.

The grand dame's vulnerability moment was bigger than ours. Our *Streisand-Streep* talented legacy actress waited for me to finish the pitch, but I can tell your hero she had fallen in love with the story and the character by page two of the presentation. She started with that, adding some comments *aplaudiendo* our story and characters. And then she said it: "*Do you think any one of those ejecutivos caspa would buy the story of the most successful matador who ever existed being gay? You have balls, I love it. Yes, I will be Carmen Orozco. I'm with you in this*". She truly connected with the story and her character, and what is more important for your hero, she truly connected with the storytellers. Maybe that was one of the reasons why she opened her heart the way she did. She showed a level of vulnerability that made me feel for real the joy and pain of every grand dame of the stages that ever existed. After saying *'Yes, I'm in,'* she decided to let us know the reality of her situation. It was way worse than what the *TMZ-style* people was saying. She wanted us to realize the challenges she was facing. From health, to finances, to love, to motherhood. She spoke with honesty about the things that passion in pursuit of a successful on-screen career can bring to a woman, for good and for bad. Her words touched me deeply, and at the same time made me feel privileged. I couldn't ever consider or imagine that I would listen to the life challenges of a superstar artist from the artist's own mouth. Another undreamt dream added to the list.

Once the creative-romantic connection was established, the contract was signed, and the series was sold -Yes, we did it! All because a not-that-*caspa* smart executive saw the possibilities of the drama of a gay matador as we did, with only a little collateral damage: Instead of the main matador being the unfaithful Concha's gay husband, the network suggested to move the gay character to their son. *Cosas del negocio* (showbiz shit)- Rewind! Once your hero has signed with the star and the outlet, they must maintain the **Respect** part and the **Prove It** part as fresh as if the contract still needs to be signed. No ups and downs in your hero's performance are allowed ever, but when dealing with showbiz legacy faces, it is mandatory to keep the *Respect* and *Prove It* apps always updated. Vulnerability, honesty, and trust are also required, but let your hero know that during production, the balance in the relationship between the creator and the face on the screen is going to be delicate. Your hero needs to add a new keyword: **wisdom**, make them added that one to *intuicion, tacto,* and *cojones.*

Let's talk about the perks of working with legacy stars now. I have under my belt six legacy names as very important characters in scripted content, both actors and actresses. Not one of them, ever, failed in this one, but first, a re-fresh: Can your hero remember and repeat **the showbiz golden principals**? (*Always on time + Performing at your best + Making it happen regardless*). Well, the legacy talent can remember that, because they 'are' that. They are the showbusiness' three golden principals in human shape. They won't fail on the golden principals, and if they do, *mucho ojito* (trouble is coming). Big lesson for your showrunners heroes: If a legacy face is late on set once, it is a message, not a mistake. Ask your hero to figure out who the message is for and what it is about, and do it fast, or things will get worse by the hour.

One of the best perks of working with legacy stars is the effect that their presence and attitude on set have over the rest of the team. Ask your hero not only to be there, but also to record with their phone the moment their legacy star walks the set for the first time. I didn't record it when I witnessed that; I couldn't even think about my phone. I was really impressed. Not only for the silence of the crew, their smiles, their pride in sharing creative work with the talented icon, but also for the immediate feeling I had. A combination of excitement and fear: '*Oh shit, we are raising the bar just with her showing up here. This is good.*' Yes, it was good, but it was also demanding. And all of that was only a small part of what I saw, the team saw, and we all felt.

If your hero wants to measure the on-screen talent experience, look at the talent when they are first on set, and pay attention to their eyes and movements. A legacy star only requires a quick, wide-angle panoramic look to get everything. And I mean everything. The lighting approach, the set décor, the spaces to move on and off scene, the position of the cameras, the jib, the dolly, the people, and of course the mood. They get all of that in seconds. A legacy star has been the only focus of our communal work, the only center of multiple teams creative and physical effort so many times, that they could probably do any job on those sets as well as everyone. Taking advantage of that experience is your hero's responsibility.

Back to legacy actors' perks and the grand dame's entrance on set. This kind of figure immediately brings higher standards and work ethic procedures to the team. That's how it works. Some of your star's crew members will behave so well than your hero won't recognize them. *Ya vereis* (you will see). Legacy superstars bring discipline, preparation, and professionalism. They also bring wisdom and understanding, accompanied by calm. Their sense of calm is freaking contagious. *Tienen el culo pelao* (slang for 'they've seen it all'). Tell them about crises, tight schedules, creative conflicts, or technical meltdowns. They've been there, done that, and survived it all. And no, they don't panic in those situations. Not only will they not panic on your hero's set, but they will also inspire and mentor. Ask your hero to catch that wave! And I mean the wave of knowledge they bring. The legacy talent level of wisdom in storytelling has been –in all my experiences– mind-blowing. They know a lot more than any one of us creators would expect. Legacy actors understand structure, rhythm, and tone better than anyone else. I had to keep my director mouth closed during several dialoged scenes, because our legacy star had better rhythm than I did for the conversations between the two super villains. *'Cubillo, calla y observa'* (keep your mouth closed and let her do) said the voices in my head during the second take.

Your hero needs to open –widely– whatever part of their bodies is needed to make the magic happens –eyes, ears, minds, hearts, or more.– The Legacy star brings the possibility of magic, but the detonator is in your hero's hands. When the legacy talent connects with the character and the story, your star must listen, learn, and support. After that, they can decide to incorporate –or not at all– the legacy's star suggestions, but only after the lessons. The time to elevate the creation to never expected altitudes is around the corner; make your hero try to catch it.

Legacy stars will also connect with the leaders of the departments that are key for them. First will be the cinematographer, and let your hero know, the director of photography and the lighting team will fall in love and defend the legacy superstar with their lives. After the DP, what is coming next is the relevant stuff related to your hero legend's comfort in both, in front of the lenses and while on set. Usually hair and make-up, wardrobe, logistics and so on. For your star's interest! The legacy people will become mentors and inspire each one of those department leaders involved, which is a nice side effect for your hero's production. Supporting emerging talent and teaching what they know is in the legacy stars' factory settings. Your hero must take advantage of that. Their presence in your stars' project will also bring perks beyond the studio. Their notoriety and the fact that they are cultural icons is going to bring to your hero's' creative romance a very positive side effect: Credibility and audience interest. Extra press and spectators attention. Just their name in the credits is enough to elevate your hero's show's profile.

What do you guys think? Based on those amazing perks described in the previous lines, what's up with the Legacy Stars' challenges about '*fragile personality, emotional volatility, easily manipulated by men (husbands, managers, or studio bosses), past trauma, self-esteem issues, fear of aging, desperate comebacks, diva attitudes, and a life of regrets or mental disease*'? Are they real? Is all of that just the public perception of the term 'Grand Dame of the Stages'? Well, in my own experience, the challenges are real. All of them, in different degrees from 0 to 100, BUT –this time is in caps because it matters a lot– BUT the legacy stars will hide it all to your hero, their teams, and to whoever is needed for the cause of your heroes' content. Make your star remember this forever: On-screen legacy people are pros. They *are* the golden principles. They make it happen regardless of their own drama. If your hero is thinking '*if it is like that and the legacy star performs on set, there is no real reason for concern*', tell them they are wrong. The legacy people's drama won't affect the shooting, but it will affect them, and when that happens, the creation is compromised.

When there are high digits in the legacy star's '*0 to 100 scale of personal challenges,*' bad things are going to happen, regardless. And your hero is in part right. The legacy star will show up and act on set, at least until the moment their drama affects them hard, and they can't hide it nor perform the same way any longer. Usually, by that time, it will be too late for your hero to fix it.

The only way to deal with those side effects is through the already mentioned wisdom, *intuicion, tacto,* and *cojones.* If your star won't be spending enough time with their legacy creative spouse during production, they must rely on the legacy talent's close circle. Luckily, they are going to be your hero's team members. They must ask them to keep track of the emotional state of their creative spouse and communicate fast. The experience with the Spaniard *Streisand-Streep* legacy actress taught me how important it is for them to have someone they trust on production. The 'trust' required is going to happen with time, but it is better to have that trusted person beside the talent as soon as possible. We were very lucky in that 'trust' department. Our legacy actress had known the other executive producer since Lola was twenty something. They worked together when my peer was a young production assistant, and of course the legacy talent remembered her perfectly. Thanks to Lola I learnt about the first crisis of our legacy star, just a couple of weeks before shooting the first scene.

I'd like for your hero now to breathe deeply and remember my comments about how the *Uncertainly Factor* and *On-Screen Talent* are connected in ways we don't understand. The laws of physics of the entertainment industry rule their own way, and when the *Uncertainty* and the Talent things travel together, the storytelling experience could be a matter of life and death. We had that kind of situation during our legacy superstar's first crisis, only two weeks before starting production. The reason behind it: Some of the iconic actress *personal challenges' indicators* reached 100, due to unexpected news in her painfully public private life. With those three digits hitting our talent *escala de marrones* (challenges' scale,) Lola received a call from the Legacy star's agent with news about suicidal attempts. Yes. Your hero is right. WTF! The biggest WTF ever, and a nine points earthquake in my body and soul. It's like the 9/11 attacks, I'm going to remember where I was for the rest of my existence. To make it more dramatic, the attempts and the call came during *el Puente de La Virgen de Agosto*, two weeks where nothing works in Spain, and nobody is at home. Kind of Thanksgiving shit, but under 100 degrees.

Thanks to every god in heaven, when we knew about the whole thing, she was ok, she was sedated, and she got her shit together before the agent's call. I only remember something about jumping, windows, and pills, but TBH, I couldn't pay attention to the specifics when Lola was explaining me. The shock and the fear were too big. For a star like our *Streisand-Streep*, in times of deep pain and blurred vision, being part again of an audiovisual creation becomes both a path to redemption and an abyss to fear. Dealing with those two sides effects of the role your hero is providing will increase digits on the *personal challenges' scale*. There is no way to avoid it. Your hero may need to re-enforce, re direct, and help to release the pressure on their legacy star to move those digits down. The medicine for that? Back to basics: the story you both are telling, the passion you both share, and the creative romance you both have. It worked in our case, despite how extreme it was. Our *Streisand-Streep* grand dame had another episode, I have to say probably due to our storytellers' ambition. We decided to shoot the most complicated scene first; we were Coppola kind of ambitious. The scene was a house party like the opening scene of *The Godfather*, with one difference: Coppola had three shooting days and almost $800,000 in today's money for the scene. We had 6 hours, and that amount was the whole episode's budget. Due to the crisis we experienced two weeks before with our iconic legend, it wasn't a good idea to start production with that scene, on location, and with stress. We should've started shooting on set, in the studio, with the comfort and the calm required, but our ambition blinded us. The consequence was a last-minute downfall on the legacy star's self-esteem counter, up to the red zone, but far from real risks. It caused just a 90-minute delay. Nobody knew about it but the three of us: the legacy actress and the two EP's, Lola and me. The following day, when I witnessed her entrance in set and what she caused, and I told myself *'This is what you should've done yesterday asshole'*. You can save your hero that moment of frustration.

FYHI –yes, For Your Hero's Interest– the required romance between creators and on-screen legends *no es fácil* (it's not easy), but it is rewarding. Very. Probably some of the best experiences your star is going to have in their showbiz career will come from those marriages. If they can make it, have them enjoy the ride! Wisdom, intuition, tact, and *cojones* are the ingredients.

Young and Talented: Old Challenges, New Blood, Grandiose Future.

From the legacy stars to the young cubs of the acting scene, your hero will need to enamor all ages, all genres, and all personalities in their creative marriages. When dealing with young on-screen talent –I mean young adults 14ish to 25ish– the advice for your hero is the same as with the grand dames, the A listers, or the pro-athletes: Earn their trust first, direct or manage second. But in this case, it requires a couple of fine tune set-up adjustments.

Your hero wants to know first who the young talent is, as an artist and as a human being, and that is something that talented kids still don't know in most of the cases. The shorter way for your hero to get good intel is by paying a lot of attention and giving freedom and security to their talented young stars. Ask your hero to encourage and respect the on-camera talent's voices. Make them try to know the young blood better as artists first. Their answer to a question like "*What does your version of this moment feel like?*" will tell your showrunner hero a lot about the cub's potential, background, and personality. Your star must also keep the set a sacred playground, a place where it's okay to ask questions, to miss, and to try again for the common cause of the story. A place where nothing but the story matters. Your hero will do better if they set the tone from the beginning: Creative, professional, curious, and open. Storytelling open, and emotionally open. No shaming allowed, no sarcasm allowed, but I'd recommend a lot of humor. If your hero can make 'Curiosity and Respect' the culture on set *-of course, starting with their own-*, they are going to make on-screen friends forever, help to grow the next generation of award winners, and succeed in their own storytelling goals, which is the whole point of these pages.

If during the journey your hero sees an on-screen cub asking a lot of questions, being curious, and spending time with crew members, chances are they have found a gem. I had that experience in my first Big Leagues drama as a director. The day I saw the curious cub in an upstairs studio control room (no talent ever goes there), learning about each team member's position, I knew we had the right actor in the project, and a great candidate for the next one. Not only because of his performance on set, but because of his level of passion –and efforts!– for the common cause of storytelling.

Now, here's an important exception to consider with the youngsters! The creative marriages with fresh on-screen talent are totally different. It doesn't matter what your hero's part in the storytelling process is– creator, showrunner, producer, director, or whatever; they are now dealing with cubs, and it is their responsibility to inspire, teach, and guide. Period. It is not only about the creation anymore, it is also about their growing. I take working with young actors or young crew members very seriously, and I'm asking your hero and you to do the same. We are all setting work-ethic standards and human values to the faces behind the future blockbusters. Your hero wants to leave a good seed in each one of those promising stars. Some of them are the next generation of legacy icons. Ask your heroes to do their part properly.

A few short-format tips for your hero to deal with young blood and old challenges. First, mentorship over management; ask your star to be the guide, not just the boss. Next, celebrate growth, not just execution. Also, feed the artist, not the ego. "*You nailed it*" it is not enough with the young talent. Ask your hero to praise their risk-taking and to teach the cubs how to evaluate their own work with questions as: "*How did you feel in that take?*" That attitude will give your star more tools to help the cub and make the product better, simultaneously. Also, have your hero look for the first signs of potential greatness, for those on-screen cubs who are looking everywhere and asking questions, wanting to know more about everything, or spending their time between scenes with different departments. Those are the symptoms your star is looking for.

Chances are your hero will work with a very famous and successful on-screen cub, yet they're still a cub. Let your hero know that this one is a tricky marriage. See if your star can imagine an on-screen character putting together a combination of an A-lister and a grand dame inside a teenager's brain and body. That would be close to the real experience. If that happens, if they are dealing with young and already famous on camera kids, let your hero know that when the young A-list talent is alone with the mirror, at the end, the question they ask to themselves is always the same: "*Who am I now?*" Fame messes with their internal compass, and that is impossible to avoid. Another law of the physics of the show business.

When fame hits, we all would confuse public validation with artistic and personal growth. Your hero will face the consequences of the young superstar's natural lack of balance, and the costs of the internal fight between their Ego vs. their Confidence. They're now juggling interviews, brand deals, fans, and social media pressure. They may think not only that they are still performing well, but also that they deserve special treatment. A difficult scenario when they are not being good enough for your hero's story. In those cases, have your star remind their on-screen famous cub that the set is a protected space from outside shit, the sacred playground where nothing but the story matters. Fame doesn't change the storytelling process, nor the novice's duties. Make your star try to ground the cub back into the craft and out of the fame, at least while on set. Redirecting the young talent's energy towards telling the best story possible is the best advice I can give. The *Shared Passion* thing is again your hero's best ally.

There are other side effects from the marriages with A-list cubs. Peer jealousy can also creep in, f**king up the whole set dynamics. After that, sooner or later, your hero's notorious novices are going to succumb under the pressure of fame, which will worsen their emotional instability even more. The best home remedy I can give to your star is '*do things right, be fair, be wise, inspire*'. The remedy and the prevention of the early fame side effects come from the same practices: A healthy production culture, human connection, vulnerability, and respect.

On-Screen Talent in the Unscripted Labyrinths

The gods of storytelling wanted me to become an expert in unscripted content, and one of the first thing I learnt was the power the genre carries to completely transform the lives of those who are in front of the lenses. For good and for bad. Very bad in some cases. That is the first lesson for your hero's romances with on-screen never again unknown people. It is a lifechanging experience. This time the changes are for them, not that much for your hero. Dealing with newbies on camera is in some ways like dealing with young talent. You must take care of them also as human beings. In the unscripted scene case, the on-screen talent has no idea about what is coming, so you must take care of them more, guys, ok? Of course, anyone who goes to a reality show audition is pursuing passion and/or notoriety, yes, you and your hero are right on that, but that fact does not alter the rule: Protect your talent. Their dreams for fame or their unique lifestyle are your hero's stories. Do not let your camera talent down. Ever. There's no excuses.

Make your star aware that any unknown human's life is going to change after a reality show. No exceptions. In the past, the public didn't know how much, but now it is different. I caught the Reality TV wave in the very beginning, in the times where the candidates had no idea about the consequences that those brief 15 minutes of fame could bring to what felt a 'normal life' before the show. Normality was over, and they didn't know it. Things are quite different today. Nowadays there are non-A-Listers *de todo el puto abecedario* (I think you guys got the Spanish, don't you?), people who make their living from season to season from the same or similar reality franchises. Professionals of the Reality TV lenses. I must advise your hero that doesn't change the approach. It is the same as with the newbies, but more difficult. Even though some of them are already *grand dames* of the unscripted celebrity scene, your hero must protect their talent. From themselves too, which is a bit difficult.

Apart from some genuine A-listers, everyone else navigates the daily demands of the abecedary of fame by combining professional activities, personal lives, passions, invitations to events, scandals, celebrity friends, podcast collaborations, panels, awards shows, trips to exotic destinations, new toys, their kids' graduation or worse than all of that. The point is that in the current times, the fame scale behaves in surprising ways and the *Non-A Listers* are on the hunt, trying it all. The content platforms are in the same hunt, but from a different side. Streamers and broadcasters prefer already famous people doing their own spectacular thing multiplied exponentially or doing challenging things they have never done before. For that reason, there are a lot of chances for your hero to end up on a project with a bunch of *Listers* from the whole abecedary, with a bunch of different backgrounds and activities. This picture is difficult to imagine if your hero hasn't had that experience. The other prey platforms and networks hunt is outstanding or ultra-exotic lifestyles. People living in impossible places or doing impossible things. People who already are, or want to be, among the 0,1% of humans on earth. Have your hero think about shows such as *Alone, Naked & Afraid, Life Below Zero, or The Deadliest Catch*. Let's break down for your hero the secrets to creatively enamor, marry, divorce, and survive both the real Real Housewives and the deadly catchers.

Real Housewives, Real Issues

Now, a question for you and your hero: do you prefer realities with individuals? Or with groups? My answer is unequivocal; I like shows with dynamics over individuals. Especially as a creator, I prefer shows with pre-existing conditions in the participants. It was love at first sight. After a few seasons producing realities with a group of individuals cast separately –that needed two weeks together to start creating interesting dynamics– I was lucky enough to run the first season of the franchise *Confianza Ciega* (Blind Faith). The show was an ancestor of the current *'Love Island'*, where three existing couples were testing their love and faith, while living separated in a resort, and being tempted by an army of *seductores y seductoras* from the opposite sex, whose beauty exceeded the mainstream parameters.

I had two life-changing epiphanies while running that show. First, while we were in the control room, cheering and celebrating how we made the female participant believe that her boyfriend was cheating on her, I felt happy for me, for the team, for the new show format, and for the storytelling, but dirty as shit as a creator. *Sucio*, that is the word to use here. For the first time in my career, I was hurting people in the name of storytelling. Our cheating scene was fake; her tears were real. I had to remind myself a million times that the couples volunteered and wanted to test their love, but I also decided that I would avoid hurting anyone else for the cause of content. If there are tears in my shows, the ultimate goal is healing. The second epiphany came while shooting the moment the couples saw each other after the seduction test, on the last day of the experience. This time I didn't feel dirty, I felt lucky. OMG guys, while shooting the encounter of the couples one by one, it stroked me like a revelation, with chills included, and the feeling was growing with each duo encounter and conversation. Everyone on the team was salivating in front of the monitors, amazed with each word coming out of the recently born reality stars. They showed themselves as we never saw before. We witnessed their most intimate dynamics and roles, and we felt their real love in a revealing and refreshing way. All of that in front of the cameras. Orgasmic. Having on-screen faces with pre-existing conditions is the best storytelling tool for unscripted. Period.

When creating Reality TV content, couples, family members, and groups with existing tensions, ambitions and unresolved history, are a guarantee of conflicts and relatability. Participants can't hide the pre-existing tensions; they will come up immediately, and with them, audiences will see themselves in the screen. As your hero see, a win, win, win. *The Holy Trinity* in action. Product, clients, and profits in a happy orgy.

But to get there –and I mean the orgy– your hero must be clear on this one: These types of shows rely on chemistry, conflict, and alliances. Individual charisma is important, but it's not enough to succeed. The flashy social media character could become less active than a medusa, floating in the waters of content without catching any storyline's currents.

Among the wide range of Reality TV sub-genres, it is good for your hero to explore those that have more impact, more seasons, and more versions –with or without negotiating format licenses, but that's another book. The mother of all those shows, and the father of the sub-genre call 'lifestyle drama reality' are *The Real Housewives of Orange County,* a series that scandalized the screens in 2008. Time for your hero to pay attention to a number: Over 1,600. That is the number of episodes that have aired so far from *The Real Housewives* franchises only in the USA. If we add similar shows as *Rica, Famosa, Latina; Love & Hip Hop,* and *Basketball Wives,* the number of US episodes is over 2,000. And still on the go. Crazy.

If your star is into unscripted –either documentary or reality, not relevant– there are clearly a few possibilities for them to end up in need of a creative romance with both sub-species, the groups and the individuals. Let's put the focus on the groups with pre-existing conditions now. I'm sure your hero has watched at least one of the +2,000 Real Housewives episodes after the ladies from OC made their entrance. Your star already knows the precedence of the sub-species. They all are, or pretend to be, abecedary listers, often connected to fame-adjacent social circles, and I mean married or dating celebrities, heirs of famous families, *primos segundos,* or similar. The point is that they are already part of social scene, and that means they have some level of notoriety, influencer energy, and connections. They may have already been suffering from social pressure, but not to the public scrutiny at the scale they are facing with your hero's show. For your star to know, for some mystery, those on-screen faces cannot visualize the consequences of the impact, despite seeing it every day in others. Weird, but they won't put themselves there. It's a symptom of the virus. The newborn reality stars will panic after the first episode is out and the social media storm starts. This is a rule in the 'lifestyle drama reality' sub-genre: The rapid transition from "nobody" to household name in niche pop culture, will take your hero's on-screen talent to the edge of anxiety, depression, body dysmorphia, and of course, social media harassment.

It is a well proven fact: Identity becomes distorted for the now real reality celebrity; many struggle to separate the character from self. Let your hero know, there's a condition call *'reality fame dependency'*, and it is as addictive as Fentanyl. We all know cases of reality luminaries chasing relevance through escalating drama, sometimes with terrible outcomes.

With the kind of picture described, if your hero still wants to creatively marry a real housewife -or similar- here are the top tips to take care of the artistic romance between vision and camera lens.

- **Manage But Don't Manipulate**

I'm a hard believer of this one. I love reality, and I work on reality precisely because la *realidad siempre supera a la ficcion* (reality always surpasses fiction). No creator will write a better storyline that the one that pure reality brings. Not your showrunner hero, nor their writers or producers. After choosing the right cast, the secret of this genre is the ability to match the characters and real-life events of the group of protagonists based on those amazing dynamics your hero sightsaw in the cast auditions. There is no need for staging, pre-production, or forced drama. It won't work, or better said, it will work every now and then, but both sides of the screen will feel the fakeness, the on-screen faces, and the audience. Not good for your hero's creation. Staging in unscripted is a death sentence. Sometimes it takes a couple of seasons, but it is usually faster. Your hero's show will have no soul, it won't connect. If your star has studied the battlefield (characters-goals-challenges-dynamics-real life events), it is only a matter of planning interactions, calculating consequences, and being ready for the real thing to happen. I define that approach as *poner detonantes para que las cosas pasen de forma natural* (set triggers so that things happen naturally). Your hero must oversee and guide emotional arcs, but don't push trauma or lies for content. Manipulation leads to fakeness on screen and to serious damages for the talent, including mental health crises, lawsuits, or wild public criticism. Keep you star out of it.

- **Invest In Talent Coaching & Branding**

This is a win-win again. For your hero's show, and for their talent. Have your star help the talent develop consistent personal brands and guide them on navigating public persona vs. private self. Fame comes fast. If the talent is lost managing the consequences, fame will flame out or turn toxic. Not good for your hero's creation. A stable personal brand supports both the show and the reality star.

- **Mediate Social Media Strategically**

Needless to say, your hero must coordinate the timing of show drops with the talent's posts and coach their on-screen faces on tone, polemics, and rules of engagement. Coach! No manipulation. These stars live and die by online relevance. They are going to post regardless. Making good use of the fact is your hero's best marketing tool. But do it with care, guys! It can go off-script fast.

- **Prioritize During and Post-Show Talent Support**

In my experience, having mental health professionals on the team is mandatory in the reality genre. First to guide your hero through the auditions stage and then to offer access to therapy to their on-screen stars. The cast also needs Public Relations guidance and legal counsel. If your hero cannot get the resources for all the above, someone above them is not practicing the Holy Trinity system. Make them be aware of it. Things do not look great; I can tell you that already.

A Real Housewives Real-Life Experience

Let's test my theories about on-screen talent in real life and see what your hero's final opinions are. The gods of showbiz are to blame for my insane showrunner-roadrunner luck. Thanks to them I've done a lot of miles, but I've also caught a lot of waves. The wave of the real housewives also caught me, thanks god, with 10 years of experience on my back. It was here, in America. I became the executive producer-showrunner of the *Estrella TV* series call *Rica, Famosa, Latina*. Before jumping into how to enamor crazy Latino women, another crazy thing for your hero, you need some context and lessons. There's no option for any on-screen romance if your hero is not hired or if their show is not commissioned, so first things first: *Enamorar al jefe*, gain trust, be hired, and start working. My story with *Rica, Famosa, Latina* and *Estrella TV* shows how dramatic storytelling romances can go. With both bosses and on-screen talent.

A question now for you and your hero: in love-related matters, are you the type that goes on and off? Several breakups and reconciliations with the same person? Not my case, I can consider the *some years later* option, but I don't do the back and forth. Not in love, but business is different, especially if it comes with passion and curiosity. My creative romance with *Rica, Famosa, Latina* and *Estrella TV* started with the boss, of course. See how much storytelling passion this guy –the network owner and CEO– and the one writing these words shared. Ready? Let's go.

We knew each other for a while, and we already had the storytelling connection. Years later, I let them know I was living in the States. The guy called me, and I joined their #1 show 'Rica' for the second season, and here is where the drama part starts: A few months later, close to the finish, I was fired after giving my all and having pretty good results. It was both, *un descanso y una putada* (a relief and a stab in the back). But then magic happened. The network CEO called me again for the third season, a surprising and exciting reconciliation. We talked, and we got an agreement for the development and production stages. The boss wanted new faces, and I started suggesting names to join the real housewives group. I especially insisted on one of them, sightseeing the surprising ratings results she would bring. The boss decided not to cast her for season three. I think he was scared, *y con razon* (and he was right). Another dose of drama: Close to the end to my second season we broke up again, but this time it was me who quit. Surprise!! *Descanso y putada*, again. A few months later he called me back for the fourth season. We spoke and we reconciled again, but now he was convinced about the on-screen talent I suggested for two seasons already. As your hero can see, showbiz magic can happen up to three times *como minimo* (at least). 'Magic' being shared passion and storytelling connection. Of course, the following breakup was only a matter of time. Time passed, and it came, but this time I didn't quit, and he didn't want to fire me. This time it was the on-screen talent I brought who forced the network to kick me off. I told you before, this sub-genre is the mother and the father of the whole invention. As a content creator, your hero will learn a lot with a few crazy on-screen ladies around. Latinas or not.

The romance with the boss was complicated, but nothing compared to the romance with the new real housewife member. In the following lines your hero will learn through my experiences with just one lady of the group. This is the moment for them to realize the dimension of the challenge this genre brings. Ask your hero to multiply this 'just one lady' experience by the number of faces in their shows and wish them good luck.

Yes, you and your hero were right when you thought that not all the ladies in those franchises were already 'friends' before the screens. Usually some of them are, but we creators need to complement the group properly, and sometimes that requires 'importing' ladies from other parts of the world and trying to make it work. That was the case with that *Rica, Famosa, y Latina* lady I was suggesting casting for two seasons. She was living in both Mexico City and Miami. She was very Latina –Cuban Mexican– very famous, but not very rich. For your hero to know, when adding characters that are obviously not coming from the same circles than the rest of the ladies, the storyline matters. In most cases neither the content producers nor the ladies would dig deep into the fact, but the narrative must be solid and make real sense. So, we built our story for her. Why does a mature triple threat actress, showgirl, polemist, *santera*, party legend and gossip queen move to Los Angeles? We decided it was because of her new business initiative, and having three actresses in town within the housewives group already made sense for the newbie to re-connect with the mature Hispanic artists. At least it made sense from the audience's perspective. The truth is that they weren't friends at all, even worse. We brought her and gave her a very good life. We set the newbie up in an amazing house that we rented empty, and our art director –another genius mastermind mind– made it the coolest house she ever had. The decisions about the household and the home décor were the first storylines of the new cast member and the beginning of her connection with the rest of the housewives. The setting up a business storyline would come later.

The reasons we gave on screen were completely made up, but the reality of the production was different. This lady came only for money, and she took the reality show as a performing gig, like a real pro. But after a few shooting days with the rest of the cast, the newbie –and her manager– got the *reality star virus,* and they started to badly muddle public persona with on-screen performing with her own private self. The *reality star virus* is a disease that will deeply affect your hero's creation, and the side effects are difficult to handle.

I followed the procedures described in the chapter, all of them, *prometido!* After connecting about storytelling –TBH, not too deeply– I lay out for the new real housewife the storylines that affected only her, those based on her activities. She loved the stories, the house, the art-director, and everything else. She was happy. But things changed fast. That is important for your hero. In the unscripted labyrinths, events speed up wildly. It is like a time machine, minutes will last seconds. Things happen fast. Too fast! Despite knowing and loving the plan, somehow the recently born reality star decided in a few days that I was lying to her, manipulating her, and wanting to destroy her public image. Shit, from 0 to 100 in days. The cast member I pushed for two years to bring, the one who owed me convincing the network CEO, the one I gave the most positive storylines of the season, an amazing house, and a Hollywood life again. My first girlfriend would still be here with the kind of treatment I gave her! My creative romance was in crisis with the most important on-screen face of the show.

To get into the side effects and the home remedies in that situation, I first needed to understand how the hell she got to that conclusion. Why was she not trusting me anymore? Who was poisoning her ears? The unscripted labyrinths have their own set of diseases. I think in her case it was because of how fast the virus described affects. Spending time –on and off set– with the rest of the real ladies was enough for her to start mixing up her public persona with on-screen performing with her own private self. If you add to the mix the pre-existing conditions of the actress, showgirl, polemist, *santera,* party legend, and gossip queen, it's going to be *un cacao de cojones para cualquiera* (one hell of a shitshow for anyone). But I know she also decided not to trust me because some members of my own crew stabbed us in the back. Badly.

Yes, that is one of the important learnings for your hero in this chapter. If your star's teams in unscripted shows are not tight enough, solid enough, and wise enough, the egos and agendas of the cast and crew will flourish, accompanied with real shitty issues. There will be intents to manipulate storylines, people, and more. From both camps and in both directions. Double agents in every room. More and more every day. The *Rica, Famosa, Latina* team wasn't tight, nor solid, nor wise. They didn't serve the holy trinity. They couldn't!

They were surviving, and as a showrunner I had no real power over them. they belonged to the network/studio; I brought just a handful of people to the project. The majority were a mixture of professionals (or semi-pros) coming from a variety of backgrounds from news to telenovelas, all servants of a tyrant famous for his bad practices and under the constant threat from the dictator. Yes, your hero is right, the perfect environment for betrayal. The question for your star is, why do they think I went back there twice after suffering all of that in my first season in *Rica*? And nope, it wasn't only for money. I did it because I loved that kind of storytelling more than my own mental health, as stupid as it sounds.

I hope you guys got it: Cast isolation is key, especially from the team. Your hero's' crew must swear in front of the holy trinity and the showbiz gods. In unscripted, cast is that sacred. It's my norm, but it wasn't the case with the Cuban Mexican scandalous actress and the rest of the *Ricas*. My fault. I accepted to work in a toxic environment, thinking that I would've had what it takes to change it or overcome it. Stupid asshole I am, you guys must learn from that, no dreamed storytelling *merece la pena* (it is worth it) if your hero feels they are in a toxic place. Big period here.

When my two seasons ambitioned new real housewife lost trust in me, the only way to connect with her was using a proxy. I decided to do it through an ambitious story producer, part of the tyrant's network/studio servers. He shared origin with the half Cuban lady, which I thought would ease the approach, but I was wrong. There was no need for approach. First, the producer was already having more conversations with the talent than I did. Second, the on-screen real lady was having real mental health issues with dramatic side effects. Third and last, IDK what your hero thinks, but probably the smart also-Cuban producer who smelled how much ratings the lady would bring was also guilty of feeding her ears with who knows what about me and my plans.

Her relevance as a villain in the show was too high to risk her. Huge! But it came with a price. She would lose her shit very often, and not only in front of the cameras –*which was good for the show*– but also everywhere else. She was also clearly dealing with her own issues through substances. Whatever it was, the virus, the poison, the substances, the egos, or the agendas, one day she left me a voice message during a psychotic breakdown –or a dope binge, one of the two– and I knew my days were over.

After a few of those wild voice messages –and a couple of surreal conversations with her manager– my phone rings showing the network feudal master number: 'It is either you, or her, and you know I can't let her go'. That was all. I left. Very important for your hero! If it is between the on-screen talent and you, the upstairs gods will always choose the talent. Always! As your hero and I would do. In *Rica*, at the end, the crazy Cuban Mexican lady tortured all of them for two more seasons, the Cuban-producer became co-executive producer of the show, and the abusive dictator owner of the network lost the network and a lot more, once his servers went to the authorities and sued him. I told you; the real housewives shit is the orgy of the *uncertainty factor* gods. If your hero deals with 'forces of nature' such as our lady, they'll need wisdom and patience. Some people have more energy than they can handle, and they will need to keep up or avoid them. Good luck! There are good lessons in both paths.

Panels, Judges, Coaches, Y Derivados

Time for the talent competition on-screen faces now. These panels are another on-screen niche where your stars are going to enamor all kinds of abecedary listers and on/off-screen backgrounds. It's a complicated and interesting romantic battlefield.

Here's your first tip for your star when dealing with the on-screen faces of the so-called *Talent/Reality Competition* genre: They must respect and strengthen the basic roles of the on-screen characters. Your hero will probably have super-famous hosts and judges on the show, but the real protagonists in these shows are the participants, not the panel or the presenters. The show is the story of the contributors' journeys, their transformations. Their personal growth arcs are what really matter. *Ojo!* That doesn't mean the unknown participants will have more screen time than the celebrities on set. Nope, it's not about that, be clear with your hero. Rather, it is about roles in the story your hero is telling.

Yes, easy so far. We have been seeing this in talent shows for decades already, where the panel's part is criticizing, giving advice, judging, and sometimes deciding the future of the participants, along with entertaining the audience and especially boosting conflicts. Yeah, that's the description of a talent show panel 'by the book'. Good luck with it. If your hero follows that ordinary narrative, forget creating anything special. Your star's content will be another mediocre talent show, not the story of an amazing transformation journey from nobody to pop star, master chef, or celebrity dancer.

Have your hero think about these lines for a second, maybe they will agree with me. If the protagonists are the participants pursuing the dream, what would be the best way for the other two characters of the story to own a solid part of it? And I mean, for the hosts and the judges, what roles would your hero ambition for those two groups in a story about talent, will, resilience, and evolution? How can those two groups have the best part possible in the winner transformation journey? How can those panelists be key in the talent show winner's story arc? And please don't allow your hero the obvious joke. No, it is not just 'voting for them when judging.' It is about being at the participant's side during the journey. Make your hero stop and read again. Being by the contributor's side means 'pushing the contestant to be better.' The panel's role? Guide, teach, correct, give wisdom, support and experience to the protagonists. You are right, guys, it feels like the opposite of what we are accustomed to.

When the Dutch creative genius who invented *The Voice* started calling the panel 'coaches' instead of 'judges', I saw some light, and I found a reference to explain to everyone my peculiar point of view about panels: The panel must push the evolution of the participant, and they can do that in many ways and with different doses of criticism, compassion, humor, advice, tone, attitude, *y demas*. That is the second concern for your hero, but tell them that it must be done according to the panel member's background and personality.

The first concern for your star's storytelling –and their connection with the on-screen panelists' faces– is their role in the story. The big picture. Make your hero go back to the basics. Force your star to pause and look at the *show premise* and *the story to be told* with a wider perspective. In that pause ask them to not yet consider names for any role, just the story to be told. When they are clear on the premise and the story, they can approach the panel and start their creative romance. Where to start? Exactly there, making the panel 'own' their role as those who are *'pushing the participant to be better in the pursuit of their dreams'* journeys. As guides, teachers, strict coaches, wise professionals, or *autenticos cabrones*. I don't care, that's not relevant yet. If your hero can convince the panel to give support and wisdom to the protagonists –in their own way– your star is going to enjoy a great ride.

The approach is valid for all the panel members' backgrounds and personalities, but it requires something from your hero's side too, and it is important. It demands AUTHENTICITY. Yes, with caps again. A degree of commitment that won't allow your hero to impose anything on the panel – *eliminations included!*– but to commit with the judges to the best possible *'Pushing The Participant To Be Better'* they can find in every scenario. Authenticity is required on both sides of the creatively-romantic connection –the faces that tell the story, and those who build it– It works in both directions, and it is your hero's best ally for greatness.

Yes, you and your protagonists are translating my words correctly. I am telling you *'ask your panel for total commitment, give your panel total freedom.'* All in the cause of pushing the participant to be better. I haven't found a greater tactic than that, despite the risks. BTW! Dealing with those risks is the cherry on top of unscripted content. Ex-bosses, mentors, and peers that developed those world-wide talent competition formats –along with the most talent competition storytellers– must be *retorciendose en la silla* (writhed in pain) while reading these words. Yes, that's what I think. Commitment and freedom are the best storytelling tools. That is what I learned after +50 episodes in the genre, it is what I would recommend, and it is what I will do the next time. It became a contract negotiation thing in my case. No AUTHENTICITY, no Daniel.

FYHI: Here are important reasons behind reaching that level of *cabezoneria* (stubbornness) from my side. Would your star be so strict with their approach to the panel power to reject a job offer? No, they won't. I wasn't either. I joined the 'talent/reality competition showrunners club', adopting the ways of the creators, producers, and exhibitors: Final decisions are ours; on-screen panel faces are just *muñecos*. Most of the times, someone else puts in *los muñecos* everything coming out of their lips. They are *on-screen mouths* instead of on-screen hearts and brains. A sad misuse of their talents.

That was the case in my debut in the genre, and it was a success, but not because of the panel. After that, I put together a few seasons of a variety of disciplines, following the way of the predecessors with a painful learning: Panels do not decide, therefore, panels don't implicate. Final outcome? Panels are not adding value to the show as they could. I have experienced a few of them: panels evaluating stars dancing for their causes, models in search of the magazine cover that will change their lives, and cooks who wanted to be chefs. Enough disciplines and enough seasons to try a variety of strategies, and to be honest, I am not satisfied with my panelists' part in those stories. They could've done so much better. My fault. But then the light came, in the form of a conversation with one of the mastermind creators of *The Voice*. It was the first talk between the Dutch guy and *servidor*, when he perfectly articulated –in no more than 20 seconds– things that I knew, but didn't put together. He made the perfect elevator pitch to explain what a talent show panel should be, and here is my version for you: The role of a panel is pushing the participants to be better. Period.

The best demonstration of the *ideal panel masterclass* was watching *The Voice* on air the first season. Until those NBC episodes, I never have had so much fun and engagement with a panel. Never in my life. As storyteller I had envy, TBH, a lot. The mastermind minds that produced the show were able to link their vision with the on-screen faces with the fastest and best route ever created. The results are part of the recent history of television. *The Voice* rescued NBC and put it back on top of the game, thanks to a panel of talent show judges once a week. Really? Shit. Showbiz magic, no doubt.

The key to the show's success was 'freedom'. Those A-lister coaches were completely involved in the participants' success. I was lucky enough to make the first adaptation of *The Voice* in Spanish –La Voz Kids for Telemundo.– A great ride overall, but one of the most Kafkaesque situations of my f***ing career. A-lister panels are complicated. With *La Voz* we experienced the two extremes. let's go with the easiest first.

Scene one. Rooftop of the Mondrian hotel in Miami. Prince Royce and his manager already seated, the Dutch creator of the show, his executive producer, and me –representing the network– approaching the table to convince him to be on the show's panel. The highlight of that meeting for me is how Prince Royce's energy, expression, and body language changed during the conversation. From '*I shouldn't be here wasting my time*' to TOTAL –yeah, caps here too– total communion with the premise (*helping talented kids to pursue a music career*) with the show and with us. Prince Royce's eyes, smile, and energy when we left the rooftop is one of the best memories I have of this craft. For real, you could feel the magic flowing through the five people sitting there.

Prince Royce was in, coach one done! Good name to start with. I cannot tell you about the meeting with coach three, Paulina Rubio. Never happened. She was cast through cash –and *yellow convertible*s, remember the comment? When producers and network creative execs talked with her, the deal was closed. Prince Royce needed to know 'what' before deciding, Paulina needed to know 'how much'. Not a good sign. If your hero's panelists don't even need to know about the show, they should reconsider. In *La Voz* each panelist/coach ran a team of minors –Btw, shooting conditions with kids are wild, and expensive. A few days before the finale, one of the kids' coaches was caught on camera –high as shit– peeing between two yachts outside a Miami mansion. Do you need to know who that member of the panel was? Yes, the one that didn't give a shit about the premise, the show, and the rest. Imagine the earthquake the following morning. A day to remember! If your hero thinks that dealing with the consequences –press and media shock, her team's kids, the kids' parent, attorneys, and more– was the Kafkaesque moment, they are wrong. Kafka was in spirit at the pier during that party, no doubt, and the next morning in the studios and the offices upstairs, but Kafka came in person to the stage the day of the finale.

I guess Paulina never left her mansion after peeing, Idk, but her next call-sheet was the finale, and nobody was able to contact her after the pics came out. 72 hours after the peeing incident, the studio was crowded, the kids were nervous –the families more– and everything was ready to proclaim the first winner of *La Voz Kids*, everything but Paulina Rubio. Her call time was two and a half hours before starting. She never came. The show was pre-recorded live on tape –this is important– and right at the time we were supposed to start, Kafka came in person. I don't know if any other *The Voice* franchise finale –of any other talent show finale on earth– has started shooting when a member of the panel finally let them know that 'she was on her way'. Super-surreal. After two hours waiting for her –remind your hero that kids have very limited shooting time by law– The network *mero mero* –the good master gardener Mr. Emperador Romano– told me '*Daniel, time for magic, you must start.*' He was right. During the waiting time, I approached the EP and the director and asked them to start figuring out how to shoot the show in a way that would allow us to insert Paulina shots in editing. I did it when I felt Kafka's presence, just preventing, and then my boss forced me to start taping. It was a one-of-a-kind XXL-size event. Huge. Celebrity guests on stage and on the tribunes. Press. The whole network upstairs offices ecosystem was there, the best clients, the city politicians, everybody. Crazy. Well, we knew she was on her way –and my boss was freaking out– so, countdown for take-off without one of the astronauts. I guess Kafka was sitting on Paulina's rotating chair, laughing his ass off at me. She made it for segment two. In the first 30 minutes of the finale, no shot of the three superstar A-lister coaches, just close-ups or back shots. Imagine the drama due to the delay and her absence, besides the empty chair in the middle of the freaking stage. Changes in the show rundown, in the scripts, in everything! It was a lot, and somehow, we made it. We added a few of her fake close-ups in those first 30 minutes, and we were all happy when we finished and she left. She was a good name, but obviously not suited for a show with kids. From Prince Royce's glowing smile when he understood the commitment, to seeing Kafka in person through a lady who was never interested. Those are my two biggest memories of an amazing experience. I hope it is clear for all. Your hero needs authenticity on the panel more than A-list faces. If you are curious, yes, of course, Prince Royce's team won the show.

You have enough about on-screen talent side effects and home remedies to digest. It is now on you to remember that love for storytelling and immaculate ethics are the fabric of the connection with the faces in front of the lenses. Your star must build the bridge between concepts and screen hand by hand with their *muñecos*, and that fact places them in a more delicate position in the relationship. Your hero must act first to make the creative romance possible, and then to keep it healthy, no matter the way –couples therapy, romantic road-trips, swinger-clubs, or whatever is required– all while protecting their on-screen faces and hearts. Remind them they will also be protecting their creation.

CHAPTER 12

And The Oscar Goes To?

THE SHOW MUST GO ON: ALIGNMENT AND ENLIGHTENMENT

Notes

CHAPTER 12

The Show Must Go On: Alignment And Enlightenment

Seeing what we have imagined come to life on a screen gives a high like no other. When that happens with more harmony than drama, when the mastermind minds involved recognize each other, if there is altruism –you are there for the cause of content, not just the cause of money– and there is authenticity, good shit pours over us –a very welcome feeling, btw. When there is alignment, there will be enlightenment. In those cases, not only are the three persons of the *Holy Trinity* happy, but also the one in the mirror. In those cases, the magic of this craft also creates personal connections that transcend time and circumstances. In certain projects, the team becomes family forever.

'*The Show Must Go On*' is the third golden principle of our business. It is going to happen with or without your hero, but now they are ready to be the one in charge. So far, your star has gone through quite a bumpy journey. The best lessons come from mess-ups, and I made a few. Through them, your characters have learned the tools to keep the 'show on' under extreme circumstances. As the last stop of the ride, I'd like for them to see a sample of 'easiness.' What happens when everything works? Good things for us, and for the rest of the *Holy Trinity*.

There was this experiment we made with a daily talk show named *Suelta La Sopa*. During its development, I made the mistake of trying a female co-host, but I changed direction when it was obvious that our host Jorge Bernal was the solo on-screen quarterback. A few weeks after launching, my vision was taking shape without my presence. The team I had put together, the workflow, and the model continued working and evolving without requiring me to keep it moving. It was a perfect machine, like German engineering. With time, the mastermind minds behind the camera and Jorge kept the show on screen for 8 years. We had put together something great that was able to continue growing until some asshole decided to kill it (network nonsense, again). Within weeks, a competitor took it to his network, where it continued leading under a different name. Do the numbers: 5 days per week, 11 months per year, 8 years – and counting. Big profits for the producers and the network, and a good number of creative souls flourishing and making their living. A testimony of creative flow, alignment, and enlightenment.

As the audience, your hero will also be able to detect alignment and enlightenment in others. I am witnessing how a YouTube creator is making his way to the social media Big Leagues under my spectator eyes in months. A guy with one passion –which is not storytelling– a lot of knowledge, and the *cojones, trabajo, y vision de la jugada* (balls, work, and vision) to make his passion audiovisual content at the right time. He grew his YouTube experiment from nothing to 100k subscribers –with an average of 300k viewers per video– in less than two Formula 1 seasons. His name is Paul Tracy. The YT channel is F1 Unchained. I don't know him, but I am seeing him walking the walk. As a viewer, this F1 fanatic case is for me a perfect example of how to apply the 'passion, balls, work, and vision' your hero has in the tank. I knew with his first video that Paul would achieve a bunch of undreamt dreams; I'm sure it is already happening.

That is just one small case that proves how show business has been in deep transformation for a decade plus already. If we look at the traditional Big Leagues of entertainment, the evidence is painful. The transition is not like an apocalyptic burn down, but it is the end of an era, don't fool yourself. The relevance and the economics of the traditional model are over. Part of the OG showbiz establishment will catch up, part won't. The 'content creation' and the 'entertainment' industries are one in essence, at least for us audiovisual storytellers.

These are very special times for other reasons. Creativity doesn't run the show currently, but the world is facing a time of transformations like no other. Something impossible without us. The non-creative part of the planet needs us to create the future that is coming. As creative mastermind minds – and as storytellers– the opportunity is gigantic, as is the responsibility. That's why these are my last set of questions for your hero: What would they like to do with the opportunity? How is their creation going to make the world a better place? What do they want to do with their creative power? I'm asking because at the end of the day, if show business feels like an eternal happy hour, we –the creators– are the lemon in the cocktails. We are indispensable, true, but we are also squeezed until the last drop and thrown into the trash. When I realized this tragic end, I decided that for the time I am still giving my creative juice, it will be for good and with fun. As one of those *friends-that-became-family* says, "for the rest of my time doing this *voy a dar por culo, pero para bien*" ('I'll be a f**king pain in the ass, but for 'the good'). *Pues eso.*

The ride is over, guys. Thanks for your time and efforts. All my best for the journey, and a call to action too. You all know how this world works now. The *followers, likes, and views* dictatorship forces us creators also to be some kind of social media talent –something I am not. Challenging to know that this book –and the following journeys– are going to be almost impossible without that. That is the reason why I am asking you all for help. If your hero has enjoyed it, push them to be proactive, share this wisdom, and ask for more. The one writing this shit has exchanged 'dream-making' for 'dream-helping.' So, thanks for sharing, and FYI, if you need help with your creation, and your creation is for good, feel free to reach out. Let's make this world better together.

CONTENTS

www.ingramcontent.com/pod-product-compliance
Lightning Source LLC
Chambersburg PA
CBHW070656190326
41458CB00052B/6910/J